THE ARDEN SHAKESPEARE

GENERAL EDITORS:
RICHARD PROUDFOOT, ANN THOMPSON
and DAVID SCOTT KASTAN

THE SECOND PART OF
KING HENRY VI

THE ARDEN SHAKESPEARE

All's Well That Ends Well: edited by G. K. Hunter
Antony and Cleopatra: edited by M. R. Ridley
As You Like It: edited by Agnes Latham
The Comedy of Errors: edited by R. A. Foakes
Coriolanus: edited by Philip Brockbank
Cymbeline: edited by J. M. Nosworthy
Hamlet: edited by Harold Jenkins
Julius Caesar: edited by T. S. Dorsch
King Henry IV, Parts 1 & 2: edited by A. R. Humphreys
King Henry V: edited by John H. Walter
King Henry VI, Parts 1, 2 & 3: edited by A. S. Cairncross
King Henry VIII: edited by R. A. Foakes
King John: edited by E. A. J. Honigmann
King Lear: edited by Kenneth Muir
King Richard II: edited by Peter Ure
King Richard III: edited by Antony Hammond
Love's Labour's Lost: edited by Richard David
Macbeth: edited by Kenneth Muir
Measure for Measure: edited by J. W. Lever
The Merchant of Venice: edited by John Russell Brown
The Merry Wives of Windsor: edited by H. J. Oliver
A Midsummer Night's Dream: edited by Harold F. Brooks
Much Ado About Nothing: edited by A. R. Humphreys
Othello: edited by M. R. Ridley
Pericles: edited by F. D. Hoeniger
The Poems: edited by F. T. Prince
Romeo and Juliet: edited by Brian Gibbons
The Taming of the Shrew: edited by Brian Morris
The Tempest: edited by Frank Kermode
Timon of Athens: edited by H. J. Oliver
Titus Andronicus: edited by J. C. Maxwell
Troilus and Cressida: edited by Kenneth Palmer
Twelfth Night: edited by J. M. Lothian and T. W. Craik
The Two Gentlemen of Verona: edited by Clifford Leech
The Winter's Tale: edited by J. H. P. Pafford

THE ARDEN EDITION OF THE WORKS OF WILLIAM SHAKESPEARE

THE SECOND PART OF KING HENRY VI

Edited by
ANDREW S. CAIRNCROSS

LONDON and NEW YORK

This edition of *King Henry VI, Part II*, by Andrew S. Cairncross,
first published in 1957 by
Methuen & Co. Ltd
Reprinted with minor corrections 1962
Reprinted 1965

First published as a University Paperback in 1969
Reprinted twice
Reprinted 1985

Reprinted 1988, 1994
by Routledge
11 New Fetter Lane, London EC4P 4EE
29 West 35th Street, New York, NY 10001

ISBN 0 416 47210 9 (hardback edition)
ISBN 0 415 02685 7 (paperback edition)

Printed in England by Clays Ltd, St Ives plc

CONTENTS

PREFACE

THE original Arden edition, by H. C. Hart, was based on premises so different from mine, as to the authorship of the play, the sources, the relation of the texts, and their authority, that very little of his has remained, even in the Notes. Collation has been automatically reduced, and a great deal of the Chronicle and other material more conveniently collected in the Appendices.

Hart worked on the fundamental assumptions of Edmond Malone's classic "Dissertation". No modern study of the play, however, can escape the influence of that other classic of the long-drawn controversy, Professor Peter Alexander's "Shakespeare's *Henry VI* and *Richard III*". Without his work, the research involved in this edition could never have been undertaken. I have had, in addition, the inestimable advantage of frequent discussions of the problem with him; and his pertinent questions have shaped even those modifications of his theory which I have felt impelled to adopt in its consolidation.

One such modification is the theory that the printers of the First Folio deliberately used one or more editions of the Bad Quarto, wherever feasible, as the "basis" for their text. This is essentially a new problem, and, in this untrodden country, I must crave the indulgence due to the explorer, and suspension of judgement from those to whom the altered landscape of the play and its textual history may seem a little strange. No one can be more conscious than myself how provisional are my conclusions, and how much remains to be done.

The state of the text, often corrupt beyond recovery, may, I hope, excuse and justify the attempts I have made where possible to restore at least something of what it must have been. In the nature of the case, many of the textual decisions have had to be of a personal kind, but I have tried to restrain within due limits the liberty of emendation that the situation seems to demand.

I owe a great debt to the painstaking and balanced criticism of my theories and material by Dr Harold Brooks; to many helpful suggestions and critical remarks from Dr J. C. Maxwell; and to Dr Ernst Honigmann for comments on the Introduction. Of Professor

Una Ellis-Fermor, I can only repeat Professor Kenneth Muir's remark, that she has been "all that a General Editor should be".

ANDREW S. CAIRNCROSS.

UDDINGSTON
GLASGOW
December 1954

NOTE TO THE 1962 REPRINT

I have taken this opportunity to make a few minor improvements and corrections.

I am now inclined to suggest that the MS. copy (cf. xxxii, xxxix, xlvii) was not Shakespeare's autograph, but a transcript of it, made for the F printers; and that the share assigned to compositor B may in fact have been set by another compositor, such as E.

A. S. C.

ABBREVIATIONS

Abbott	E. A. Abbott, *Shakespeare Grammar*, 1869.
Boswell-Stone	W. G. Boswell-Stone, *Shakespere's Holinshed*, 1896.
Brooke	Tucker Brooke, *King Henry the Sixth, Part Two* (Yale), 1923.
Chambers, *E.S.*	Sir Edmund K. Chambers, *The Elizabethan Stage*, 1923.
Chambers, *W.S.*	Sir Edmund K. Chambers, *William Shakespeare*, 1930.
Dodsley	*Old English Plays* (4th edn), edited by W. C. Hazlitt, 1874–6.
Fabyan	*The New Chronicles of England and France*, ed. Henry Ellis, 1811.
Fox	John Foxe, *Actes and Monuments*, repr. 1843–9.
Franz	W. Franz, *Shakespeare-Grammatik*, ed. 1909.
French	George R. French, *Shakespeareana Genealogica*, 1869.
Hall	Edward Hall, *Chronicle* (*Vnion of the two noble and illustre famelies of Lancastre & Yorke*), ed. 1809.
Hardyng	John Hardyng, *Chronicle* (continued by Grafton), ed. Henry Ellis, 1812.
Hart	H. C. Hart, *Henry VI* (Part 2), Arden edn, 1909, 1931.
Hol(inshed)	Raphael Holinshed, *Chronicles*, repr. 1807 (vol. 2), 1808 (vol. 3; vol. 4).
Homilies	*Certain Sermons or Homilies*, 1844.
Mirror	*The Mirror for Magistrates*, ed. Lily B. Campbell, 1938.
Mirror, Add.	*Parts added to The Mirror for Magistrates*, ed. Lily B. Campbell, 1946.
Noble	Richmond Noble, *Shakespeare's Biblical Knowledge*, 1935.
Onions	C. T. Onions, *A Shakespeare Glossary*, ed. 1951.
Partridge	Eric Partridge, *Shakespeare's Bawdy*, 1947.
Rothery	Guy Cadogan Rothery, *The Heraldry of Shakespeare*, 1930.
Schmidt	Alexander Schmidt, *Shakespeare-Lexicon*, 1886.
Scott-Giles	C. W. Scott-Giles, *Shakespeare's Heraldry*, 1950.
Sh. Lib.	*Shakespeare's Library*, ed. W. C. Hazlitt, 1875.
Sternhold and Hopkins	*The whole Book of Psalms* (in metre), ed. 1628.
Sugden	Edward H. Sugden, *A Topographical Dictionary to the Works of Shakespeare and his Fellow Dramatists*, 1925.
Wilson	J. Dover Wilson, *Henry VI* (New Shakespeare), 1952.
CP.	*Book of Common Prayer.*
MP.	*Modern Philology.*
OED.	*Oxford English Dictionary.*

Ph. Q.	*Philological Quarterly.*
PMLA.	*Publications of the Modern Language Association of America.*
RES.	*Review of English Studies.*
SB.	*Studies in Bibliography* (University of Virginia).
Trans. N.S.S.	*Transactions of the New Shakespere Society.*

Elizabethan authors are cited from the following editions:

Greene	Plays: J. C. Collins, Oxford, 1905.
	Prose: A. B. Grosart (Huth Library), 1881–3.
Jonson	C. H. Herford, Percy and Evelyn Simpson, Oxford, 1925–50.
Kyd	F. S. Boas, Oxford, 1901.
Lyly	R. W. Bond, Oxford, 1902.
Marlowe	C. F. Tucker Brooke, Oxford, 1910.
Nashe	R. B. McKerrow, Oxford, 1904–10.
Peele	Alexander Dyce, 1828–39.
Shakespeare	William Aldis Wright, Macmillan, 2nd edn. 1891–3.
Spenser	J. C. Smith and E. de Selincourt, Oxford, 1912.

The abbreviations for Shakespeare's plays, and customary terms, are from Onions's *Shakespeare Glossary.*

INTRODUCTION

I. HISTORICAL

THE TEXTS

The three parts of *Henry VI* were originally published, as we know them, in the first collected edition of Shakespeare's plays, the First Folio (F), in 1623. The general entry in the Stationers' Register, however, did not include the second and third parts. Entry was probably considered unnecessary because of the previous appearance of an inferior version of each, in quarto form (Q).[1] The quarto of the second part was entered on 12 March 1594, and published the same year by Thomas Millington under what must have been its original title:

> THE / Firſt part of the Con- / tention betwixt the two famous Houſes of Yorke / and Lancaſter, with the death of the good / Duke Humphrey: / And the baniſhment and death of the Duke of / *Suffolke*, and the Tragicall end of the proud Cardinall / of *Wincheſter*, with the notable Rebellion / of *Iacke Cade: / And the Duke of Yorkes firſt claime vnto the / Crowne.* / [device] / LONDON / Printed by Thomas Creed, for Thomas Millington, / and are to be ſold at his ſhop vnder Saint Peters / Church in Cornwall. / 1594.

The following year, 1595, the same publisher, without entry, issued a similar inferior version of the third part as:

> The true Tragedie of Richard / *Duke of Yorke, and the death of* / good King Henrie the Sixt, / *with the whole contention betweene* / the two Houſes Lancaſter / and Yorke, as it was ſundrie times / acted by the Right Honour- / able the Earle of Pem- / brooke his ſeruants./ [device] / Printed at London by P. S. for Thomas Milling- / *ton, and are to be ſold at his ſhoppe vnder / Saint Peters Church in / Cornwal.* 1595.

These versions may be called for convenience *The Contention*

1. Copyright was at that date secured by entry in the Stationers' Register, and belonged to the entering printer or publisher, not to the author or acting company. See e.g. A. W. Pollard, *Shakespeare's Fight with the Pirates* (1917; *Shakespeare Problems Series*, 1920, 1937), p. 33.

(*Cont.*) and *The True Tragedy* (*Tr. Tr.*). A second quarto (Q2) of each was issued in 1600 for Millington without material alteration. In 1602 Millington assigned the copyright to Thomas Pavier, who brought out a third (undated) edition[1] (Q3) in 1619, this time with the two parts combined under the title of *The Whole Contention*, as part of an attempt to publish a pirated collection of plays, mainly Shakespeare's.[2] Jaggard was the printer, as he was of the First Folio.

COMPARISON OF THE TEXTS

We may anticipate by saying that *The Contention* (Q) shows all the characteristics we now associate with reported texts, or "bad quartos". The main structure and the characters are, with minor exceptions, the same. Q is about one-third shorter, and lacks many passages present in F; and F lacks some passages present in Q. A few passages, I suggest, are alternatives, and have been rewritten, probably at the censor's request; while the remainder of the Q text varies from verbal identity to paraphrase of F.[3] The order of words, lines, and whole passages, often varies considerably. Q often makes nonsense of complicated speeches; is inferior in metre, grammar, syntax, and dramatic effect; and substitutes phrases "recollected" from other plays. F contains "authorial" stage-directions, and the names of *Bevis* and *John Holland*, probably those of actors, occur in the stage-direction at IV. ii. 1. There is an occasional change due to the Act of Abuses of 1606, e.g. *Ioue* for *God* at IV. x. 57. F is thus likely to have been derived from a stage manuscript, possibly Shakespeare's autograph; Q to be a "memorial" version of the text as Shakespeare originally handed it over, but modified by a number of "cuts" to reduce the acting time or the cast of the play. The same is true, substantially, of the relation between *The True Tragedy* and *3 Henry VI*, except that there is little or no rewriting due to censorship or other causes.

THEORIES OF F AND Q

The two main theories of the relation between F and Q are based on revision and mutilation respectively. The revision theory argues that Q, the text of which is generally admitted to be corrupt, repre-

1. The First Folio and its text will be referred to as F (subsequent Folios are derivative); the first, second, and third quartos as Q1, Q2, and Q3, and all together as Q (where the texts are identical). Q1 is quoted from the *Cambridge Shakespeare* (1891–3), vol. IX, by page only.

2. See Pollard, *Shakespeare Folios and Quartos* (1909); Chambers, *W.S.*, I. 133 ff; R. Crompton Rhodes, *Shakespeare's First Folio* (1923), chap. 3.

3. For illustrative parallel passages, see below, pp. xxii, xxviii, xxx–xxxvi and Appendices 4 and 5.

sents an original two-part play which was later revised by Shakespeare to produce the F text. Revisionists differ as to the original author or authors, but find them in the group comprising Greene, Nashe, Marlowe, and Shakespeare himself; Shakespeare's alleged revision, i.e. F, being written either single-handed, or with the assistance of one or more of the others. The mutilation theory, on the other hand, maintains that F represents Shakespeare's original composition, of which Q is merely a reported and debased version. Both theories, as will appear, contain elements of truth, but neither has yet accounted adequately, or with general acceptance, for all the peculiar features of the texts and their relation to each other.

THE REVISION THEORY

Already in 1725 Pope, in the Preface to his "Shakespeare", had assumed that the quarto versions of *The Merry Wives*, *Henry V*, and *Hamlet* had been "new writ, improved, or enlarged" in their F equivalents. In 1734, Theobald extended this revision theory to *Henry VI* (for the First Part of which, however, there is no quarto) on the ground of style.[1] In this he was following the trail blazed by Edward Ravenscroft in 1687, when he said of *Titus Andronicus*, "I have been told by some anciently conversant with the stage, that it was not originally his, but brought by a private author to be acted and he only gave it some master-touches to one or two of the principal parts or characters." Warburton (1747) even held that *Henry VI* was "certainly not Shakespeare's".[2] Farmer, in his "Essay on the Learning of Shakespeare" (1767), applied similar phrases to *The Taming of the Shrew* (allegedly based on *The Taming of A Shrew*) —"re-touched and polished"; and thought *1 Henry VI* to be "previous to our author".[3]

JOHNSON AND TYRWHITT

A reaction, in favour of the mutilation theory, came with Dr Johnson, who answered Theobald and Warburton thus: "From mere inferiority nothing can be inferred; in the productions of wit there will be inequality . . . the diction, the versification, and the figures, are Shakespeare's."[4] Affirmatively, he asserted what, with the substitution of "actor" for "auditor", has become the modern, memorial, version of the theory; "there is no reason for supposing them [the quartos] the first drafts of Shakespeare. I am inclined to believe them copies taken down by some auditor who wrote down,

1. In Boswell's *Malone*, xviii. 557–97; 3. 2. *Ibid.*, 548.
3. See Nichol Smith, *Eighteenth Century Essays on Shakespeare*.
4. Boswell's *Malone*, xviii. 548–9.

during the representation, what the time would permit, then perhaps filled up some of his omissions at a second or third hearing."[1] This idea seemed to be confirmed by a reference in Heywood[2] to the use of shorthand in the reporting of his plays. Further confirmation was discovered the following year by Tyrwhitt[3] in the famous attack on Shakespeare, in which Robert Greene parodied a line from *3 Henry VI*. So complete did the case for mutilation now seem that Edmond Malone, who was later to become the champion of revision, accepted the theory.[4]

GREENE'S ATTACK ON SHAKESPEARE

Greene's allusion appeared in 1592 in his pamphlet entitled:

> *Greenes, Groats-worth of witte, bought with a million of Repentance. Describing the follie of youth, the falshood of make-shifte flatterers, the miserie of the negligent, and mischiefes of deceiuing Courtezans. Written before his death and published at his dyeing request.*

This pamphlet contains a letter headed:

> *To those Gentlemen his Quondam acquaintance, that spend their wits in making plaies, R. G. wisheth a better exercise, and wisdome to preuent his extremities.*

Greene addresses himself particularly to three playwrights. Though he does not name them explicitly, he provides allusions that make identification reasonably certain. The first is Marlowe, the "famous gracer of Tragedians"; the second, "yong *Iuuenall*, that byting Satyrist, that lastly with mee together writ a Comedie", is probably Nashe (but may be Lodge); while the third is identified by the phrase "by sweet S. George" as George Peele. All three are warned, from Greene's own experience, not to depend on playmaking and the players, who have deserted him in his extremity. "Trust not then (I beseech ye)", he concludes, "to such weake staies; for they are as changeable in minde, as in many attyres."

The venom of Green's invective, however, is reserved for Shakespeare, the actor who not only belongs to that unreliable profession, but has even had the audacity to write plays himself. The style of these plays is ridiculed by the quotation, or rather parody, of a line from one of them, *3 Henry VI*. His three friends are warned particularly against this "upstart":

> Base minded men all three of you, if by my miserie you be not

1. *Ibid.*, 549. 2. *Ibid.*, 549–50. 3. *Ibid.*, 551–2.
4. "An Attempt to Ascertain the Order of Shakespeare's Plays." First version, in Steevens's *Shakespeare* (1778), vol. i. Revised edition (1787, 1790) in Boswell's *Malone*, ii. 288 ff.

> warnd: for unto none of you (like mee) sought those burres to cleaue: those Puppets (I meane) that spake from our mouths, those Anticks garnisht in our colours. Is it not strange, that I, to whom they all haue beene beholding: is it not like that you, to whome they all haue been beholding, shall (were yee in that case as I am now) bee both at once of them forsaken? Yes trust them not: for there is an vpstart Crow, beautified with our feathers, that with his *Tygers hart wrapt in a Players hyde*, supposes he is as well able to bombast out a blanke verse as the best of you: and beeing an absolute *Iohannes fac totum*, is in his owne conceit the onely Shake-scene in a countrey . . . whilest you may, seeke you better Maisters; for it is pittie men of such rare wits, should be subiect to the pleasure of such rude groomes.[1]

Greene then passes on to warn two more of his friends, and any others who may be tempted to take up his profession, against the actors:

> In this I might insert two more, that both haue writ against these buckram Gentlemen: but lette their owne workes serue to witnesse against their owne wickednesse, if they perseuere to maintaine any more such peasants. For other new-comers, I leaue them to the mercie of these painted monsters, who (I doubt not) will driue the best minded to despise them: for the rest, it skils not though they make a ieast at them.

Greene, as Professor Alexander points out,[2] and as Tyrwhitt understood, was simply repeating a long-standing grievance against the actors, a grievance he had previously expressed, in 1590, in his *Neuer Too Late*, using almost the same terms:

> Why *Roscius*, art thou proud with *Esops* Crow, being pranct with the glorie of others feathers? of thy selfe thou canst say nothing, and if the Cobler hath taught thee to say *Aue Caesar*, disdain not thy tutor, because thou pratest in a Kings chamber.

Roscius, the actor, is here also a crow, "beautified with our feathers", or "garnished in our colours", and of himself can say nothing, but is one of the "Puppets that spake from our mouths"—the mouths of the dramatists, who like the cobbler and Greene, supply words for his use. Greene's attack, then, was directed against Shakespeare, first as a member of a profession he disliked, and, second, as a dramatist who wrote plays like *3 Henry VI*.[3]

1. G. B. Harrison's reprint: Bodley Head Quartos, 45–6.
2. *Shakespeare's* Henry VI *and* Richard III (Cambridge, 1929), p. 43.
3. For a different view, see pp. xlii–xlv below.

MALONE'S "DISSERTATION"

All discussion of the problem of *Henry VI* must revolve round the classic "Dissertation",[1] the first real critical examination of a Shakespearean textual question. Here Malone, "after a more minute investigation" made in the course of editing Shakespeare's plays as a whole, returned to the earlier revisionist position. He found in the *Henry VI* plays the same inequality as Theobald and Warburton had done. He knew that Johnson had pronounced that from inequality no certain conclusion can be drawn. He went beyond the scope of Johnson's objection, however, to say that "the inferior parts are not only unequal to the rest . . . , but of a quite different complexion from the inferior parts of our author's undoubted performances."[2] He had no difficulty in showing that the Q versions could not be wholly accounted for as reports made by a shorthand writer or auditor during performances, as Johnson had suggested. The differences of length and matter were too substantial. He noted also a considerable number of inconsistencies—in the use of the chroniclers, in the knowledge of the classics displayed, and in references to matters of fact.

The "chief hinge" of his argument, however, was a re-interpretation, in the directly opposite sense from Tyrwhitt's, of Greene's allusion as a charge of plagiarism against Shakespeare. The quartos must therefore, he now argued, be older plays revised (and partly appropriated) by Shakespeare. The line that Greene parodied, in *3 Henry VI*, I. iv. 137,

Oh Tygres Heart, wrapt in a Womans Hide,

appeared also in *The True Tragedy*, and, since this could no longer be considered to be Shakespeare's, must have been originally Greene's own. Malone's solution of the problem, and his interpretation of Greene, he states thus:

> Greene and Peele were the joint authors of the two quarto plays . . . or . . . Greene was the author of one, and Peele of the other. . . Shakespeare having therefore new-modelled and amplified these two pieces and produced on the stage . . . The Second and Third Parts of King Henry VI and having acquired considerable reputation by them, Greene could not conceal the mortification . . . at his fame . . . being eclipsed by a new *upstart* writer . . . He . . . in direct terms, charges him with having acted like the crow in the fable, *beautified with their feathers*; in other

1. 1787; and in his Shakespeare (1790) and in Boswell's *Malone* (1821), xviii. 557–97.

2. *Ibid.*, 570.

> words, with having acquired fame *furtivis coloribus*, by new-modelling a work originally produced by them, and wishing to depreciate our author, he very naturally quotes a line from one of the pieces which Shakespeare had thus *re-written*; a proceeding which the authors of the original plays considered as an invasion of their literary property and character. This line, with many others, Shakespeare adopted without any alteration. The very term that Greene uses—"to *bombast* out a blank verse", exactly corresponds with what has now been suggested. This new poet, says he, knows as well as any man how to *amplify* and swell out a blank verse.[1]

Later, and probably under the influence of Farmer, Malone inclined to Marlowe as "the author of one, if not both, of the old dramas" (i.e. the quartos).[2]

In spite of some able protests and counterblasts, notably those of Knight,[3] Kenny,[4] and Schmidt,[5] Malone's theory of revision, in one or other of its modifications or aspects, held the field throughout the nineteenth century. The most elaborate study was that of Jane Lee,[6] who went so far as to allocate the text among the various claimants—Greene, Peele, and Marlowe—and ascribed the revision to Shakespeare and Marlowe. Of later editors, H. C. Hart[7] gave Shakespeare himself a hand, as well as Greene, Peele, and Marlowe, in the "syndicate"; and thought that Q was not itself the original version, but a garbled and imperfect reproduction of it. Tucker Brooke[8] extended the list of parallel phrases between Marlowe's plays and the two texts of *Henry VI*. On this basis, he revived Malone's later argument in favour of Marlowe's authorship of the quartos, or rather the lost texts of which they were thought to be corruptions. He contended that the treatment of plot, metre, and character were Marlowe's only, and that Shakespeare was responsible only for the F material that is not present in Q. He also laid stress on the variations introduced in the 1619 edition (Q3) of *The Whole Contention*, variations that often tended towards the F text. These, he argued, must have been due to the possession by the printer of a better copy of Marlowe's original, and were difficult to account for on any other hypothesis.

1. *Op. cit.*, xviii. 571. 2. Boswell's *Malone*, ii. 311 ff.
3. *Pictorial Shakespeare* (1839), vii. 399.
4. *The Life and Genius of Shakespeare* (1864). 5. *Anglia*, III (1880), pp. 1 ff.
6. *Trans. N.S.S.* (1875–6), 219–79. 7. Arden edn, 1909–10.
8. *Trans. Connecticut Acad. of Arts and Sciences* (July 1912), 17. 141–211; Appendices to *Yale Shakespeare*, 1923.

THE MEMORIAL THEORY

With the twentieth century, Shakespearean criticism was revolutionized by the work of A. W. Pollard and Sir Walter W. Greg. Using the now familiar methods of critical bibliography, they concentrated on the variant versions (quartos and folios) of certain plays. Pollard[1] made a useful working division of the Shakespearean quartos into good and bad. The good quartos, which agree substantially with F, he supposed to have emanated from the company itself; the bad, which are textually corrupt, he held to be pirated or surreptitious versions issued without authority. The bad quartos were those of *Romeo and Juliet* (Q1), *Henry V*, *The Merry Wives*, *Hamlet* (Q1), and *Pericles*. Sir Walter Greg followed this with a detailed study of the quarto of *The Merry Wives*,[2] and showed that it was an attempt at reconstruction from memory of the text found (with modifications) in the First Folio. He identified the probable reporter, or pirate, as the actor who had played the part of the Host.

Professor Peter Alexander,[3] developing the work of J. S. Smart,[4] was responsible for extending Greg's theory to *The Contention* and *The True Tragedy*, and finally establishing their true nature as bad quartos. His main thesis was that they could only be explained as "memorial" versions of *2* and *3 Henry VI*, and not as earlier plays (or reports of such plays) which were later revised by Shakespeare. QF parallels with the work of Greene, Peele, and Marlowe, on which the revision theory had argued for their authorship, could be simply accounted for as imitations of their work by Shakespeare, or of Shakespeare's by them; or by their common use of current stage vocabulary. Similar parallels found in Q only were "recollections" erroneously incorporated in their versions by reporters who had acted in plays by the various dramatists concerned, and whose memories had been deceived by false association of ideas and phrases. In addition, Professor Alexander thought that the reporters must have had in their possession certain transcripts—a few written "parts", such as the Armourer's (*2 Henry VI*, I. iii); scrolls containing, for example, the "articles" (I. i); and some pages of manuscript including stage-directions as well as dialogue. The Greene reference he explained in the sense first adopted by Tyrwhitt, as implying Shakespeare's authorship of *3 Henry VI*, and therefore, by implication, of *2 Henry VI*.

The occasion for the piracy could be deduced from the ascrip-

1. *Shakespeare Folios and Quartos*; *Shakespeare's Fight with the Pirates*.
2. Clarendon Press (1910). 3. *Op. cit.*
4. *Shakespeare: Truth and Tradition* (1929).

tion, on the title-page, of *The True Tragedy* to Pembroke's Men. That company is known, from a letter of 29 September 1593 of Henslowe to Alleyn,[1] to have failed about six weeks before. They had been prevented, by the plague, from acting in London during part of 1592 and 1593, and been forced to travel in the provinces, where they were unable to make their expenses. Some of the plays known to have been theirs, or versions of them, including *The True Tragedy* and *The Contention*, were published soon after, or appeared in the repertory of the Lord Chamberlain's Men.[2] It seems likely, therefore, that Pembroke's Men were forced to part with their "books" as well as their apparel. The Q versions may thus have been compiled to sell to a printer, or to enable some of the company to try their luck again for a time in the provinces, or both. The actors responsible for the piracies probably played the parts of Warwick, and of Suffolk doubled with Clifford, these being the best reported.

The memorial thesis has been generally accepted.[3] On details however, there has been some disagreement, chiefly concerning the use by the reporters of transcript material, the rôles of the reporters in *2* and *3 Henry VI*, the substantial variants between Q and F, and the purpose and occasion of the piracy.

Sir E. K. Chambers[4] justifiably remarked that he did not "see any evidence for a fragmentary transcript, or know why any such document should come into existence". He thought the reporter might have had the short "part" of the Citizen (IV. v), and on the whole was inclined to suggest that the reporter was a "book-keeper", rather than Warwick and Suffolk-Clifford, whose parts were not so much better rendered than those of the other characters. McKerrow,[5] followed later by Greg,[6] suggested that the identical, but defective, passages in F and Q were due, not to the use of transcripts, but to an attempt by the printer of F, where his "copy" was illegible, to print from an edition of Q. John E. Jordan,[7] after a detailed statistical examination of the accuracy with which the speeches of the various characters of *2 Henry VI* are reported in *The Contention*, came to the conclusion that the reporter was "the bit player who took the parts of Armourer-Spirit-Mayor-Vaux-Scales". How, he asks, could leading actors of Pembroke's Men "break", pawn their apparel, remain in London for six weeks, and then patch up a version of a play they knew, take it on tour in the

1. Chambers, *W.S.*, 2. 314. 2. *Ibid.*, 319.
3. An exception is C. T. Prouty, *The Contention and Shakespeare's "2 Henry VI"*, 1954.
4. *Op. cit.*, 1. 283. 5. *RES.* (1937), 13. 64–72.
6. *Ed. Pr.*, xvi. 7. *PMLA.* (1949), 45–6.

provinces, return to London, and sell their play, all in six months? "A single bit player", on the other hand, "could have reported the play for a new company of provincial actors as well as for a printer" and would be more interested than the major players of a company in the £2 or so that a printer would give for his version.

Madeleine Doran,[1] who, almost simultaneously with Professor Alexander, advocated the memorial nature of *The Contention*, suggested that it might have been put together, quite legitimately, by a section of the company travelling in the provinces without a prompt-book. Her main attention was directed to a group of passages where memorial report was inadequate as an explanation of the relationship of the texts. Here she found "verse printed as prose, prose printed as verse, and, chiefly, verse wrongly divided—which indicate revision in the text itself". In almost all of these "revisional areas" the material was the same in Q and F, but the wording differed. They included the "petitioner" scene (I. iii), the conjuring scene (I. iv), the hawking-Simpcox scene (II. i), and some of the Cade scenes (IV. ii, v, vi, vii). Revision must have been done, she thought, on the prompt-book, and some of it in the margin, so that the printer found it difficult to reproduce the correct lineation. In short, she combined in her theory elements of both mutilation and revision.

PROFESSOR J. DOVER WILSON AND REVISION

While the main Shakespearean critics accepted, substantially, Professor Alexander's theory, there has remained a strong section of resistance, especially in America, among critics who considered the theory inadequate to account for certain features, in particular the use of different chronicles and the inconsistencies.[2] The main restatement of the revision theory has, however, come from Professor J. Dover Wilson.[3] Accepting the memorial theory, he has set aside Q and the FQ variants, and concentrated on the internal "inconsistencies" in F, and on a re-examination of Greene's attack.[4] He finds the three parts of *Henry VI* to be of composite authorship, by Greene (who did the "plotting") and Nashe, perhaps Peele, afterwards revised by Shakespeare. For this view he finds confirmation from parallels of phrase and style with the other works of the three original authors; from the inconsistencies of style, incident, use of the chronicles, and knowledge of the classics;

1. *Henry VI* (University of Iowa Studies, 1928), 28–9.
2. E.g. C. A. Greer, *PMLA.* (1933), 48. 655 ff; C. T. Prouty, *op. cit.*
3. New Shakespeare, *1, 2, and 3 Henry VI*, Cambridge, 1952; and see my review in *RES.*, IV (April 1953), 157–60.
4. *Shakespeare Survey*, IV. 56–68.

and from his clear establishment of the fact that Greene had in mind—as Malone saw—a passage in Horace's Third Epistle, in which a reference to the fable of the crow is used to convey a charge of literary plagiarism. Chettle's testimony to Shakespeare's "honesty",[1] Professor Wilson further argues, would be superfluous unless as a reply to a previous accusation of theft. That contemporaries so understood it he finds to be corroborated by the lines of R. B. in *Greene's Funerals*, published in February 1594:

> Greene, gave the ground, to all that wrote upon him,
> Nay more the men, that so Eclipst his fame:
> Purloynde his Plumes, can they deny the same?

The present position, then, is that both sides of the controversy have established something—the mutilation theory that Q is mainly a memorial version made by Pembroke's Men in 1593–4, compiled with the help of written material of some kind; the revision theory, that there are inconsistencies between F and Q not yet explained, and peculiarities of both which lie beyond the scope of mutilation. While this difference of opinion remains unresolved, the question of authorship is also in dispute.

II. TEXTUAL

THE COPY FOR Q

Is it, then, possible to reconcile the opposing theories? I offer the following brief outline of the origin and relations of the texts as a contribution to a more comprehensive solution of the problem. It depends on certain factors hitherto little or not at all noticed, namely (*a*) the sporadic use in the printing-house of Q3 (and perhaps Q2) as copy for parts of F, (*b*) the rewriting, at the command of the censor, or for other reasons, of about three hundred lines of the original text, after the performances reflected in Q, and (*c*) a recognition of Shakespeare's debt to Hall rather than Holinshed for his basic material, and of his simultaneous use of various chronicles.

Very few, I think, now deny that Q is a report of *2 Henry VI*—as it is substantially given in F—and by a group of actors who played in it. Q has all the recognized features of such a report—abbreviation, transposition of material, the use of synonyms, recollections external and internal; with inferior metre, and verse wrongly divided as prose.[2]

The external recollections[3] throw some light on what may be

1. See further, p. xliii below. 2. See the parallel extracts in Appendix 5.
3. Three are noted in the margin in Appendix 5; for others, and for explanation of their nature, see Appendix 3.

taken as the repertoire of Pembroke's Men, or their predecessors, about 1592–3. They include items from *1* and *3 Henry VI*, *Richard III*, *The Spanish Tragedy*, *Arden of Faversham*, and *Edward II*; which suggests that Shakespeare, Kyd, and Marlowe were the chief dramatists then writing for the company. Other recollections can be traced to various sources, or belong to the stock dramatic vocabulary of the time; others, again, will no doubt be identified in future; while some may derive from plays now lost. One is of special interest as proving, what has been taken for granted, that the same group of actors was responsible for both *The Contention* and *The True Tragedy*, or that these versions had at least one reporter in common:

F:	Q:
Away my Lord . . .	*Away my Lord*, and flie to London straight,
We shall to London get . . .	*Make hast*, for vengeance comes along with them,
But fly you must . . .	Come *stand not to expostulate*, lets go.
2 Henry VI, v. ii. 72, 81, 86	*Contention*, 568
Away! for vengeance comes along with them: Nay, stay not to expostulate, make speed . . .	*Awaie my Lord* for vengeance comes along with him: Nay *stand not to expostulate make hast*, . . .
3 Henry VI, II. v. 134–5	*True Tragedy*, 602

The text familiar to the reporters had been "cut". A number of long F passages leave no trace at all in Q. This cutting was probably done by the author before the "parts" were issued to the actors, in order to shorten the play and lighten the task of the principal members of the cast. A good example is the elimination of the first half of York's speech, I. i. 215–36, which disappears entirely from Q, in favour of the second half, I. i. 237–60, which Q has reproduced almost perfectly. Nothing essential is lost by the omission; and it is interesting to note that the two sections begin with almost identical lines,[1] so that cutting was easy and continuity preserved. The cutting would be done, of course, in such a way as to leave the passages standing in the prompt-book, where they might be indicated only by marginal lines; and the marked passages would then be omitted by the scribe who made out the "parts" for

1. *Aniou* and *Maine* are given to the French, 215
Aniou and *Maine* both given unto the French? 237
For the same cutting device, cf. *R 3*, II. ii. 89–100.

the actors. In the same way, the cast has been reduced by the omission of a few minor characters, such as Southwell (I. iv) and the bishop who was sent to the rebels (IV. iv. 9).

THE Q3 VARIATIONS

Much has been made,[1] in support of a revision theory, of certain Q3 variants which are closer to F than is Q1 or Q2. For this reason, and also because of its probable relation to F as copy,[2] Q3 requires a brief notice here. Q2 was printed, naturally, from Q1, adding the usual quota of new errors and not always successful attempts to correct old ones. Collation shows that Q3 was likewise printed mainly, if not entirely, from Q1 and produced its own independent crop of variants. Pavier, it seems, was specially conscious of the defective nature of the text, and went to some trouble to have it improved. In particular, as C. A. Greer[3] has shown, the genealogy in II. ii was amended from the 1615 edition of Stow's *Chronicle*, but so unintelligently that several new errors were introduced, and few of the old eliminated. Throughout the text of Q3 there was, moreover, a consistent editorial effort to restore the lineation of verse that had been printed as prose, to regularize imperfect metre and modernize language. This tinkering[4] may be illustrated by the versions of III. ii. 28, which exemplify also the dependence of Q3 on Q1, and the unauthentic nature of the Q3 variants generally:

Q1: Dead in his bed, my Lord Gloster is dead.
Q2: Dead in his bed my Lord, Gloster is dead.
Q3: Dead in his bed, my Lord of Glosters dead.
F: Dead in his Bed, my Lord: Gloster is dead.

Or compare, at III. ii. 279:

Q12: Tell them we thank them all for (Q2 for all) their louing care,
Q3: Tell them we thanke them all for their kinde care,
F: I thanke them for their tender louing care.

All through the Q3 text, words are freely inserted, omitted, or altered in this way for metrical reasons.

Q1 inconsistencies, real or apparent, were dealt with by the same conjectural procedure. For example, where Q1 reads, II. i. 82–3 (*Cont.*, 525):

1. By Tucker Brooke, *loc. cit.* 2. See below, pp. xxiii ff.
3. *PMLA.* (1933), 48. 655–704.
4. This is a consistent feature of plays in the 1619 Pavier collection. Many of the modernizations were taken into F. The matter requires detailed study.

King. Thou . . . thee.
Humphrey. Where wast thou borne?
Poore man. At *Barwicke*, sir, in the North.

the prefix "*Humphrey*." was accidentally omitted in the printing of Q3, and his speech was continued to the King. The editor, therefore, thought it necessary to alter "sir", in the following line, to "please your Maiesty". Q3 thus reads:

King: Thou . . . thee:
Where wast thou borne?
Poore man. At *Barwicke* please your Maiesty in the North.

Some such error or misunderstanding must, it would seem, be responsible for the peculiar substitution of York for Winchester at I. i. 56–7:

Q12: Vnckle of *Winchester*, I pray you reade on.
Cardinall. . .
Q3: My Lord of Yorke, I pray do you reade on.
Yorke. . .

When faced by gaps in the type of its Q1 copy, or gaps arising in the press,[1] Q3 might either acknowledge defeat, and print, as at II. iv. 73 (Q1 This is sodeine.) "This is ——"; or it might hazard a bold but quite unauthoritative conjecture (v. ii. 66), thus—

Q12: So Lie thou there, and breathe thy last.
Q3: So, Lie thou there, and tumble in thy blood,

The only other major variations, confined mainly to the first two acts, cannot be so accounted for. There are two complete lines, and two short passages, which fit into their context; they are versions of material present in F, and have therefore some *prima facie* claim to authenticity. It would seem, however, as if Pavier or Jaggard either reverted to the original manuscript from which Q1 had been printed, or used an example of Q1, not now extant, in which these lines, omitted by the printer, had been re-inserted by a press-corrector. The suggestion of omission in printing is strengthened by the similarity of words or letters before and after the omissions. The printer's eye, as often happened, passed from the first to the second, omitting the intervening matter. The first passage (I. ii. 25 ff; *Cont.*, 514), reads:

Q1: . . . in two, and on . . .
Q3: . . . in twa[ine by whom I cannot gesse:

1. Cf. also III. ii. 224: thee downe Q3; thy soule Q1, 2, F; and IV. x. 82: beare it Q1; beare it with me. Q2; beare it to the King Q3; beare . . . to the King. F.

But as I thinke by the Cardinall. What it bodes
God knowes;] and on the ends were plac'd
The heads of *Edmund* Duke of *Somerset*,
And *William de la Pole* first Duke of *Suffolke*.

In Elizabethan script, the *aine* or *ine* of *twaine* would be hardly distinguishable from *and*, and, especially if, as is likely, they occurred at the same point in the line, the transition would be easy. A similar explanation could cover the second passage (I. ii. 61 ff; *Cont.*, 515) with its repetition of "go before". Of the single lines, one, I. iii. 80, is in F, slightly modified, and is almost certainly authentic; the other[1] may be memorial.

Even though it may be doubtful, therefore, what exact cause led to this or that variation in Q3, the general attempt of the publishers to improve their text in such ways as are suggested above seems an adequate explanation. To seek there for evidence of a general revision or recourse to a better copy, as does, for example, Tucker Brooke, is quite fruitless. Q is basically a report; and Q1, with the possible addition of the major variations just mentioned, the substantive Q text.

The Q text, however, does not consist entirely of reported matter. At some points F and Q are bibliographically much too close for that; at others they differ too substantially. These resemblances and differences have never been satisfactorily explained within a consistent theory of the texts; and it is this failure, as much as anything, that accounts for the vitality of the revision hypothesis.

CENSORSHIP

The variations of substance that so troubled Malone and still hamper progress towards a solution of the problem may be set down quite simply to the action of the censor as the main agent. This action might come from either of two sources—the censorship of printing, or the censorship of the theatre. The ecclesiastical authorities, under the Privy Council, dealt with printing, and took stringent action against the publication of political and religious matter likely to be offensive to church and state, not sparing books already in print.[2] This action was later supplemented by the Act of Abuses of 1606, which required the purging of oaths. Authors and publishers, of course, might anticipate censorship here, and do their own purging. This seems to have been done, though most imperfectly, with the F text of *2 Henry VI*.[3] Q, how-

1. See collation at III. i. 359.
2. See e.g. Pollard, *Shakespeare's Fight*, and A. Hart, *Shakespeare and the Homilies*, 154–218.
3. See notes to IV. x. 57, V. iii. 29.

ever, seems to have escaped censorship in the press, though it is perhaps noteworthy that after 1600 it was not reprinted for nineteen years. The main F variants obviously derive from a period long before publication in 1623, and it is therefore to theatrical censorship, as exercised by the Master of the Revels, that we must look for their explanation.

It would seem that the degree of theatrical censorship varied with the political and religious atmosphere of the time. Between 1593 and 1595 (probably), we have the well-known example of *Sir Thomas More*. On the manuscript submitted to him, Edmund Tilney, the Master of the Revels, wrote at the top of the first page, "leave out ye insurrection wholy and ye cause theroff, and begin with Sir Tho. Moore at ye mayors sessions, with a reportt afterwardes off his good service don. being shrive off London, uppon a mutiny agaynst ye Lumbardes, only by a shortt reportt, and nott otherwise, att your own perilles. E. Tyllney."[1] The insurrection scene, however, as Brooke points out, and the other parts to which Tilney took exception, were not left out, but merely recast, generally by pasting a new version over the old. Apart from the theme of insurrection to which Tilney objected, a number of reflections on the Court and a reference to the "netherland of hell" offer a sufficient explanation. One can imagine Queen Elizabeth's attitude to the lines (IV. iv. 79 ff):

> As for the prince in all his sweet-gorgde mawe,
> And his ranck fleshe, that sinfully renewes
> The noones excesse in the nights dangerous surfeits . . .

A similar period of suppression seems to have affected both the press and the stage about 1599–1600. Already, in or before 1597, the "abdication" scene in *Richard II* had been removed, probably on the stage as well as in the early quartos.[2] Most of the excisions from *2 Henry IV* (1600) refer to Richard II and his fate, and contained matter and situations that could be applied too easily to Elizabeth's own circumstances.[3] Members of the nobility seem also to have brought their influence to bear towards excision of unflattering references to their ancestors or namesakes. The best-known case is that of the alteration, imperfect, of *Oldcastle* to *Falstaff*, and *Brooke* to *Broome*, in deference to the family of Cobham.[4] A parallel, probably under James I, may be found in the total excision of the

1. *Shakespeare Apoc.*, xlvii ff and 418 ff. Cf. *Barnavelt* (ed. Frijlinck), xviii–xxiii; *Game at Chesse* (ed. Bald), Intro., pp. 19–25.

2. Hart, *op. cit.*, 158–9. 3. *Ibid.*, 187 ff.

4. Cf. Hart, *op. cit.*, 184, and *3 H 6*, I. ii. 40, where "to Edmund Brooke, Lord Cobham" (Q), is reduced to "vnto my Lord Cobham" (F).

"clock" passage in *Richard III*,[1] where Buckingham (James's favourite's title) was slighted by the king.

An examination of the variant QF passages[2] in *2 Henry VI* suggests that many probably originated from the same cause, at one or more of such periods of intensive censorship. Q shows that the original versions reached the stage and remained unaltered probably until the end of 1593 at least Some of them thereafter disappeared entirely, and must have been very thoroughly deleted or pasted over in the prompt-book,[3] since there is no trace of them in F, just as there is no memorial trace of the F variants in Q. Such are the indecent passages in IV. ii and IV. vii; and the reference to the bastardy of Winchester in II. i,[4] the absence of which leaves a gap in the metre. Most of the others touch obvious danger-points politically, or use language that might be considered derogatory to the Queen, the Court, or certain members of the nobility. And in almost every case the F, or later, version (when there is one) says much the same thing, at the same length, but in a more harmless way—which suggests that the entire disappearance of the Q version from the F text was due to the same method of revision as in *Sir Thomas More*, the pasting in of a slip of paper containing the new lines. The danger-points included Ireland (then in rebellion), claims to the Crown, the question of succession, threats of rebellion, and references to particular noble families (e.g. Buckingham[5]) in particular connections, and places with unpleasant associations for the Queen, such as Kenilworth.[6] Compare, for example, the "wild Onele" passage, with its suggestion that the Queen (or King) was not taking strong enough measures to prevent English bloodshed in Ireland; the question of York's rebellion; the participation of Eleanor Cobham[7] in the conjuring and conspiracy and the insulting treatment of her afterwards; the general attitude of the characters to King Henry; the replacement of Buckingham by Suffolk in the unpopular business of levying soldiers for Ireland;[8] and the elimination of the Queen's responsibility for the levies and for Humphrey's murder and for receiving Suffolk's head.

The recasting may be adequately illustrated by one short passage, V. ii. 19–30:

1. IV. ii. 103–20; and see Griffin in *RES.* (1937), 13. 329.

2. See Appendix 4.

3. I make no distinction, for *2 H 6*, between prompt-book and "foul papers"; see below, pp. xxxii ff.

4. Cf. a similar deletion in Fabyan, 533; Winchester was, of course, one of Queen Elizabeth's ancestors.

5. Cf. above.

6. Cf. the excision of the Richmond reference in *R 3*, IV. ii. 103–20; and Griffin in *RES.* (1937), 13. 329.

7. Cf. p. xxvi above.

8. Cf. Hart, *op. cit.*, 207.

Q:[1]

Yorke. Now, Clifford, since we are singled here alone,
Be this the day of doome to one of vs,
For now my heart hath sworne immortall hate
To thee and all the house of Lancaster.
Cliffood. And here I stand, and pitch my foot to thine,
Vowing neuer to stir, till thou or I be slaine,
For neuer shall my heart be safe at rest,
Till I haue spoild the hatefull house of Yorke.
Alarmes, and they fight, and *Yorke* kils *Clifford*.
Yorke. Now Lancaster sit sure, thy sinowes shrinke,
Come fearefull Henry grouelling on thy face,
Yeeld vp thy Crowne vnto the Prince of Yorke.
Exet Yorke.

F:

Clif. What seest thou in me Yorke?
Why dost thou pause?
Yorke. With thy braue bearing should I be in loue,
But that thou art so fast mine enemie.
Clif. Nor should thy prowesse want praise & esteeme,
But that 'tis shewne ignobly, and in Treason.
Yorke. So let it helpe me now against thy sword,
As I in iustice, and true right expresse it.
Clif. My soule and bodie on the action both.
Yor. A dreadfull lay, addresse thee instantly.
Clif. *La fin Corrone les eumenes*.
Yor. Thus Warre hath giuen thee peace, for y[u] art still,
Peace with his soule, heauen if it be thy will.

Allowing for the division of the first F line by the printer, the two versions will be seen to consist of twelve lines each, and to be to the same general effect. The mutual insults of Q have, however, disappeared, with their mutual hate, and with them the insult to the King, and the whole question of yielding the crown. In their place, we have expressions of antagonism, but qualified by mutual compliments. There is much virtue in a "But that". It may be noted, further, that F has not troubled to insert the necessary stage-directions[2] and that the F passage is correctly divided. The pasting of a new slip over the older text in the prompt-book seems to be the natural explanation of all the phenomena.

While many of the variant passages can be reasonably ascribed to censorship, other factors may have had some influence. It is difficult, for example, to see any reason for censorship in the alteration

1. *Camb. Sh.* vol. ix, p. 567.

2. Cf. the *marginal* insertion of the S.D. at III. ii. 5, where similar recasting has occurred, and the superfluous inclusion of Suffolke in the S.D. at III. ii. 13.

of Margaret's lines at I. i. 24–31, and it is much more likely, in this case, that nothing more is involved than vamping by the Q reporters, and that the variations are merely "recollections" from other plays.[1] However that may be, there is no doubt that most of these passages have been substantially altered in form, and that the Q version was unacquainted with that of F, of which it bears no trace, even memorial. The simplest explanation, and the only one that seems to fit all the facts, is the radical alteration of the prompt-book.

The total extent of the alterations was rather less than 300 lines. Neither from its extent, nor from the nature of the variants, can this be called revision in any literary or dramatic sense. There is no apparent dramatic point, and no substantial alteration to plot or character, although the process of alteration has indeed left a few "inconsistencies" in the play. And if, as seems likely, the changes were made to order, there is still less ground for speaking of revision.

TRANSCRIPTION

The Q text has one other remarkable feature. At a number of points, it shows such close bibliographical links with F that the two must have had some common basis of transcription. Transcription includes, as McKerrow pointed out,[2] both copying by hand, and setting up in type of one text from another. The question is, what kind, or kinds of transcription?

Possession by the reporters of manuscript material, in the form of "parts", scrolls, or transcripts of pages of the text, was suggested by Professor Peter Alexander.[3] He indicated three longer passages in particular—II. i. 114–49; II. iii. 59–102; and IV. v. 1 to IV. vi. 6—which are almost identical in stage-directions and in speeches by a number of characters *in succession*; and a few similar fragments, such as the articles of peace (I. i), the questions to the Spirit and the answers (I. iv), part of York's speech (I. i. 237–60), the Armourer's part (I. iii), the five lines addressed by Duke Humphrey to Eleanor (II. iv. 10–14), and an isolated stage-direction (II. i. 67).

The written material available to the reporters, however, was almost certainly confined to the second, or uncut, half of York's speech, I. i. 237–60. This document—the actor's "part"—was slightly defective,[4] the third line ending "fertill England" (Q) instead of "fertile Englands soile" (F). That this was the version the

1. See Appendix 4; note e.g. poore Margaret, *3 H 6*, III. iii. 30, *R 3*, I. iii. 30; lauish . . . tongue *1 Tamb.*, 1511, *Arden*, IV. iv. 155, *1 H 6*, II. v. 47; England's king *2 H 6*, I. iv. 46, II. ii. 62, etc.

2. *RES.* (1937), 13. 64.

3. *Op. cit.*, 82 ff.

4. I attribute this to an omission by the scribe who wrote out the "part".

reporter knew seems to be confirmed by his repetition of the same version of the phrase, in error, at III. i. 87–8:

(*a*) I. i. 238–9:

Q: Cold newes for me, for I had hope of *France*,
Even as I have of fertill England.
F: Cold newes for me: for I had hope of France,
Even as I have of fertile Englands soile.

(*b*) III. i. 87–8:

Q: Cold newes for me, for I had hope of France,
Even as I have of fertill England.
F: Cold Newes for me: for I had hope of France,
As firmly as I hope for fertile England.

This possible possession of a copy of one of his speeches suggests that York should be added to the number of the reporters. A review of his performance throughout Q, with due allowance for possible "cuts", and for the heavy and complicated matter of many of his speeches, tends to corroborate the suggestion. If, alternatively, his speech is memorial,[1] it is, on any theory, good enough to justify the same conclusion.

The other "transcript" passages, however, do not agree as closely as one is entitled to expect, even after allowing for the printer's errors, and for changes in the original text. They bear the marks of memorial origin. At II. iii. 64, for example, the quarto adds "And be merry"—an anticipation of line 68; transposes the knave and the honest man in lines 84–5, while lines 83–8 are, on any hypothesis, very badly reproduced, yet are followed by speeches practically identical in F and Q. So in the articles of peace, I. i. 49, "of the next month" (F "of May next ensuing") is a recollection, or anticipation, from the Herald's announcement to Gloucester at II. iv. 71. The following short extract from IV. vi should be sufficient to illustrate and dispose of the pure transcript theory:

Q: *Cade*. Now is Mortemer Lord of this City,
And now sitting upon London stone, We command,
That the first yeare of our reigne,
The pissing Cundit run nothing but red wine.
And now henceforward, it shall bee treason
For any that calles me any otherwise then
Lord Mortemer.

F: *Cade*. Now is *Mortimer* Lord of this City,
And heere sitting upon London Stone,
I charge and command, that of the Cities cost

1. "fertill England" in Q at I. i. 239 being, in that case, a recollection from III. i. 88.

The pissing Conduit run nothing but Clarret Wine
This first yeare of our raigne.
And now henceforward it shall be Treason for any,
That calles me other then Lord *Mortimer*.

It might be possible to excuse the Q variants singly—"now" in line 2 as a printer's or scribe's error from line 1; the omission of "charge and" before "command"; even of the phrase "of the Cities cost". The transposition of the fifth F line, however, the insertion of "*any* other*wise*", and the substitution of "red" for "Clarret" (which occurs—in the wrong place—in the second main "transcript" passage)—all these demand rather much of the incompetence of a scribe or printer. They can, however, be reasonably attributed to a moderate reporter.

If, then, transcribed pages and scrolls are inadequate as an explanation of (all but one of) the remarkable correspondences between F and Q, what is the alternative? McKerrow's second form of transcription—the setting up in type of one copy from another, and his observation[1] of the use of Q "copy" for at least one passage in F, contains the germ of a theory, which, more widely extended and suitably adapted, offers the key to the problem. For IV. v. 1 to IV. vi. 5, and for *3 Henry VI*, IV. ii. 1–18, he suggested, on the basis of common errors and common mislineation of verse as prose in Q and F, the use of Q copy by the printers of F. He suggested that the F manuscript must have been defective at these points and that recourse was had to Q to fill the gaps. Such recourse, however, he believed to have been "only as far as necessary"; the person responsible "took the trouble to take from the manuscript whatever was legible", thus accounting for the alterations. The particular quarto used, he thought, was Q1. As to method, "in some cases the actual printed text was corrected and used for the compositor to work from". His view has been adopted by Sir Walter W. Greg[2] and Professor J. Dover Wilson;[3] all three extending it to cover some stage-directions elsewhere in the play.

Investigation shows, however, that while McKerrow was right about the use of Q copy, this use was much more extensive than he suspected, covering about a quarter of *2 Henry VI*; that it was not due to, or limited by, defects in the manuscript, but was practised wherever Q and manuscript ran close enough together to make Q copy seem feasible and profitable; and that the edition used was not Q1, but Q3, with perhaps some help from Q2.[4]

In other words, the correspondences between F and Q are not

1. *RES.* (1937), 13. 64–72. 2. *Ed. Pr.*, xvi. 3. *3 H 6*, p. 122.
4. See further p. xxxvii below.

attributable to anything in the character and provenance of Q, but must be sought in the nature of the copy for F. Q remains a report of a cut version of an original, was compiled with the help of an occasional "part", and retains a number of original passages (in reported form, of course) that were later modified or removed for reasons principally of censorship.

THE "COPY" FOR F

It is obvious that the printers of F had at their disposal a manuscript of the play, in which were preserved the many passages cut before the performances reported in Q. We may assume that this manuscript had been altered to satisfy the censor. We may now go a step farther, and claim that it was a theatrical manuscript in Shakespeare's own hand. Theatrical, because of the appearance in the F text of the names Bevis and John Holland for the two rebels in IV. ii; Shakespeare's, because certain slips of memory which can only have been his—*Nell* or *Elianor* for *Meg* or *Margaret* four times in III. ii—were left standing, though they must have been corrected, or cut, on the stage. Bevis and Holland were almost certainly the names of actors; Bevis, though otherwise unknown, appears in Q at II. iii. 88 in what is obviously a topical reference, while Holland appears in the "plot" of *2 Seven Deadly Sins.*[1] The presence of the names could be ascribed to the prompter, but, since they are repeated as speech-prefixes throughout the scene, they are more probably the author's. For present purposes, it comes to the same thing. The question of "fair copy" or "foul papers" does not seem to arise here. Shakespeare's autograph, as one is entitled to expect from the testimony of his friends Heminge and Condell to the unblotted papers,[2] became the prompt-book, and, with the prompter's notes,[3] and the various modifications due to the censor and other causes, provided the copy for the First Folio.

But this manuscript was not the sole copy for F. With the manuscript in their hands, the printers, as I have suggested, followed the practice they are known to have used elsewhere, both in the Quartos and the Folio. They preferred printed copy, even corrected printed copy, to manuscript.[4] There was a double gain—legibility and speed. And the labour of correction was generally not

1. Chambers, *W.S.*, I. 44, 288.

2. In their address "To the great Variety of Readers", prefixed to the First Folio. Cf. Greg, *Shakespeare's First Folio*, p. 183. There are, of course, such well-known exceptions as *The Merry Wives of Windsor*, probably printed from a scribal transcript: see Greg, *op. cit.*, 335.

3. E.g. Bed put forth, III. ii. 145. Contrast the authorial S.DD. at e.g. IV. ix. 9.

4. Alice Walker, *Textual Problems of the First Folio* (Cambridge, 1953), 132–3.

excessive; at some points, indeed, where the Q text looked accurate, or the corrector was inclined to scamp, there might even be no labour at all.

As with several other plays, then, the editor or printer's reader looked out an exemplar of Jaggard's own Q3, and probably also one of Q2.[1] The quartos, as they stood, were of course unsatisfactory copy, and, over a large part of the text, impracticable. But there were many passages where the quartos could be brought into line with the manuscript by a few corrections and marginal additions. Longer passages missing from Q, or badly corrupted by the reporters, could be restored by the insertion or attachment of slips of paper[2]—another form of "transcript". If the correction or amendment were carefully done, the text of the manuscript should be accurately reproduced, or so it seemed. Unfortunately the amendment was sometimes imperfect (or imperfectly interpreted by the compositor), or negligible, and where this happened, F derives from a mixture of Q and manuscript, or even from Q alone.

This is why the text is of two distinct kinds. Those passages not represented in Q and therefore taken by F direct from manuscript, are in general clear, and metrically regular; those, however, where Q and F run parallel, present the irregularities and inconsistencies which have provided the basis for a theory of revision done by marginal or interlinear alterations.[3] That theory was a natural one in the circumstances. It does not account, however, for *all* the phenomena. What is wanted is a theory of amendment, not of Q into F, but of memorial Q copy brought into line with the manuscript as copy for F.

The evidence for this theory of Q copy—evidence beyond the reach of a "revision" theory—is to be found in the exclusive agreement of F with Q3 (or Q2) in obvious errors, unauthoritative readings, and indifferent variants—errors of fact, similar lineation of prose as verse, wrongly divided verse, and variants of all kinds peculiar to Q3 (or Q2), and therefore in almost all cases certainly conjectural or erroneous.

Take for example the following exclusive F agreements with Q3, too many for editions of such divergent origin. Since these have been added by Q3 to Q1 by chance, error, or "sophistication", they can hardly be attributed to anything but F use of Q3 copy.

	Q1; Q2 (subst.)	Q3	F
I. i. 50	Duches (Dutches)	Dutchesse	Dutchesse (=Duchies
II. i. 25	doate (dote)	do't	doe it (=dote)

1. See below, p. xxxvii. 2. Or, of course, printed direct from MS.
3. Such as Miss Doran's theory; see p. xx above.

	Q1; Q2 (subst.)	Q3	F
II. iii. 34	erst	ere	ere
II. iii. 67	affeard	affraid	afraid
III. ii. 19	against	'gainst	'gainst
IV. ii. 48	for the	the	the
IV. ii. 142	testifie	testifie it	testifie it
IV. iii. 6	Thou	and thou	and thou
IV. x. 41	neuer shall	shall neuer	shall nere

To these must be added a number of errors where all the texts agree. Here it is easier, from the sense and the regularity of the metre, to identify an error than to suggest the correct reading. For example:[1]

I. i. 252:
Till Henrie surfetting in ioyes of loue, . . . (*surfeit in the*)
And Humfrey with the Peeres be falne at iarres:

IV. x. 42:
That *Alexander Iden* an Esquire of Kent, (omit *an*)
Hall: Alexander Iden, esquire of Kent

II. i. 29–30:
Glost. As who, my Lord?
Suff. Why, as you, my Lord, (read *yourself*)
An't like your Lordly Lords Protectorship. (read *Lord-Protectorship.*)

Common QF mislineation of verse may be illustrated from one typical example:

II. i. 134–5:
Q: My Maisters of saint Albones,
Haue you not Beadles in your Towne,
And things called whippes?

F is substantially the same, and is identically divided. The passage is generally recognized as blank verse and printed by editors as two lines, divided after "not". Similar identical lineation, of prose as verse, has already been noticed in IV. vi.[2]

The stage-directions[3] tell the same story of F debt to Q copy:

IV. iii. 1 S.D.:
Q1: Alarums to the battaile, and sir *Humphrey Stafford* and his brother is slaine. Then enter Iacke Cade againe and the rest.

Q3: *Alarmes to the battell, wherein sir Humfrey Stafford and his brother are both slaine. Then enters Iacke Cade againe, and the rest.*

1. Cf. also II. i. 124–46, IV. iv. 21–4 and collation. 2. Above, pp. xxx–xxxi.
3. Cf. also S.DD. at II. i. 59, III. i. 1, III. ii. 31, III. ii. 235, IV. ii. 104, 115.

F: *Alarums to the fight, wherein both the Staffords are slaine. Enter Cade and the rest.*

The F use of *both* and *wherein* shows clearly, through the editing, its debt to Q3, in which alone of the quartos the words appear.

The amending process itself may be illustrated from one of the worst-printed columns in F—p. 126, column 1—where the influence of the Q copy has left some of its clearest marks.[1] At II. i. 25–6, Q3 reads:

. . . church
men so hot? Good vnckle can you do't. (Q1 doate. Q2 dote?)

The reading "do't" has, of course, no authority; it is simply an attempt to "improve" the sense. A missing line from the manuscript was restored by the amender, probably in the space at the end of the Q3 line, after "do't.", and probably in two sections to fit the space. This insertion the F compositor unfortunately understood to be required after "vnckle" instead of after "do't", with the following result:

Church-men so hot?
Good Vnckle hide such mallice:
With such Holynesse can you doe it?

He ought clearly to have printed something like:

Church-men so hot? Good uncle can you dote,
[To] hide such malice with such holiness?

The process of insertion can also be clearly seen, through lack of the necessary consequential adjustments, in IV. vi. 8 ff, where F follows Q2, even to the lineation:

Q2: *Cade.* Zounes knocke him downe. *they kill him.*
Dicke. My Lord, there's an Army gathered togither
Into Smithfield.

F: *Cade.* Knocke him downe there. *They kill him.*
But. If this Fellow be wise, hee'l neuer call yee *Iacke*
Cade more, I thinke he hath a very faire warning.
Dicke. My Lord, there's an Army gathered together
in Smithfield.

In F, it will be remarked, Dick Butcher appears twice—as *But.*, and as *Dicke.* The *But.* speech has been added, but someone, perhaps misled by the second "*Cade.*", which he took for a speech-prefix, omitted to cancel the existing Q "*Dicke.*" in the same speech.

1. Cf. above, p. xxxiv (for II. i. 29–30). For another misplacement, see III. ii. 407, and collation.

"*But.*" is the constant F prefix; "*Dicke.*" the constant Q form of it.

Similarly, the superfluous "*War.*" in F at v. ii. 8 may be explained by the failure to remove it when the intervening speech of Clifford in Q was deleted.

Where the F editor, amending in this way, came on a gap or series of gaps in Q, he seems to have tried to bridge it by writing the missing lines in the margin if there was room, which would produce short lines and a chance of mislineation in printing; or he might be forced to copy the passage on a slip of paper for insertion, and here too he might disregard the lineation, or write in such a way as to confuse the compositor. This seems to be the explanation of some mislining in F, for it is generally at such points that it occurs. From the same causes, a compositor might occasionally print prose as verse, by following the lineation of the slip. This may explain the F verse-lining of the prose at iv. vii. 124 to iv. viii. 5. The probable use of a single insertion or slip may be illustrated from ii. i. 83–95:[1]

Q1:
Poore man. At *Barwicke* sir, in the North.
Hum. At *Barwicke*, and come thus far for helpe.
Poore man. I sir, it was told me in my sleepe,
That sweete Saint Albones should giue me my sight againe.
Hum. What are lame too?

F:
Simpc. At Barwick in the North, and't like your Grace. } Q, amended
King. Poore Soule,
Gods goodnesse hath beene great to thee:
Let neuer Day nor Night vnhallowed passe,
But still remember what the Lord hath done.
Queene. Tell me, good-fellow,
Cam'st thou here by Chance, / or of Deuotion,
To this holy Shrine?
Simpc. God knowes of pure Deuotion,
Being call'd / a hundred times, and oftner,
In my sleepe, / by good Saint Albon:
Who said; Symon, come; / come offer at my Shrine,
And I will help thee.
Wife. Most true, forsooth:
And many time and oft / my selfe haue heard a Voyce,
To call him so.
} Slip (with verse mislined)
Card. What, art thou lame? } Q, amended

The passage, it will be noted, is preceded by identical stage-directions, and followed by a long passage dependent on Q copy.

In general, the amendment, as in the case of other quartos that served as basis for F, was done with considerable care and in detail. Sometimes, however, perhaps because he was hurried to keep up

1. Cf. also i. iv. 23–6, 58–72; ii. i. 24–54; ii. ii. 32–51.

with the press, or because a passage seemed to require no amendment, the corrector overlooked a part of the Q text. The result is that a F passage which looks "good" on the surface, and has hitherto been accepted as good precisely because F and Q agree, is really "bad". Such a passage, for example, as II. i. 124 ff, is open to suspicion for this reason, and because of the presence of verse rhythms in the prose of which it appears to consist. The ease with which the blank verse may be restored by omission of stock "memorial" particles and phrases confirms the diagnosis, but suggests at the same time that the passage has in fact been reasonably well reported.[1]

A detailed collation of the three quartos and the First Folio confirms the evidence of mislineation, common errors, etc., and indicates that the main printed copy for F was Q3. An exception, however, seems to emerge at IV. v. 1–IV. vii. 1 S.D., where Q2 was almost certainly used; and it is possible that the following page of Q2 served as copy for IV. vii. 1–45 (hang'd). The Q2 pages concerned are G1^{v} and G2^{r}. The first contains the identical lineation of prose as verse that has long been recognized as proving its derivation in F from Q.[2] It also furnishes proof of amended Q copy for F in the duplicate F speech-prefix *Dicke.* / *But.*[3] The main variants are:

	Q1	Q2	Q3	F
IV. v. 10	I will	I will	will I	I will
12	Exet	exeunt	Exit	Exeunt
IV. vi. 3	Cundit	conduit	Cundit	Conduit
13	a fire	on fire	a fire	on fire

and a number of spellings, but some of these at least must be due to the special preferences of the F compositors.[4] On the other hand there are no signs of exclusive Q3F agreements. Evidence at other points is too scanty or indecisive for a conclusion, but another example may be E4^{v} and F1^{r} (III. ii. 299–355; 356–407 I go.). So far as one can judge, the use of the alternative quarto belongs to complete quarto pages, and to one side of each page; and on the Q3 corresponding reverse side, the amended quarto presents difficult copy, because of heavy amendment, considerable or numerous omissions, or rearrangement of passages.

If a tentative solution may be offered, suggested rather by other bad quartos, especially *The True Tragedy* and *Henry V*,[5] it is that, where Q copy, as amended, was likely to present excessive difficulty for the compositors, the F amender, where he wished to avoid

1. See also IV. iv. 21–4; II. i. 77–80, 108–23; I. ii. 75–6; I. i. 57–60, 66–8.
2. See above, pp. xxx f. 3. See above, p. xxxv. 4. See below, p. xxxviii.
5. See my article in *Studies in Bibliography*, VIII (1956), pp. 67–93.

excessive transcription, had recourse to a scissors-and-paste technique. This would afford a notable relief to his labours in the handling of re-arrangement and the insertion of numerous small (or large) omissions; and can be shown by experiment to be a perfectly feasible device. The use of one side of a quarto page in this way would naturally entail resort to another quarto exemplar for the other side of the page thus mutilated. It is probable that a modification of this procedure may be seen almost at the beginning of the play, where a Q3 page, of which the top half of one side and the lower half of the other were useless as copy, was neatly cut across between two lines, so that the "good" halves were both used to the fullest extent possible. The last nineteen lines of A4^{r} (from I. i. 208) are used, and the last nineteen lines of A4^{v} witness an abrupt end of amended text at I. ii. 2. A long insertion, of twenty-two lines, was required, and a further cutting of the page would make way for it very conveniently.[1]

All these phenomena, it will be noticed—use of two quartos, scissors-and-paste technique, and the use of Bad (as distinct from Good, or Doubtful) quartos—point rather to the printing-house, than to the theatre, as their point of origin. There is, however, no relation with the known stints of the two F compositors, A and B, who were responsible for this text.[2] The use of the Q copy seems to be determined by the Q page, not by the F column; and in any case, since most of the play relied on Q3, while the F text was set up almost equally by A and B, there is no question of using different quartos merely to allow compositors to work simultaneously. The factors that called Q2 into play must therefore be related rather to the ease or difficulty of the copy.

Detailed collation, together with a consideration of the other signs of Q copy, suggests that Q was used at approximately the following passages:

> I. i. 1–74; I. i. 208–I. ii. 2; I. ii. 70–81; I. iv. 22 S.D.-79 (end); II. i. 16–153; II. ii. 1–65; II. iii. 22–38; II. iii. 59 S.D.–II. iv. 14, 70–86; III. i. 1 S.D.–57 (mainly 36–44, 56–7); III. ii. 26–85, 187–411 (end); IV. i. 44–139; IV. ii. 84–IV. iii. 8; IV. iv. 19–24; IV. v. 1 S.D.–IV. vii. 5; IV. x. 24–44; V. i. 136–48, 192–216; V. ii. 1–8; V. iii. 28–33 (end).

1. On the whole subject of corrected Q copy for F, see further my treatment of *Lear* in *RES.*, VI. 233 (July 1955), pp. 252–8; and of *Henry V* in *Studies in Bibliography*, VIII (1956).

2. The stints were as follows:

B	m2^{v}–m3^{v}	I. i. 1–I. ii. 79
A	m4^{r}–n3^{r}	I. ii. 80–III. ii. 60
B	n3^{v}	III. ii. 61–186
A	n4^{r}	III. ii. 187–305
B	n4^{v}–o3^{v}	III. ii. 306–end.

These passages include, of course, many lines and series of lines restored to the Q text by marginal or interlinear insertion or by attached slips of paper. They are passages, however, throughout which there is evidence that Q, in whatever degree, was used as amended copy.

The copy for F, then, seems to have been Shakespeare's autograph, used as a prompt-book, with a few prompter's notes added, a few passages completely excised, others recast; and used partly as direct copy, partly through the medium of Q3 and probably Q2, amended with varying degrees of care, but sometimes not at all. The stage-directions, in particular, were often taken straight from Q, with slight editing, and are thus unlikely to reproduce exactly what was in the prompt-book.

USE OF THE CHRONICLES

It was Malone who originated the business, still flourishing, of trying to test Shakespeare's authorship and the presence in doubtful plays of other hands by the investigation of sources in different chronicles. In a note to *Henry V*,[1] I. ii. 76, where Shakespeare, following Holinshed, spoke of Lewis the tenth, in mistake for Lewis the ninth, as Hall had it, Malone remarked, "Here therefore we have a decisive proof that our author's guide in all his original plays was Holinshed, and not Hall." The assumption was that the use of one chronicle excluded the use of any other. Malone was able to argue that anything common to F and Q must have been taken over by Shakespeare when he was "revising" *The Contention* into *2 Henry VI*. Fortunately for his argument, he did not look far enough into the passages peculiar to F to discover that some of these also were peculiar to Hall. In the same way, many recent critics have attempted to found a case on the sources of matter which occurs only in F or Q.[2] It may be said at once that Shakespeare, in all three parts of *Henry VI*, drew on *both* Hall and Holinshed, and that *The Contention* also exhibits passages peculiar to each chronicler, so that, if they were written by another dramatist, *he* likewise used both. In fact, variation in the chronicle sources is not a decisive test of single or multiple authorship. Professor J. Dover Wilson's similar attempt[3] to argue that *2 Henry VI* had Grafton at the back of it whereas *3 Henry VI* had Hall, and that this suggests a difference of authorship, is equally fallible, even if it were well founded in fact.

1. Boswell's *Malone*, xvii. 270, n. 4.

2. See e.g. McKerrow, *RES.* (1933), 9. 157–69; C. A. Greer, *PMLA.* (1933), 655–704; *Ph. Q.* (1934), 13. 324–32 (L. King); *PMLA.* (1935), 50. 745 (L. King); *PMLA.* (1936), 51.

3. New Shakespeare, *3 H 6*, xxi.

Professor Wilson—like Hart,[1] who also favoured Grafton as a source—has overlooked the use of Fox's *Actes and Monumentes*, and has been led astray by Boswell-Stone.[2] There is, in fact, nothing in Grafton that cannot be accounted for from Holinshed, Hall, and Fox.[3] Hall is the chief source; there is more material exclusive to Hall than to Holinshed in all three parts of *Henry VI*.[4] Hall and Holinshed (2nd edn, 1587) were often used side by side. In the first scene, for example, Margaret's marriage settlement, as reported in *The Contention*, declares that Henry should "wed and espouse the ladie Margaret . . . and crowne her Queene of England, ere the 30. of the next month. Item. It is further agreed betwene them, that the Dutches of *Anioy* and *Maine*, shall be released and deliuered ouer to the King her fa." In *2 Henry VI*, which is substantially the same, the phrase "of the next month" becomes "of May next ensuing"; "released and deliuered" is unchanged. Now this last expression is from Hall alone; Holinshed has "deliuered"; and "next", which is common to F and Q, comes from Holinshed alone; Hall writes "the xxx. daie of May"; while Holinshed has "the thirtith of Maie next following". Both F and Q, therefore, are indebted to both Hall and Holinshed.

The extent of Shakespeare's debt to Hall has been underestimated. Here Boswell-Stone quotes Holinshed as the source; a more careful collation would have indicated Hall. For, in one scene alone (II. ii), *2 Henry VI* follows Hall exclusively in at least three decisive phrases—"in captivity", "after Edward the third's death", and "Edmund, Anne, and Elianor".[5] The miracle of St Albans, the collocation of the "commons" with the "good Duke", as well as the (exclusive) spelling *Hume*, are from Fox.[6] The conflicting accounts of Clifford's death Shakespeare adopted also from Hall (223, 251), one as from his main dramatic source, the other in a casual collective reference.[7] For the general interpretation, Hall and Fox are certainly a more direct source than Holinshed. Other chroniclers must also have been consulted, or familiar, such as Fabyan ("the keyes of Normandy" I. i. 113)[8] or Hardyng ("what cruelty ye can", IV. i. 132); and the popular poetic version, "The Mirror for Magistrates".[9]

1. Arden edn, 1909, 1931.
2. *Shakespeare's Holinshed* (1896).
3. See my review in *RES.* (1953), 4. 14. The only exception I know is the Q "Alice" (not in F) at II. ii. 37.
4. See refs. above.
5. Ed. 1809, pp. 23, 2, 2.
6. Ed. 1844, vol. III, p. 713 (see Appendix I).
7. *2 H 6*, V. ii; *3 H 6*, I. iii. 47; *3 H 6*, I. i. 9.
8. See also notes to IV. iii. 10; IV. vii. 1; IV. x. 11, 24.
9. See also note to I. i. 141, 179; I. ii. 49; II. iii. 28; II. iv. 19 (and head-note); IV. vii. 119.

And Shakespeare's acquaintance with Hall was not new or limited to the period covered by *2 Henry VI*. He shows intimate and easy familiarity with the whole chronicle. It was from Hall, more than from any other source, that he drew his interpretation of the Plantagenet dynasty, the chain of nemesis from Richard II to Richard III, and his conception of the leading characters in the drama. But more particularly, it was from his familiarity with Hall that he was able to draw material from any part that was needed or suitable for any other part. Thus the genealogical material came from the reign of Richard II in Hall, the praise of Henry V (I. i. 77 ff) from the last year of Henry V and the first of Henry VI,[1] the suggestion for the Clifford scenes from the material for *3 Henry VI*. This range of familiarity, which is even better exemplified in *3 Henry VI*, is not the result of an *ad hoc* study of Hall as a source, but of a long acquaintance, extending back no doubt to early youth.

"INCONSISTENCIES"

Similar "inconsistencies" with which Shakespeare is charged, or which are made the basis of revision theories of *2 Henry VI*, stand on the same footing. "The contrast between erudition and sheer ignorance" that Professor Wilson finds in *Henry VI* is somewhat exaggerated, and proves nothing. Shakespeare's reference to Ascanius, instead of Cupid masquerading as Ascanius, might, as he thinks, be due to a misunderstanding of a passage in Chaucer; it might equally be due to Virgil himself, where the subsequent history of Ascanius drops the impersonation; or it may be just another lapse of memory. In this, however, Shakespeare was no better, and no worse, than his more learned contemporaries. Nashe,[2] for example, makes a double error in a reference to Io (for Europa).

Other inconsistencies, as we have seen, derive from the use of Q "copy" in the printing of F. Others, again, were caused by the censor's demand for recasting certain passages, and to Shakespeare's failure to tie up completely all the loose ends occasioned by this procedure.[3] The main inconsistencies are, of course, the variants, and these we have seen good reason to attribute mainly to the censor's operations. In all, they afford no adequate ground for a general theory of revision, or of multiple authorship.

Shakespeare's use and knowledge of the chronicles was not always accurate. On the one hand, he showed at times a pardonable ignorance of the exact genealogy of his characters; the Mortimers, for example, were a constant source of confusion.[4] Sometimes he

1. Hall, 112, 114–15.
2. McKerrow, *Nashe*, 4. 18; cf. also the confusion over Scylla in *Dido*, 5. 1. 247.
3. See e.g. notes to IV. iv. 9; IV. x. 39.
4. II. ii. 38–42 and Appendix 2.

must have read in haste, as when he misapplied a statement about Ruthven to Mortimer;[1] sometimes he took over the inconsistencies of the chronicles themselves.[2] On the other hand, the telescoping technique of the *Henry VI–Richard III* tetralogy required the taking of some liberties with exact historical truth, but without altering the truth of substance or the general impression conveyed. Thus York's term of office in Ireland is split in two,[3] Queen Margaret is made contemporaneous with the Duchess of Gloucester, and two Warwicks are combined in the conquest of Anjou and Maine.[4] Such historical "inconsistencies" are thus no argument for revision.

AUTHORSHIP

There is thus no foundation for the idea that Shakespeare did not write the whole of *2* and *3 Henry VI*. And there is positive proof that he did. The main testimony, apart from Greene's own, is that of Heminge and Condell, who owned (as argued above), a censored autograph prompt-book, and sent it to the printers. They had been Shakespeare's fellows for over twenty years, and almost certainly from the date at which he wrote these plays. Any doubts as to their competence to provide a good text of these, as of other plays, are now being recognized as more appropriately directed against the publishers of the First Folio. The Epilogue to *Henry V* is equally suggestive—unless we are to deny that play likewise to Shakespeare—in alluding to the reign of Henry VI,

> Whose state so many had the managing,
> That they lost France and made his England bleed:
> Which oft our stage hath shown; and, for their sake,
> In your fair minds let this acceptance take.

On the negative side, the absence of the plays from the list of Francis Meres (1598) and the inferences drawn from Shakespeare's reference to *Venus and Adonis* (1593) as the first heir of his invention, will nowadays carry little if any weight.

MALONE AND THE "UPSTART CROW"

So we return to Malone. Professor J. Dover Wilson thinks that this "chief hinge" of Malone's argument still holds, and that Greene was making a definite charge of literary plagiarism. Professor Wilson has indeed succeeded in tracing Greene's allusion to Horace's Third Epistle, and Malone, in quoting Horace's "furtivis coloribus", showed that he took the allusion. And the Hora-

1. *Ibid.* 2. Above, p. xl. 3. I. i. 193, and n. 4. I. i. 114, 206, etc.

tian passage does indeed refer to the bombast of Titius and the "plagiarism" of Celsus.

"Plagiarism", however, is a wide and loose term, and this interpretation of Greene, now that Malone's supporting evidence of inconsistencies has vanished, wants closer examination. If Greene, the arch-plagiarist,[1] makes such an accusation—which would be in itself surprising—why does he not make it more directly, instead of leaving it to be deduced? Does a classical allusion necessarily carry with it always its full original connotations and associations? If "our" feathers refers to Peele, Nashe, and Marlowe, what has happened to Marlowe's share in the authorship, for which Tucker Brooke made just such a case from parallel phrases? Why did Greene ask his fellow-dramatists to "let these Apes *imitate* your past excellence", rather than *appropriate* it?

It may be, of course, that Greene was so conscious of his own practice of plagiarism that he preferred to leave the accusation indirect. The Horatian echo, however, as far as it carries the implication of theft, is in fact applied to the *actors* by Greene, who calls them "those Puppets that spake from our mouths, those Anticks garnisht in our *colours*".

Professor Wilson's use of Chettle's testimony to Shakespeare's "honesty" to imply a previous charge of dishonesty is likewise beside the point. Shakespeare has been charged with ingratitude and desertion ("beholding . . . forsaken"), cruelty ("Tygers hart"), and generally with names like "peasant", "rude groome", "monster", not to mention over-weening pride ("the only Shake-scene"). As Professor Wilson observes, we may infer some harsh treatment of Greene by the players—whether really harsh or justified, matters little—and perhaps by Shakespeare in particular. The charges need mean no more; but Shakespeare's insistence, through his friends and Chettle, on his "honesty", is not a reply to the charge of plagiarism—he could have mentioned it definitely—but to being treated as "no gentleman". "Honestus", to these Elizabethans so familiar with their Horace, meant "decent, gentlemanly"; and "uprightness of dealing" has not quite the same business flavour as it has today.

Plagiarism, besides, as Professor Wilson is very conscious, was not regarded as an abnormal practice; it was an accusation that Greene least of all men could bring, and it would hardly call for such an apology as Chettle's, or the pains that Shakespeare obviously took to extract it. The real plagiaristic charge is rather

1. See e.g. Introduction to "The Debate between Pride and Lowliness" (ed. J. P. Collier, 1841), on its relation to Greene's "Quip for an Upstart Courtier".

different, and is not incompatible with the Horatian allusion.

It is instructive to compare Greene's attack with the very similar one made by Nashe three years earlier, in his preface to Greene's *Menaphon*, and not improbably inspired by Greene himself. There, one main line of attack is directed against the "bombast of a bragging blank verse", and the "vainglorious tragoedians, who . . . embowell the clowdes in a speach of comparison"; and the "plagiarist" who feeds "on nought but the crummes that fal from the translators trencher" or "the Italionate pen, that of a packet of pilfries . . . in disguised arraie, vaunts *Ouids* and *Plutarchs* plumes as their owne". Returning to the latter subject, he goes on to attack those (including Kyd, and perhaps, as I think, Shakespeare) who borrow "handfulls of tragical speaches" from "English *Seneca*", who is "let bloud line by line and page by page". Again he speaks of certain gentlemen who have "trickt vp a companie of taffata fooles with their feathers". Here, then, in the same context of bombast and feathers, we have the reference specifically directed to actors, and the plagiarism limited to occasional phrases and speeches from classical authors, particularly Shakespeare's favourites Ovid and Plutarch.[1]

It seems that this was the sense in which Shakespeare took any suggestion of plagiarism that may have been read into Greene's words by such contemporaries as R. B.[2] This may be the explanation for the removal from *2 Henry VI* of the phrase about "Abradas, the great Masadonian Pyrate"[3] which he had picked up from Greene's "*Menaphon* or *Penelope's Web*",[4] and which appears in Q, and its replacement, in F, by "Bargulus the strong Illyrian pirate",[5] from Cicero's *Offices*. If so, then the plumes that Shakespeare recognized as borrowed from Greene must have been very few indeed.

It is in this sense that plagiarism is specially applicable to Shakespeare. His enormous receptivity, and his faculty for picking up words and phrases here and there, need no elaboration. They are nowhere better illustrated than in this very play. There are verbal echoes and borrowings in plenty from the Bible, the Homilies, the metrical Psalms, the Prayer Book, from Ovid (in the original rather than Golding's translation), Aesop, Virgil, Lucan; and in English, from *Tamburlaine*, *The Spanish Tragedy*, *Jack Straw*, from Greene himself, as well as from the chronicles of Hall, Holinshed, Fabyan, Hardyng's Grafton, and possibly others. There are likewise many words, phrases, and even lines or sentences that he uses in common with other dramatists, so that it is, *ceteris paribus*, impos-

1. See e.g. note to IV. i. 138–9. 2. Above, p. xxi. 3. *Cont.*, 548.
4. Grosart, vi. 77, 78; v. 197. 5. IV. i. 107.

sible to decide who, if anyone, is the borrower. Take, for example, the phrase at II. i. 18, "The treasury of everlasting joy" and compare it with Spenser's "the threasury of joy" from "Astrophel", published in 1595. Did Shakespeare know it in manuscript, or did Spenser derive it from a performance of *2 Henry VI* (it is not found in Q), or did both take it from a common source? Yet this is precisely the type of evidence on which Professor Wilson, quite conscious of the danger, is driven to rely for proof that Greene and Nashe had a hand in the text. By parity of reasoning, Spenser had a share in the play, or Shakespeare had a hand in *The Faerie Queene*.

Professor Wilson's interpretation of Greene is thus left without external support, and is, in itself, no Atlas for so great a weight. With his final effort, it is fairly safe to forecast that the revision theory, as we know it, will be decently buried, and that something like the theory outlined above towards a reconciliation of the opposing schools of thought will take its place.

It is worth returning, in conclusion, to pay a tribute to Malone, who was logical enough to see the force of the evidence on both sides, and honest enough to advocate in turn, though without being able to reconcile, two opposing theories; and who carried such conviction that critics have been limited ever since to doing little more than adopt one of his theories or the other. And, in the event, both, now that they can be seen not to be irreconcilable, are still found to be necessary factors in a comprehensive explanation of the phenomena.

DATE

The only certain limits for the date of *2 Henry VI* are the publication of the second edition of Holinshed in 1587 and Greene's attack in 1592, before 3 September. The limit is slightly narrowed by the fact that the theatres were closed in that year from 23 June.[1] On the other hand a series of probabilities converge to suggest a date early in 1590, with *3 Henry VI* and *Richard III* not long after. Shakespeare was indebted, in *2 Henry VI*, to Greene's *Penelope's Web* (S.R. 26 June 1587) or *Menaphon* (S.R. 23 August 1589), Spenser's *Faerie Queene*, Books 1–3 (January 1590; S.R. 1 December 1589), and possibly to Lyly's *Pappe with a Hatchet*[2] (*c.* October 1589). The latest of these, *The Faerie Queene*, furnishes Hart[3] with a few source phrases, none of which is singly very cogent. But both *1 Henry VI* and *Richard III*, written, I assume, respectively before and after *2 Henry VI*, supply better.[4] On the other hand, *The Troublesome*

1. Chambers, *W.S.*, I. 287.
2. See notes to IV. vii. 81, 85; and McKerrow, *Nashe*, IV. 461.
3. *2H6*, Old Arden edn, xl ff.
4. *1H6*, Old Arden edn, xxvi ff; *3H6*, xxvi.

Raigne of King John, published in 1591, is full of echoes of various plays, which include *3 Henry VI* and *Richard III*. From the former we have, among others, the "scandal of retire" (II. i. 150; *2 T.R.*, vi. 33) and from the latter

> Set down, set down the load not worth your pain! *2 T.R.*, vi. 1
> Set down, set down your honourable load— *R 3*, I. ii. 1

And if, as seems probable, Marlowe had *Henry VI* in mind in composing *Edward II*[1] (perhaps performed in London Christmas 1592; Marlowe d. May 1593) for the same company, this would confirm the date. Until this is further investigated, it seems not unreasonable to assume 1590 as the date of *2*, and probably *3*, *Henry VI*.

CONCLUSIONS AND SUMMARY

The probable textual history of *2 Henry VI* may now be briefly reconstructed. Shakespeare wrote the play as part of a carefully planned tetralogy, probably in 1590, for Pembroke's Men, or their predecessors. His main source was Hall's *Chronicle*, but he was also indebted to Fox's *Actes and Monuments*, to Holinshed (2nd edn, 1587), with a few suggestions from Fabyan and Hardyng.

A few cuts in personnel and extensive cuts in the text were made, probably at once, but in any case before the play came to the knowledge of the reporting actors; a few speeches being transferred to other characters of the play. It is reasonable to suppose that the cuts were made by Shakespeare himself.

The play in this state proved very popular, and was probably heard, like its successor, by Robert Greene, and, like its predecessor, by Thomas Nashe, in or before 1592. Late in 1593, or early in 1594, the play was "reported" by a group of Pembroke's Men for a provincial tour, and the report sold to Thomas Millington, who entered it on the Stationers' Register on 12 March 1594, and published it under what must have been its original title, *The Contention* . . . The reporting group relied on memory except for the uncut part of York's speech (I. i. 237 ff), of which they had retained a copy. The group included the actors who had played Warwick, Clifford, and York, and the smaller "bit-parts", doubled, of the Armourer, Bolingbroke, the Mayor, Vaux, Scales, or perhaps the First Citizen. The repertory with which they were familiar included a number of Shakespeare's plays, Marlowe's *Edward II*, the anonymous *Arden of Faversham*, and Kyd's *Spanish Tragedy*.

At some time, or times, thereafter, Tilney reviewed the prompt-copy and ordered the recasting of a number of passages for reasons

1. Cf. Alexander, *op. cit.*, 203 ff.

mainly political. Shakespeare either deleted these or replaced them by passages of equivalent length, which were written on slips and pasted over the originals. He also altered, then or earlier, the phrase about Abradas, as a result of Greene's attack.

For his attempt at a collected volume of plays, in 1619, Pavier had some "corrections" made in *The Contention*, by reference to Stow's Chronicle (edition of 1615).

For the First Folio, Heminge and Condell handed over the prompt-book, in Shakespeare's autograph, as amended for the censor, and with an occasional note by the prompter. According to their usual custom, Jaggard and his associates (including Pavier) attempted to ease and speed their work with the help of one, possibly two, of their editions of *The Contention*, used where feasible after amendment from the prompt-book.

THE TEXT

If these arguments on the true nature and origin of the First Folio text are well-founded, it falls into two fairly distinct categories:

(*a*) The larger part of the text, where Q copy was not used, either because Q was too "bad" for amendment or because the text was peculiar to F, and where the copy must have been a play-house manuscript. F is thus the only, or the superior, substantive text here, and an editor's duty is to adhere as closely to F as possible.[1] With several provisos, however. One is to discount the peculiar habits and failings of the two compositors, A and B, which have now been to some extent analysed.[2] Both, but particularly B, were guilty of omissions; and in many places the Q text, however bad it may be, does help to restore what is almost certainly the true but omitted reading.[3] Again, the "revision" of a number of passages at the request of the censor provides a choice between two versions of the same substance, one early and "bad", in Q, the other late and "good", in F.[4] There is no doubt that the F form is to be preferred on both counts, though it does not fit with absolute precision into Greg's first rule[5] for presenting a critical text "in the form in which we may suppose that it would have stood in a fair copy, made by the author himself, of the work as he finally *intended* it".

Whether omissions can be restored or not, their occurrence is generally obvious in a play written so largely in verse; and the

1. See e.g. II. i. 91; III. i. 328; IV. ii. 81.
2. See especially Alice Walker, *op. cit.*
3. See e.g. I. iii. 21, 31–2, 204; I. iv. 31; II. i. 41–2; III. ii. 13; IV. i. 48, 113; IV. iv. 48.
4. See above, pp. xxvii f. 5. *Ed. Pr.*, x.

same is true of small interpolations,[1] which can be dealt with by removal.[2] Again where simple literal or minim misprints occur, as commonly with A, there is a reasonable chance of recovering the true reading.[3] It is when we come to the misreadings by B of his manuscript copy that we enter the realm of conjecture. His known erratic habits, however, do help to justify at least some conjectures where the process of corruption cannot be bibliographically explained, but where the sense and fitness of the emendation seem beyond any doubt. Such I take to be "pap with a hatchet" for F "the help of hatchet" at IV. vii. 85, and "sword" for F "soule" at V. i. 10, as well as the conjecture "plenteous" for F "because" at IV. vii. 59.

Compositor B also seems to have had some ability in "recollection", for he not only copies by the eye from the line immediately above,[4] but allows his reading to be affected by a similar word a dozen lines earlier, e.g. "But", IV. vii. 67, becomes "Kent", from 57, and "rebel", IV. viii. 13, is printed "rabble" from the direction at the head of the scene.

(*b*) Some of these considerations apply to a certain degree, of course, to the whole text. The remainder of F, however, raises a widely different set of problems. Here F was set up from Q copy sometimes amended from the manuscript, sometimes imperfectly amended, sometimes not amended at all. This means that much of the inevitable corruption is latent. Sources of correction may be found, if the corruption is discoverable, in the sense,[5] the metre,[6] comparison with the Chronicles and especially Hall,[7] in the variants of Q2 and Q3 from Q1 and from each other,[8] and in parallels with the reporters' stock vocabulary as exhibited in other bad quartos.[9]

The particular process of amendment used will also have a considerable bearing on the types of errors that found their way into F, and the sort of correction it is legitimate to adopt. It is fairly clear that amendment was done marginally, or inter-linearly, or on separate slips, and that deletions and insertions were made as necessary. This implies that such common types of error are likely to be found as inadequate or excessive deletion, or correction and

1. How considerable these could be, is shown by Alice Walker, "The Folio Text of *1 Henry IV*", in *Studies in Bibliography* (University of Virginia, 1954), VI. 45–59.
2. E.g. I. iii. 219; III. i. 137; III. ii. 118.
3. E.g. I. iv. 23; III. i. 211; III. i. 260.
4. Or below; see e.g. IV. i. 32, collation, and note.
5. E.g. I. i. 252.
6. E.g. I. i. 209; III. ii. 407.
7. E.g. I. ii. 75–6.
8. E.g. II. iii. 34, 67; IV. ii. 142; IV. vi. 13.
9. E.g. II. ii. 9.

misplaced insertion; and the evidence confirms this.[1] Fortunately these errors, given a recognition of their mode of origin, suggest in most cases their own correction.

But some readings must remain optional. In a passage, for example, where Q was amended to provide the F copy, and Q3,F agree against Q1,2, it may be uncertain whether (*a*) Q1,2 are correct, and F has been misled through following a Q3 error or conjecture, or whether (*b*) Q1 was corrected in proof, and Q3, followed by F, derived its reading from the correction—a correction which, even so, may or may not give the authentic reading.[2] Some weight in the decision will go to the degree of amendment of Q which is obvious in the context, to the bibliographical factors likely to have produced the Q3 divergence, to the evidence, if any, for disturbance or correction of the Q1 text from which Q3 was printed. Again, where Q has been used as F copy unamended, and an isolated variation occurs in F,[3] it is sometimes difficult, if not impossible, to decide whether this is an intentional amendment or a conjecture or a printer's error. The balance of probability, however, is against a Q3,F or Q2,F variation from Q1.

The final result is of course unsatisfactory, but in the nature of the case it must be so. The main source of satisfaction, perhaps, is to know the worst, to see how it happened, and do the best possible to repair some of the damage. That is possibly better than deceiving ourselves over the real nature of the text, and expending our energies on fruitless attempts to solve problems that never were.

III. LITERARY

The definitive literary verdict on *Henry VI*, so far as it goes, is Johnson's:

> These plays, considered, without regard to characters and incidents, merely as narratives in verse, are more happily conceived, and more accurately finished than those of King John, Richard II or the tragick scenes of King Henry IV and V . . .
>
> Of these three plays I think the second the best. The truth is, that they have not sufficient variety of action, for the incidents are too often of the same kind; yet many of the characters are well discriminated. King Henry, and his Queen, King Edward, the Duke of Gloucester, and the Earl of Warwick, are very strongly and distinctly painted.[4]

This verdict has the merit of recognizing the elementary fact that the artist is limited by the nature of his material. And, of all

1. E.g. II. i. 25–6.
2. See e.g. IV. iii. 6 (Thou: and thou); I. i. 8 (then the: twenty).
3. II. i. 131 (his/it).
4. In Boswell's *Malone*, 18. 549.

literary material, chronicle history is the most recalcitrant to free artistic fashioning. The critical and imaginative interpretation of historical trends was not yet, and the chronicles had in general little more unity than was imposed by a king, a hero, or a conflict. The reign of Henry VI, in any case, was too long, its events too rambling and fortuitous, to be easily digested into drama; its king too insignificant to play the hero; and its personal relations too superficial and external for profound psychological treatment. Shakespeare was tied from the outset to a series of political events—treaties, lists of "articles", orations, and battles—scattered in disconnected array over a very long period, intermingled with all sorts of irrelevant incidents, and generally devoid of any central figure or theme of development.

Shakespeare might further appear to be limited by accepting without question what his chronicles told him. This, however, was no limitation dramatically; it is not the historical facts that matter, but what he made of them. We know, for example, that Suffolk was, in fact, a good administrator, the Cardinal a not unfavourable character, Humphrey of Gloucester not "the good Duke" of Hall and Fox, and that Henry suffered from fits of insanity.[1] But Shakespeare drew them substantially as they appear in the pages of Hall.

But he had the compensation of finding ready to hand, in Hall, a general scheme of cause and effect, a predestinarian interpretation already imposed on the events. The leading theme of crime and punishment was there, beginning, where Hall began, from the original sin of Henry Bolingbroke in the forcible deposition and murder of Richard II. The story of Henry VI, in Hall and Shakespeare, is thus but one variation on the evils of weak government, intestine broils,[2] and the French influence, and the just retribution on the house of Lancaster for broken faith and rebellion. And behind it, for the Elizabethans, lay the fear of civil war and anarchy that would inevitably follow rebellion, disputed succession, and national disunity.

Now Shakespeare was, in 1590–1, an adept in the art of planning, and in this respect *2 Henry VI* will bear comparison with almost any other of his plays.[3] Having set out to write the epic of York and Lancaster, he would and could impose a further unity. Without a hero, for the moment—unless we remember *Respublica*

1. See e.g. C. L. Kingsford, *Prejudice and Promise in Fifteenth Century England*, 1925; A. W. Ward, *Collected Papers*, 1921.

2. Cf. Hall, 1.

3. Contrast e.g. Chambers, *W.S.*, 1. 286, "loosely constructed".

of the Morality plays in the background[1]—he proceeded to tighten the structure by adding new causes and effects to emphasize the prevailing nemesis, and by omitting ruthlessly a mass of detail that would not subserve his purpose.

He first shed off the events grouped around Talbot and Joan of Arc and the loss of France, much of it overlapping the material for *2 Henry VI.* The centre of the succeeding action he found in the "fatal marriage",[2] based on a breach of trust, of Henry with another Frenchwoman, Joan's successor, and its consequences for English unity. Added to the original crime, this brought a further aggravation of Lancastrian misfortunes, beginning with the loss of Anjou and Maine and then the rest of the French possessions. The marriage is linked naturally with the fall of Humphrey, whose alternative marriage proposal "was not heard", while Suffolk's was "condiscended unto. . . Whiche facte engendered suche a flame, that it never wente oute, till bothe the parties with many other were consumed and slain, to the great unquietness of the kyng and his realme".[3] Suffolk, Margaret, and the rest, each for his own reasons, combined to overthrow Humphrey. The succeeding tragedies follow with the irony and inevitability of fate. "The Quene", says Hall, "mynding to preserve her husband in honor, & her selfe in aucthoritie, procured & consentid to the death of this noble man, whose onely death brought to passe that thynge, which she woulde fayne have eschewed . . . : if this Duke had lyved, the Duke of Yorke durst not have made title to the crowne: if this Duke had livyd, the nobles had not conspired against the king, nor yet the commons had not rebelled: if this Duke had lyved, the house of Lancastre had not been defaced and destroyed."

Shakespeare seized his centre of action squarely, placed it firmly in the forefront, and grouped round it, in the opening scene, the various internal factions, clearly framing the attitude of each, and reflecting the weakness of Henry and the anarchy of the commons. With the introduction of the Duchess, in the second scene, the action is well under way.

Both for filling out his "cast", and for variety of incident and flexibility of staging, Shakespeare felt it necessary to add a number of subsidiary events that lay scattered and often irrelevant about the chronicles. Such are the Armourer scenes, the conjuring, Iden's

1. See further A. P. Rossiter, *Woodstock* (1946), Introduction; E. M. Tillyard, *Shakespeare's History Plays* (1944).

2. Cf. the similar breach in *3 H 6*, on the marriage of Edward and Lady Gray.

3. Hall, 204; *2 H 6*, I. i. 43 ff. 4. Hall, 210.

triumph, and the miracle of St Albans. Or he expanded a hint from Hall—the questions to the Spirit, the Margaret–Suffolk affair, and the death of Clifford. In each case these events were used to tighten and multiply the links between the main scenes, and increase the general effect of unity and causation. From another angle, he increased this effect by telescoping the events of the ten odd years of the Chronicles into a continuous series in apparently natural and rapid succession. Chronology suffers, but the problem of dramatic time disappears.

Eleanor begins the series. Her fall took place, in fact, before the arrival of Margaret, but the two women are made contemporary. Her ambitions and conjuring are used in the play to mark the first stage in Humphrey's fall; while the conjuring itself links up the fates of the King, Suffolk, and Somerset. The Armourer scenes, quite detached in Hall, are tied in with the treason of York, and with the Queen and Suffolk; and used, with the miracle and the question of the regency, to illustrate the judgement of Humphrey, ironically placed on the very eve of his arrest. Cade is similarly linked with York, as his instrument from Ireland, and with the whole plot as the leader of the discontented and anarchical commons—the obverse of the disunited nobility.

In search of further amplification, chiefly for the alternate and minor scenes, Shakespeare seized on two hints in Hall, which he not only expanded here, but used as links with *1* and *3 Henry VI* respectively. Hall says of Suffolk that he was "the Quenes dearlynge" (219), and that Margaret "entierly loved" him (218).[1] This, with the earlier hint (207) that Suffolk, "by the meanes of the Quene, was shortely erected to the estate and degree of a Duke, and ruled the Kyng at his pleasure" is the sole foundation for their quite unhistorical love affair. Similarly, the death of Clifford at the hands of York is a backward inference and development from the *3 Henry VI* material in Hall (251), "the lord Clifford marked him and sayde: by Gods blode, thy father slew myne."

With such a varied and complicated mass of material, it is unnatural to expect unity of style. To say that variety indicates other hands than Shakespeare's is, of course, begging the question. Shakespeare was clearly artist enough to know that style, like treatment, is determined by matter and purpose. No one disputes that the contrasted styles of *Julius Cæsar* and *Antony and Cleopatra* are the work of the same man. And clearly the speeches of the aristocracy, the dialogue of the Margaret–Suffolk scenes, and the talk of Cade

1. Hall also speaks (217) of the commons' "disdain of lascivious sovereigntie whiche the Queene with her minions toke and usurped upon them."

and the rebels, require separate styles.[1] The style of *2 Henry VI* is thus necessarily "unequal", ranging from the high poetry of "The gaudy, blabbing, and remorseful day", and "Now let the vile world end", to the set oratory of "Anjou and Maine both given unto the French", and the popular humour and indecency of the Cade scenes.

The most characteristic Shakespearean feature running through all the varied styles is the wealth of association that underlies and permeates the play. It is this richness of subconscious association in which he soaked his subjects that distinguishes Shakespeare among his contemporaries. His artistic sensibility to word and phrase, and his wealth of assimilated literature, both from reading and acting, with a vivid memory, furnished him with a storehouse of imagery. It is not merely, as Clemen[2] thought about *Henry VI*, a matter of padding or epic similes, though these have their natural place as embroidery to the oratorical-epic speeches of the protagonists. It is an internal atmosphere in which the theme of the play is enveloped by a succession of figures and images, often merely implicit and hardly recognized.

We may therefore expect, in Shakespeare, large numbers of parallels, echoes, or borrowings—what Malone and his followers would call plagiarism. We find many from the other main contemporary dramatists, Peele, Greene, Marlowe, and Kyd; from the Bible (both Genevan and Bishops' versions), the metrical Psalms, the Homilies, and the Prayer Book; from the school version of Æsop, and the Latin of Ovid, Virgil, and Lucan; the mediaeval romances of Arthur and Bevis; and the Chronicles of Hall, Holinshed, Fabyan, Fox, and Hardyng. And these tend to group themselves round a few leading themes and characters.

It was, for example, characteristic of the ancients, as of the Middle Ages and the Renascence, to think of anarchy in terms of animals and appetites. And *2 Henry VI* is characteristically full of the imagery of the jungle, the chase and the slaughter-house. Suggestions were not wanting in Hall;[3] and the emblems of the nobles —the bear and the boar, for example—lent themselves to these associations. Æsop was a natural quarry. Furnivall collected a long

1. That this should be so was a principle recognized in Renaissance literary theory; see e.g. W. L. Renwick, *Edmund Spenser* (1925), 73–7, and J. E. Spingarn, *Literary Criticism in the Renaissance* (1899).

2. W. Clemen, *The Development of Shakespeare's Imagery*, 1951, translated and revised from *Shakespeares Bilder* (Bonn, 1936).

3. E.g. 114 "sheep . . . shepherd"; 119 "dog . . . snake . . . lamprey"; 208 "venomous serpentes, and malicious Tygers"; 225 "worse than a tode or scorpion"; 239 "cancred crocodyle and subtile serpent".

list,[1] which divides itself naturally into beasts and birds of prey and their victims; and into this context fit appropriately the bear-garden, creatures of ill-omen, like the raven and the screech-owl, and all ugly and venomous creatures, like the toad, the serpent, the lizard and the spider. Parallel with this run images from the un-tended garden and the genealogical tree.

The building up of Henry's "holiness" on a basis of Biblical and religious phrases is the best example of this sustained use of imagery in the field of character, and finds a later parallel in Richard's use of proverb and epigram. In much the same way, the parting of Margaret and Suffolk gathered to itself, along with the natural parallel to Lancelot and Guinevere, and to the story of Dido and Æneas,[2] associations[3] from that of Ovid and his wife, described in the *Tristia*. So the great speech of Young Clifford[4] on finding the body of his father owes much of its tragic quality to the richness of the imagery behind it—imagery shared almost word for word with *Lear* and *Macbeth*, and compounded from representations of the Last Judgement, and associations from *2 Tamburlaine*, the story of Nabal, and Ovid's *Metamorphoses*.[5]

With which we return to Johnson, who summed up the impression left on him by the treatment of images, style, plot, and character—if rather dogmatically, not the less surely—"The diction, the versification, and the figures are Shakespeare's."[6]

1. *NSS.*, 1875–6, 280 ff.
2. See III. ii. 116 ff.
3. See note to III. ii. 388.
4. See V. ii. 40 ff. and note.
5. See notes to V. ii. 31–65.
6. Johnson's *Shakespeare* (1765), 5. 224–5.

THE SECOND PART OF KING HENRY VI

DRAMATIS PERSONÆ[1]

KING HENRY THE SIXTH.
HUMPHREY, *Duke of Gloucester, his Uncle.*
CARDINAL BEAUFORT, *Bishop of Winchester, Great-uncle to the King.*
RICHARD PLANTAGENET, *Duke of York.*
EDWARD *and* RICHARD, *his Sons.*
DUKE OF SOMERSET.
DUKE OF SUFFOLK.
DUKE OF BUCKINGHAM.
LORD CLIFFORD.
YOUNG CLIFFORD, *his Son.*
EARL OF SALISBURY.
EARL OF WARWICK, *his Son*
LORD SCALES.
LORD SAY.
SIR HUMPHREY STAFFORD *and* WILLIAM STAFFORD, *his Brother.*
SIR JOHN STANLEY.
VAUX.
MATTHEW GOFFE.
WALTER WHITMORE.
A Lieutenant, a Master, and a Master's Mate.
Two Gentlemen, Prisoners with Suffolk.
JOHN HUME *and* JOHN SOUTHWELL, *Priests.*
ROGER BOLINGBROKE, *a Conjurer.*
THOMAS HORNER, *an Armourer.*
PETER, *his Man.*
The Clerk of Chartham.
The Mayor of Saint Albans
SIMPCOX, *an Impostor.*
JACK CADE, *a Rebel.*
BEVIS, JOHN HOLLAND, DICK *the Butcher,* SMITH *the Weaver,* MICHAEL, *etc., Followers of Cade.*
ALEXANDER IDEN, *a Kentish Gentleman.*
Two Murderers.

MARGARET, *Queen to King Henry.*
ELEANOR COBHAM, *Duchess of Gloucester*
MARGERY JOURDAIN, *a Witch.*
Wife to Simpcox.

Lords, Ladies, and Attendants; Herald; Petitioners, Aldermen, a Beadle, Sheriff, and Officers; Citizens, Prentices, Falconers, Guards, Soldiers, Messengers, etc.

A Spirit.

Scene: *England.*

1. *Dramatis Personæ*] Cambridge (*subst.; first given imperfectly by Rowe*).

THE SECOND PART OF KING HENRY THE SIXTH

ACT I

SCENE I.—*London. The palace.*

Flourish of trumpets: then hautboys. Enter the KING, *Duke* HUMPHREY, SALISBURY, WARWICK, *and* BEAUFORT *on the one side; the* QUEEN, SUFFOLK, YORK, SOMERSET, *and* BUCKINGHAM, *on the other.*

Suf. As by your high imperial Majesty
I had in charge at my depart for France,

ACT I

Scene I

Title.] The first part of the Contention of the two famous Houses of Yorke & Lancaster, with the death of the Good Duke Humphrey. *Q;* The second Part of Henry the Sixt, with the death of the Good Duke Humfrey. *F.* Act I Scene I.] *edd.; Actus Primus. Scœna Prima. F; om. Q.* Locality.] *Capell, Theobald,* + *edd.* Entry.] *F (subst.); Enter at one doore, King* Henry *the sixt, and* Humphrey *Duke of* Gloster, *the Duke of* Sommerset, *the Duke of* Buckingham, *Cardinall* Bewford, *and others. Enter at the other doore, the Duke of* Yorke, *and the Marquesse of* Suffolke, *and Queene* Margaret, *and the Earls of* Salisbury *and* Warwicke. *Q.*

Flourish] a fanfare, especially to announce the approach of a person of distinction.

hautboys] oboes.

1–75.] F was here set up with the help of Q3. Such passages are marked by verse which is defective (e.g. 62–9) or printed as prose, as well as by variants in spelling, punctuation, etc., due to Q. See Introduction, pp. xxxii–xxxix.

1. *As by . . .*] "The opening of this play is a direct continuation from Part I. In the last speech, Suffolk announces his departure to procure Lady Margaret; he has now returned to present her to the king" (Hart). The sources are Hall, 203–5 (Appendix 1) and Holinshed, 3. 205–8; see Introduction, pp. xxxix–xli.

Suffolk left England in Nov. 1444, and returned in April 1445.

imperial] of an empire; cf. Strype, *Annals*, 4. 516, "Elizabeth, late Queen of England, France and Ireland; by whose death . . . the imperial crown of these realms . . ."; *H 5*, v. ii. 26; and Hall, 13, "the scepter and diademe Imperiall".

2. *had in charge*] had commission to.

depart] departure. For the use of verbs as nouns, see Abbott, 451; III. i. 160 below; *3 H 6*, IV. i. 92; and *F.Q.*, 3. 7. 20.

As procurator to your Excellence,
To marry Princess Margaret for your Grace;
So, in the famous ancient city, Tours,
In presence of the Kings of France and Sicil,
The Dukes of Orleans, Calaber, Bretagne, and Alençon,
Seven earls, twelve barons, and twenty reverend bishops,
I have perform'd my task, and was espous'd:
And humbly now upon my bended knee,
In sight of England and her lordly peers,
Deliver up my title in the Queen
To your most gracious hands, that are the substance
Of that great shadow I did represent;
The happiest gift that ever marquess gave,
The fairest queen that ever king receiv'd.

King. Suffolk, arise. Welcome, Queen Margaret:
I can express no kinder sign of love
Than this kind kiss. O Lord, that lends me life,
Lend me a heart replete with thankfulness!
For thou hast given me in this beauteous face
A world of earthly blessings to my soul,
If sympathy of love unite our thoughts.

Queen. Great King of England, and my gracious lord,

8. twenty] *Q3, F;* then the *Q1, 2.* 24–31.] *F; for Q, see App. 4.*

3. *procurator*] substitute, procurer for another, proxy.

6. *Sicil*] Margaret's father, René; see Appendix 1 (Hall, 204).

8. *twenty*] see collation. Q3 must have restored from a corrected sheet of Q1. "Twenty" is in the Chronicles.

10–16. *And humbly . . . receiv'd*] contrast Suffolk's tone here with the expression of his intentions at the end of *1 H 6* (cf. Hall, 207): "Margaret shall now be queen, and rule the king; / But I will rule both her, the king, and realm." For the love-affair of Margaret and Suffolk, see further at III. ii. 299, n. below.

12. *title*] in the legal sense of "a right to, or interest in".

13. *your . . . that are*] a Latinism = the hands of you . . . that are . . .

13, 14. *substance . . . shadow*] a common antithesis in Shakespeare, e.g. *Wiv.*, II. ii. 116; *1 H 6*, II. iii. 35–7; V. iv. 133–5; *Sonn.*, 43, 53, etc.

14. *represent*] The thought is confused by the mixed metaphors, "shadow" and "represent" expressing the idea of Henry's greatness working at a distance through a substitute = "of whose greatness I was a substitute or shadow".

18. *kinder*] more natural, as in "mankind".

19. *kind*] affectionate. Note the pun.

19–22. *O Lord . . . soul*] note the religious cast of Henry's speech, maintained throughout the play.

22. *earthly blessings*] in antithesis to "soul".

24 ff.] For the alternative Q passage, see Appendix 4. It would not be

The mutual conference that my mind hath had
By day, by night, waking, and in my dreams,
In courtly company, or at my beads,
With you mine alderliefest sovereign,
Makes me the bolder to salute my king
With ruder terms, such as my wit affords,
And over joy of heart doth minister.

King. Her sight did ravish, but her grace in speech,
Her words y-clad with wisdom's majesty,
Makes me from wond'ring fall to weeping joys,
Such is the fulness of my heart's content.
Lords, with one cheerful voice welcome my love.

All [*kneeling*]. Long live Queen Margaret, England's happiness! [*Flourish.*

Queen. We thank you all.

Suf. My Lord Protector, so it please your Grace,
Here are the articles of contracted peace
Between our sovereign and the French King Charles,
For eighteen months concluded by consent.

Glou. [*Reads.*] "Imprimis, It is agreed between the French King Charles, and William de la Pole, Marquess of Suffolk, ambassador for Henry King of England,

37. *All* (*kneeling*).] *Camb.; All kneel. F.* 37. S.D. *Flourish.*] *F* (*38*); Sound Trumpets. *Q* (*38*). 43–105. *Glou.*] *F* (*Glo.*); *Hum. Q.* 43. Imprimis] *Q1;* Inprimis *Q2, 3, F.*

beyond the ability of a reporter to vamp the Q version.

24–31.] Margaret's character is apparently at variance with the later developments in *2* and *3 H 6,* and *R 3.* Dramatic consistency, however, requires that on her first introduction to England and Henry, and before she has had time to become aware of Henry's character and of the factious state of the nobility, she should speak thus. Note the rapid transition and development at I. iii. 42.

25. *mutual*] intimate; cf. *Meas.*, I. ii. 164, "our most mutual entertainment".

conference] in the usual Elizabethan sense of "conversation, communication".

27. *courtly*] belonging to the Court.

beads] prayers said with the rosary.

28. *alderliefest*] dearest of all; from "alder" or "aller", the old genitive pl. of "all", and "lief" = dear. The word was becoming obsolete; this is the only instance in Shakespeare.

29. *salute*] in the L. sense of "greet".

30. *ruder*] in the L. sense of "rougher", "too rough, unpolished".

wit] mind; intelligence.

31. *over joy*] greater, higher joy. "Over" is an adj. here (Hart).

33. *y-clad*] an archaism—the old pa. pple. with "ge-"; possibly due to Spenser's influence.

43. *Imprimis*] in the first place. For the source of the "articles", see Appendix I (Hall, 205).

That the said Henry shall espouse the Lady Margaret, daughter unto Reignier King of Naples, Sicilia, and Jerusalem, and crown her Queen of England, ere the thirtieth of May next ensuing. Item, It is further agreed between them, That the duchy of Anjou and the county of Maine shall be releas'd and deliver'd to the King her father"— [*Lets the paper fall.*

King. Uncle, how now!

Glou. Pardon me, gracious lord;
Some sudden qualm hath struck me at the heart
And dimm'd mine eyes, that I can read no further.

King. Uncle of Winchester, I pray read on.

Car. "Item, It is further agreed between them, That the duchy of Anjou and the county of Maine shall be releas'd and deliver'd to the King her father, and she

46. espouse] *F;* wed and espouse *Q.* 49. thirtieth . . . ensuing] *F;* 30. of the next month *Q.* 49–50. It . . . them,] *Q; om. F. See n.* 50–1. the duchy . . . Maine] *F;* the Dutches (Dutchesse *Q3*) of *Anioy* and of *Maine Q.* 52. S.D. *Lets . . . fall.*] *Camb.;* Duke *Humphrey* lets it fall. *Q; om. F.* 56. Uncle of Winchester] *Q1, 2, F;* My Lord of Yorke *Q3.* read] *Q1, 2, F;* do you read *Q3.* 57. *Car.*] *Q1, 2; Yorke Q3; Win. F.* 58. duchy] *ASC;* Duches *Q1;* Dutches *Q2;* Dutchesse *Q3, F;* duchies *edd.* the county of Maine] *ASC;* of Maine *Q;* Maine *F.* 59. to] *ASC;* ouer to *Q, F.*

46. *espouse*] see collation. Q "wed and espouse" does not look like a recollection; is a standard bilingualism; and Hall, 23, has "marry and espouse". Perhaps we should read with Q, and assume an omission by F.

49–50. *Item, . . . them,*] see collation. This ought, of course, to agree with 57–9. The most probable cause of the omission by F is the identical ending of the two words; the compositor's eye has jumped from one to the other.

50–1. *the duchy . . . Maine*] see collation. The Q recollection, from 109, has been corrected in F from MS. This and similar Q variants tell against the idea of the reporters' possession of a scroll containing the "articles". Cf. notes on 58, 59 below.

51. *releas'd*] given up.

52. Lets . . . fall.] Gloucester is grieved and angry that this marriage should have occurred, and to learn that it should entail the surrender of Anjou and Maine, "the keys of Normandy" (113) for which the nobles had fought so long. In the Chronicles, his displeasure arises from the fact that his own arrangement of a marriage between Henry and the daughter of the Earl of Armagnac has been set aside. Cf. *1 H 6,* v. i.; v. v. Note his development of the theme at 74.

53, 56. *Uncle*] see Appendix 2. Winchester was an uncle once removed.

58. *duchy*] The Q3 error "Dutchesse", retained in F, is evidence of F use of Q3 copy, and failure of the F editor to amend. Contrast 50 above.

59. *to*] see collation, and n. to 58. That F was failing to amend this line is shown by retention of the Q corruption "deliver'd ouer", though it was rightly reduced to "deliver'd" at 52 above.

sent over of the King of England's own proper cost and charges, without having any dowry."

King. They please us well.
Lord Marquess, kneel down: we here create thee
First Duke of Suffolk, and girt thee with the sword.
Cousin of York, we here discharge your Grace
From being Regent in the parts of France,
Till term of eighteen months be full expir'd.
Thanks, uncle Winchester, Gloucester, and York,
Buckingham, Somerset, Salisbury, and Warwick;
We thank you all for this great favour done,
In entertainment to my princely Queen.
Come, let us in, and with all speed provide
To see her coronation be perform'd.

[*Exeunt King, Queen, and Suffolk. Gloucester stays all the rest.*

62–9.] *arranged ASC; as prose Q; as verse, divided* . . . down, / . . . Suffolke, / . . . Yorke, / . . . Regent / . . . Moneths / . . . Winchester, / . . . Somerset, / . . . Warwicke. *F.* 63. Lord] *Q, F;* My Lord *ASC conj.* 64. First] *Q;* the first *F.* girt] *Q, F;* gird *Camb.* 66. in the] *Q;* I'th *F;* in these *ASC conj. See n.* 68. and York] *ASC; Yorke, and Q;* Yorke *F.* 73. S.D.] *Q (subst.); Exit . . . Suffolke. Manet the rest. F.*

60–1. *own . . . charges*] a legal expression used in state affairs, translating "suis & eorum propriis sumptibus & expensis" in e.g. Letters Patent granted to the Cabots by Henry VII, 1495 (Hakluyt, ed. 1810–12, vol. III, pp. 25–6) (Hart).

63.] a metrically defective line, probably due to the Q "copy"; cf. collation 68–9 below, and n. above on 1–75. It is worth noting that Q prints 62–7 as prose, which F arranges as verse by guess.

63–4. *create . . . Duke*] an anticipation; the title was conferred three years later. See Appendix 1 (Hall, 207).

65. *Cousin*] used loosely of collateral relatives more distant than brother or sister, and by sovereigns to noblemen. For the exact relation, see Appendix 2.

York . . . discharge] Shakespeare holds over the new appointment for fuel to the quarrels of the nobles, who divide on the question whether York or Somerset should be appointed. This allows discussion of York's conduct during his previous term: and Shakespeare further invents a connection between York and the Armourer's servant to explain the choice of Somerset by Gloucester. Cf. 42 above for the term of the truce.

65–6.] cf. *1 H 6*, IV. i. 162–3: "Cousin of York, we institute your Grace / To be our regent in these parts of France:".

66. *the parts*] *OED.* defines "part", *sb.* III. 13, as "a portion of a country, or territory; region (often with a vague collective rather than plural sense) e.g. The mixed jurisdiction in the Parts of Kesteven."

67. *full expir'd*] cf. *1 Maccabees*, I. 29, "after two years fully expired".

68–9.] see collation; note the defective metre, which F has taken over unamended from Q; cf. *H 5*, IV. iii. 51–5, in Q and F.

71. *entertainment*] reception; cf. *2 Tamb.*, 2985, "To entertain divine Zenocrate".

Glou. Brave peers of England, pillars of the state,
To you Duke Humphrey must unload his grief—
Your grief, the common grief of all the land.
What! did my brother Henry spend his youth,
His valour, coin, and people, in the wars?
Did he so often lodge in open field,
In winter's cold, and summer's parching heat,
To conquer France, his true inheritance?
And did my brother Bedford toil his wits,
To keep by policy what Henry got?
Have you yourselves, Somerset, Buckingham,
Brave York, Salisbury, and victorious Warwick,
Receiv'd deep scars in France and Normandy?
Or hath mine uncle Beaufort and myself,
With all the learned Council of the realm,
Studied so long, sat in the Council House
Early and late, debating to and fro
How France and Frenchmen might be kept in awe?
And had his highness in his infancy
Crowned in Paris, in despite of foes?
And shall these labours and these honours die?

92. had] *Grant White;* hath *Q,F.*

74. *peers*] probably a pun on "pier". "In the *Alvearie* (by John Baret, 1573) *peer* is etymologized: 'the Peeres or rather pierres & noble men which like head corner stones and pillers in a building susteine & mainteyne the royalme . . .'" (James Sledd in *MP.*, 49 (1951–2), 10). Cf. the similar speeches of York and Warwick in *1 H 6*, v. iv. 102 ff.

77 ff.] This speech is based on a passage from the first year (1422) of Henry VI (Hall 114–15, Appendix 2). Henry's coronation did not take place until 1431 (Hall, 160–1).

77. *brother Henry*] Henry V; see Appendix 2.

79. *lodge*] lie; a common sense in the Bible and the Chronicles.

80. *cold . . . heat . . .*] (Hall, 112) "No *colde* made him slouthfull, nor *heat* caused him to loyter."

summer's parching heat] cf. *Arden*, II. ii. 109 and Peele, *An Eclogue Gratulatory* (Dyce, 562b), 1589.

81. *true inheritance*] by his marriage with Katherine de Valois; cf. *H 5*, v. ii. 333, "Haeres Franciae".

82. *Bedford*] see Appendix 2.

83. *policy*] administration; craft; stratagem. The word acquired in the 16th century the sense of action, however immoral, calculated to attain a prescribed end, particularly power. Mario Praz (*Machiavelli and the Elizabethans*, pp. 14 ff.) shows how the word came to be associated with the popular conception of Machiavelli and his philosophy of government. Here, however, it probably retains its better sense, of statesmanship.

87. *uncle Beaufort*] the Cardinal; cf. 103 below.

88. *Council*] Privy Council.

90. *to and fro*] for and against.

93. *Crowned . . . Paris*] cf. *1 H 6*, IV. i.

Shall Henry's conquest, Bedford's vigilance,
Your deeds of war, and all our counsel die?
O peers of England! shameful is this league,
Fatal this marriage, cancelling your fame,
Blotting your names from books of memory,
Razing the characters of your renown,
Defacing monuments of conquer'd France,
Undoing all, as all had never been!

Car. Nephew, what means this passionate discourse,
This peroration with such circumstance?
For France, 'tis ours; and we will keep it still.

Glou. Ay, uncle, we will keep it, if we can;
But now it is impossible we should.
Suffolk, the new-made duke that rules the roast,
Hath given the duchy of Anjou and Maine
Unto the poor King Reignier, whose large style
Agrees not with the leanness of his purse.

Sal. Now, by the death of Him that died for all,
These counties were the keys of Normandy!

100. Razing] *F* (Racing). 108. roast] *Q*; rost *F*.

98. *Fatal this marriage*] The marriage, with its background of broken faith, and the introduction of a French Queen (successor, in English minds, to Joan of Arc), already in love with Suffolk, and not only without a dowry, but at the expense of Anjou and Maine, is firmly seized as the centre of the story; and serves to accentuate the weakness of the King and the factious conduct of the nobles. Cf. Marlowe, *Massacre at Paris*, 206, "Oh fatall was this marriage to us all."

For the breach of contract involved, see *1 H 6*, v. v. 25–9.

98–101. *cancelling . . . Blotting . . . Razing the characters . . . Defacing*] note the succession of cognate metaphors.

99. *books of memory*] memorandum books; chronicles; cf. Hall, 15, "the book of fame", and *1 H 6*, II. iv. 101.

100. *characters*] writing, letters.

101. *monuments*] in the double sense of (*a*) memorials, (*b*) stones erected.

103. *passionate*] emotionally excited.

104. *peroration . . . circumstance*] rhetorical discourse . . . details or instances.

105 *For*] as for.

108. *rules the roast*] domineers, takes the lead—as if presiding over the head of the table. Hall, 232, says of Margaret, "Which then ruled the rost and bare the whole rule" (Hart).

110. *Reignier* . . .] Hall, 205 (App. 1).

large style] grandiose title, namely, "duc d'Anjou, de Lorraine, et de Barre, comte de Provence et de Piedmont, roi d'Hongrie, de Naples, des deux Siciles, de Jerusaleme, et d'Arragon". He used the Imperial and the Apollotic eagle, with aureoled head, as supporters to his armorial shield (Rothery). Cf. Talbot's titles in *1 H 6*, IV. vii. 60–74, and Joan of Arc's comment.

112. *by the death* . . .] *2 Cor.*, 5. 14, 15.

113. *the keys of Normandy*] from Fabyan's Chronicle, 617; cf. 216–17 below.

But wherefore weeps Warwick, my valiant son?
War. For grief that they are past recovery:
For, were there hope to conquer them again,
My sword should shed hot blood, mine eyes no tears.
Anjou and Maine! myself did win them both;
Those provinces these arms of mine did conquer:
And are the cities, that I got with wounds,
Deliver'd up again with peaceful words?
Mort Dieu!
York. For Suffolk's duke, may he be suffocate,
That dims the honour of this warlike isle!
France should have torn and rent my very heart
Before I would have yielded to this league.
I never read but England's kings have had
Large sums of gold and dowries with their wives;
And our King Henry gives away his own,
To match with her that brings no vantages.
Glou. A proper jest, and never heard before,
That Suffolk should demand a whole fifteenth
For costs and charges in transporting her!
She should have stayed in France, and starv'd in France,
Before—
Car. My Lord of Gloucester, now ye grow too hot:
It was the pleasure of my lord the King.
Glou. My Lord of Winchester, I know your mind:
'Tis not my speeches that you do mislike,
But 'tis my presence that doth trouble ye.

131, 138. *Glou.*] *edd.; Hum. Q,F.* 134. starv'd] *F* (steru'd). 136 ff.] *F; for Q, see App. 4.*

114. *Warwick*] Richard Neville, who became Earl of Warwick in 1449, four years after the date of this scene, and is generally known as the King-maker. He first saw military service at the (first) Battle of St Albans in 1455. He is here telescoped with his father-in-law, Richard Beauchamp, who died in 1439, from whom he derived the title, and some of whose exploits are here credited to him. See Appendix 2.

123. *Suffolk . . . suffocate*] another of the many puns in this play.

130. *match with*] marry.

vantages] profit, gain; cf. "without . . . any dowry", I. i. 61.

132. *fifteenth*] a tax of one-fifteenth levied on personal property; cf. IV. vii. 20. In *1 H 6*, V. v. 92, Suffolk was promised a *tenth*.

134. *starv'd*] the old form used in F (*steru'd* — cf. Ger. *sterben*) preserves more than a suggestion of the original meaning "died"; it was still in use into the 17th century.

Rancour will out: proud prelate, in thy face
I see thy fury. If I longer stay
We shall begin our ancient bickerings.
Lordings, farewell; and say, when I am gone,
I prophesied France will be lost ere long. [*Exit.*

Car. So, there goes our Protector in a rage.
'Tis known to you he is mine enemy;
Nay, more, an enemy unto you all,
And no great friend, I fear me, to the King.
Consider, lords, he is the next of blood,
And heir apparent to the English crown:
Had Henry got an empire by his marriage,
And all the wealthy kingdoms of the west,
There's reason he should be displeas'd at it.
Look to it, lords; let not his smoothing words
Bewitch your hearts; be wise and circumspect.
What though the common people favour him,
Calling him "Humphrey, the good Duke of Gloucester,"
Clapping their hands, and crying with loud voice
"Jesu maintain your royal Excellence!"
With "God preserve the good Duke Humphrey!"
I fear me, lords, for all this flattering gloss,
He will be found a dangerous Protector.

Buck. Why should he then protect our sovereign,

141. *proud prelate*] *Mirror* (Humphrey), ll. 155, 205.

143. *ancient bickerings*] wranglings, contention. The allusion is to the bickerings recorded in *1 H 6*, III. i. 1 ff. Cf. below, I. iii. 171.

144. *Lordings*] an early form of address equivalent to "Sirs!", "Gentlemen!"

150. *next of blood*] as the king's nearest brother; see Appendix 2.

151. *heir apparent*] "strictly, heir presumptive, i.e., his right to succeed was contingent upon the chance that Henry would leave no lineal heir" (Brooke).

153. *all the wealthy kingdoms of the west*] perhaps an anachronistic allusion to the golden realms of Spanish America (Brooke). A recollection of *2 Tamb.*, 2588, "all the wealthy kingdoms I subdewed".

155. *Look to it*] be on your guard.

smoothing] flattering, blandishing; cf. II. i. 22.

157–8. *common people . . . good Duke*] see Fox (Appendix 1). This idealized portrait of Humphrey has been taken over from Hall and Fox. See C. L. Kingsford, *Prejudice and Promise in Fifteenth Century England* (Oxford, 1925), and headnote to I. ii. below.

162. *gloss*] smooth, specious talk.

163, 164. *Protector . . . protect*] note the word-play; cf. I. iii. 4; II. i. 55. Henry was now 25, and Gloucester no longer Protector. The office is maintained, in the play, to give a handle for his fall and Eleanor's. Note also the first suggestion of his treason here.

He being of age to govern of himself?
Cousin of Somerset, join you with me,
And all together, with the Duke of Suffolk,
We'll quickly hoise Duke Humphrey from his seat.

Car. This weighty business will not brook delay;
I'll to the Duke of Suffolk presently. [*Exit.*

Som. Cousin of Buckingham, though Humphrey's pride
And greatness of his place be grief to us,
Yet let us watch the haughty Cardinal:
His insolence is more intolerable
Than all the princes' in the land beside:
If Gloucester be displac'd, he'll be Protector.

Buck. Or thou or I, Somerset, will be Protector,
Despite Duke Humphrey or the Cardinal.
[*Exeunt Buckingham and Somerset.*

Sal. Pride went before, Ambition follows him.
While these do labour for their own preferment,
Behooves it us to labour for the realm.
I never saw but Humphrey, Duke of Gloucester,
Did bear him like a noble gentleman.
Oft have I seen the haughty Cardinal—
More like a soldier than a man o' th' church,
As stout and proud as he were lord of all—
Swear like a ruffian, and demean himself
Unlike the ruler of a commonweal.
Warwick, my son, the comfort of my age,

167. all together] *Rowe* + *edd.;* altogether *F.* 177. Protector] *Q;* Protectors *F.*

168. *hoise*] hoist, remove forcibly.

169. *brook*] suffer, tolerate.

170. *I'll to . . . Suffolk*] the beginning of a long partnership, ending in the murder of Gloucester; cf. III. i. 137, 187, etc.

presently] in the Elizabethan sense = immediately.

172. *grief*] grievance; pain.

174. *insolence*] pride, overbearing nature.

175. *all . . . beside*] all the other . . .

176. *displac'd*] removed from his office.

177. *Or . . . or*] common Elizabethan usage = either . . . or.

179. *Pride . . . Ambition*] a modification of an old proverb, "Pride goes before, and shame follows after." Pride is the Cardinal; Ambition, Buckingham and Somerset. Cf. II. ii. 70–1. The line foreshadows the "fall" or "destruction" (*Prov.*, 16. 18) that follows pride. Both proverbs occur in *Mirror* (Eleanor), 432, 434.

181. *for the realm*] Salisbury and Warwick stand almost alone in their concern for the good of England; cf. 200, 206.

187. *demean himself*] behave.

189–91. *Warwick . . .*] see Appendix I (Hall, 231–2). Cf. I. iii. 72–4.

Glou. Brave peers of England, pillars of the state,
To you Duke Humphrey must unload his grief—
Your grief, the common grief of all the land.
What! did my brother Henry spend his youth,
His valour, coin, and people, in the wars?
Did he so often lodge in open field,
In winter's cold, and summer's parching heat,
To conquer France, his true inheritance?
And did my brother Bedford toil his wits,
To keep by policy what Henry got?
Have you yourselves, Somerset, Buckingham,
Brave York, Salisbury, and victorious Warwick,
Receiv'd deep scars in France and Normandy?
Or hath mine uncle Beaufort and myself,
With all the learned Council of the realm,
Studied so long, sat in the Council House
Early and late, debating to and fro
How France and Frenchmen might be kept in awe?
And had his highness in his infancy
Crowned in Paris, in despite of foes?
And shall these labours and these honours die?

92. had] *Grant White;* hath *Q,F.*

74. *peers*] probably a pun on "pier". "In the *Alvearie* (by John Baret, 1573) *peer* is etymologized: 'the Peeres or rather pierres & noble men which like head corner stones and pillers in a building susteine & mainteyne the royalme . . .'" (James Sledd in *MP.*, 49 (1951–2), 10). Cf. the similar speeches of York and Warwick in *1 H 6*, v. iv. 102 ff.

77 ff.] This speech is based on a passage from the first year (1422) of Henry VI (Hall 114–15, Appendix 2). Henry's coronation did not take place until 1431 (Hall, 160–1).

77. *brother Henry*] Henry V; see Appendix 2.

79. *lodge*] lie; a common sense in the Bible and the Chronicles.

80. *cold . . . heat . . .*] (Hall, 112) "No *colde* made him slouthfull, nor *heat* caused him to loyter."

summer's parching heat] cf. *Arden*, II. ii. 109 and Peele, *An Eclogue Gratulatory* (Dyce, 5626), 1589.

81. *true inheritance*] by his marriage with Katherine de Valois; cf. *H 5*, v. ii. 333, "Haeres Franciae".

82. *Bedford*] see Appendix 2.

83. *policy*] administration; craft; stratagem. The word acquired in the 16th century the sense of action, however immoral, calculated to attain a prescribed end, particularly power. Mario Praz (*Machiavelli and the Elizabethans*, pp. 14 ff.) shows how the word came to be associated with the popular conception of Machiavelli and his philosophy of government. Here, however, it probably retains its better sense, of statesmanship.

87. *uncle Beaufort*] the Cardinal; cf. 103 below.

88. *Council*] Privy Council.

90. *to and fro*] for and against.

93. *Crowned . . . Paris*] cf. *1 H 6*, IV. i.

sent over of the King of England's own proper cost
and charges, without having any dowry."

King. They please us well.
Lord Marquess, kneel down: we here create thee
First Duke of Suffolk, and girt thee with the sword.
Cousin of York, we here discharge your Grace
From being Regent in the parts of France,
Till term of eighteen months be full expir'd.
Thanks, uncle Winchester, Gloucester, and York,
Buckingham, Somerset, Salisbury, and Warwick;
We thank you all for this great favour done,
In entertainment to my princely Queen.
Come, let us in, and with all speed provide
To see her coronation be perform'd.

[*Exeunt King, Queen, and Suffolk. Gloucester stays all the rest.*

62–9.] *arranged ASC; as prose Q; as verse, divided* . . . down, / . . . Suffolke, / . . . Yorke, / . . . Regent / . . . Moneths / . . . Winchester, / . . . Somerset, / . . . Warwicke. *F*. 63. Lord] *Q,F;* My Lord *ASC conj.* 64. First] *Q;* the first *F.* girt] *Q,F;* gird *Camb.* 66. in the] *Q;* I'th *F;* in these *ASC conj. See n.* 68. and York] *ASC; Yorke, and Q;* Yorke *F.* 73. S.D.] *Q* (*subst.*); *Exit . . . Suffolke. Manet the rest. F.*

60–1. *own . . . charges*] a legal expression used in state affairs, translating "suis & eorum propriis sumptibus & expensis" in e.g. Letters Patent granted to the Cabots by Henry VII, 1495 (Hakluyt, ed. 1810–12, vol. III, pp. 25–6) (Hart).

63.] a metrically defective line, probably due to the Q "copy"; cf. collation 68–9 below, and n. above on 1–75. It is worth noting that Q prints 62–7 as prose, which F arranges as verse by guess.

63–4. *create . . . Duke*] an anticipation; the title was conferred three years later. See Appendix I (Hall, 207).

65. *Cousin*] used loosely of collateral relatives more distant than brother or sister, and by sovereigns to noblemen. For the exact relation, see Appendix 2.

York . . . discharge] Shakespeare holds over the new appointment for fuel to the quarrels of the nobles, who divide on the question whether York or Somerset should be appointed. This allows discussion of York's conduct during his previous term: and Shakespeare further invents a connection between York and the Armourer's servant to explain the choice of Somerset by Gloucester. Cf. 42 above for the term of the truce.

65–6.] cf. *1 H 6*, IV. i. 162–3: "Cousin of York, we institute your Grace / To be our regent in these parts of France:".

66. *the parts*] *OED*. defines "part", *sb*. III. 13, as "a portion of a country, or territory; region (often with a vague collective rather than plural sense) e.g. The mixed jurisdiction in the Parts of Kesteven."

67. *full expir'd*] cf. *1 Maccabees*, I. 29, "after two years fully expired".

68–9.] see collation; note the defective metre, which F has taken over unamended from Q; cf. *H 5*, IV. iii. 51–5, in Q and F.

71. *entertainment*] reception; cf. *2 Tamb.*, 2985, "To entertain divine Zenocrate".

Thy deeds, thy plainness, and thy house-keeping,
Hath won the greatest favour of the commons,
Excepting none but good Duke Humphrey:
And, brother York, thy acts in Ireland,
In bringing them to civil discipline,
Thy late exploits done in the heart of France,
When thou wert Regent for our sovereign,
Have made thee fear'd and honour'd of the people.
The reverence of mine age, and Nevil's name,
Is of no little force, if I command.
Join we together for the public good,
In what we can, to bridle and suppress
The pride of Suffolk and the Cardinal,
With Somerset's and Buckingham's ambition;
And, as we may, cherish Duke Humphrey's deeds,
While they do tend the profit of the land.

War. So God help Warwick, as he loves the land,
And common profit of his country!

York. And so says York—[*Aside.*] for he hath greatest cause.

Sal. Then let's make haste, and look unto the main.

198–9.] *Q; om. F. See n.* 208–10.] *Pope; Yor.* And . . . Yorke, / For . . . cause. / *Salisbury.* Then . . . hast away, / And . . . maine. / *Warwicke.* Vnto the maine? / Oh . . . lost, / *F.* 208. *Aside.*] *Theobald* (*before* And), *Alexander.* 209. Then let's make haste] *Pope;* Then lets make hast away *F;* Come sonnes away *Q.*

190. *house-keeping*] hospitality.

191. *Hath*] agrees with "house-keeping", or l. 189 collectively; cf. Abbott, 237.

191, 192. *commons . . . good Duke*] cf. n. to 157–8 above; from Fox.

193. *brother York*] strictly, brother-in-law; see Appendix 2.

thy acts . . .] an anachronistic duplication of York's term in Ireland, whither he is sent again at III. i. 309–10 (1449). These events occurred in 1445.

194. *civil*] proper to citizens (L. *civilis*); orderly.

195. *exploits*] military undertakings.

198–9.] see collation. The Q lines complete the qualifications of the trio, begun at 189 (Warwick) and 193 (York).

200. *Join we*] "The subjunctive of the present, followed by 'we' expressing an invitation = let us" (Schmidt).

200, 207. *public good . . . country*] cf. Marlowe, *Massacre*, 225: "rather chuse to seek your countries good".

204. *cherish*] support; foster (as a plant).

208. *greatest cause*] as representing the rival house to Lancaster. The theme is developed in his soliloquy below.

209. *haste*] F haste away. An example of imperfect amendment of Q "copy". See Intro., pp. xxxiii ff.

209–13. *main . . . Maine*] a multiple pun on the gambling term "main" (as opposed to the "by" (Bond, *Lyly*, I. 245. 16), a number called by the "caster" of the dice before it is thrown; fig. ("main chance") the most important thing at stake; main

War. Unto the main! O father, Maine is lost!
That Maine which by main force Warwick did win,
And would have kept so long as breath did last:
Main chance, father, you meant; but I meant Maine,
Which I will win from France, or else be slain.
[*Exeunt Warwick and Salisbury.*

York. Anjou and Maine are given to the French;
Paris is lost; the state of Normandy
Stands on a tickle point now they are gone;
Suffolk concluded on the articles,
The peers agreed, and Henry was well pleas'd
To change two dukedoms for a duke's fair daughter.
I cannot blame them all: what is't to them?
'Tis thine they give away, and not their own.
Pirates may make cheap pennyworths of their pillage,
And purchase friends, and give to courtezans,
Still revelling like lords till all be gone;
While as the silly owner of the goods
Weeps over them, and wrings his hapless hands,
And shakes his head, and trembling stands aloof,
While all is shar'd and all is borne away,
Ready to starve, and dare not touch his own.
So York must sit and fret and bite his tongue
While his own lands are bargain'd for and sold.

213. meant] *Q1, 3, F;* meane *Q2.* 214. S.D.] *Exit Warwicke, and Salisbury. Manet Yorke. F.* 215–36.] *F; om. Q.* 230. starve] *F* (sterue).

= overpowering; Maine; and "mean", then a homonym of "main", as still in Ireland.

216–17. *state of Normandy . . . point*] since Anjou and Maine were the "keys".

217. *Stands on a tickle point*] in a ticklish, unstable condition. Cf. *Sp. Tr.*, 3. 4. 78, "Now stands our fortune on a tickle point."

218. *concluded on*] came to a final arrangement about.

222. *thine*] York is addressing himself; cf. 231–2, below.

223–36. *Pirates . . . Calydon*] note the two epic similes, in the recognized Renascence tradition of ornament, and characteristic of the formal rhetoric of the play.

223. *make cheap pennyworths*] sell for next to nothing; give away.

224. *purchase*] in the double sense of "acquire" (legal) and "buy".

225. *Still*] normal Elizabethan sense = always, continually.

226. *While as*] "as", like "that", was often added superfluously, as a conjunctional affix, to words that are already conjunctions (Abbott, 116).

silly] poor, helpless.

227. *hapless*] unlucky.

230. *starve*] on the F form *sterve*, see n. to 134.

231. *bite his tongue*] keep silence.

Methinks the realms of England, France, and Ireland
Bear that proportion to my flesh and blood
As did the fatal brand Althæa burnt
Unto the prince's heart of Calydon.
Anjou and Maine both given unto the French!
Cold news for me, for I had hope of France,
Even as I have of fertile England's soil.
A day will come when York shall claim his own;
And therefore I will take the Nevils' parts
And make a show of love to proud Duke Humphrey,
And when I spy advantage, claim the crown,
For that's the golden mark I seek to hit.
Nor shall proud Lancaster usurp my right,
Nor hold the sceptre in his childish fist,
Nor wear the diadem upon his head,
Whose church-like humour fits not for a crown.
Then, York, be still awhile, till time do serve:
Watch thou, and wake when others be asleep,

239. England's soil] *F;* England. *Q. See n.* 248. humour] *Rowe;* humours *QF.*

233. *Methinks*] it seems to me.

234. *proportion*] relation.

235–6. *the fatal brand . . .*] Meleager, prince of Calydon, died when his mother, Althaea, in anger burned the brand on which the Fates (triplices sorores) had decreed that his life depended; cf. *2 H 4*, II. ii. 85 f. The story is told in Ovid, *Metam.*, 8. 451–526; cf. Newton's *Seneca* (Tudor trans., pp. 88–9): "Loe heere the *fatall brand*, which late the fatall sisters three / Conspyred at Meleager's byrth, such should his destiny bee, . . ."

236. *prince's heart of Calydon*] L. construction = the heart of the prince of Calydon.

238. *Cold news*] unwelcome, disagreeable, bad, news. Often used by Shakespeare in this sense; cf. III. i. 86–8, for a repetition of the sentiment by York in almost the same words.

hope of France] i.e. of the French crown.

239. *England's soil*] Q reads "England", either owing to the omission of "soil" by the scribe who copied out the actor's "part", or owing to a recollection by the pirate (York?) of III. i. 88. Tucker Brooke finds in the "addition" of "soil" a sign of revision! (*Trans. Conn. Acad.*, 1912.) See Introduction, pp. xxix–xxx.

241. *take the Nevils' parts*] ally with, join the party of. For the relationships, see Appendix 2. In actual fact, it was the Nevilles who supported York (Brooke); cf. II. ii.

244. *golden mark I seek to hit*] The centre of the target, the mark, was white. Otherwise this might do duty for "hit the gold" (Hart). In *Mirror*, p. 396, l. 175, Somerset says of York, "But to be kyng, to that *marke* was his bent."

245 *Lancaster*] Henry VI. See Appendix 2.

248. *church-like humour*] pietistic disposition; cf. I. iii. 55–64, and Appendix 1 (Hall, 208).

250. *Watch . . . asleep*] cf. Marlowe, *Massacre*, 105–6: "For this I wake, when others think I sleepe, / For this, I waite, that scornes attendance else".

To pry into the secrets of the state;
Till Henry surfeit in the joys of love,
With his new bride and England's dear-bought queen,
And Humphrey with the peers be fall'n at jars:
Then will I raise aloft the milk-white rose,
With whose sweet smell the air shall be perfum'd,
And in my standard bear the arms of York,
To grapple with the house of Lancaster;
And force perforce I'll make him yield the crown,
Whose bookish rule hath pull'd fair England down.
[*Exit.*

SCENE II.—*The Duke of* GLOUCESTER'S *house.*

Enter Duke HUMPHREY *and his wife* ELEANOR.

Duch. Why droops my lord, like over-ripen'd corn,
Hanging the head at Ceres' plenteous load?
Why doth the great Duke Humphrey knit his brows,
As frowning at the favours of the world?
Why are thine eyes fix'd to the sullen earth,

252. surfeit in the] *Hanmer;* surfeiting in *Q,F.* 260. S.D. *Exit.*] *Exit Yorke. F; Q (subst.).*

Scene II

Locality.] *Theobald.* Entry.] *F;* Enter Duke *Humphrey*, and Dame *Ellanor, Cobham* his wife. *Q.*

252. *surfeit in the*] For the QF reading, cf. *H 5*, I. ii. 110: Foraging Q1, 2; Foraging the Q3; Forage in F.

surfeit] be satiated, sick from excess.

254. *fallen at jars*] become involved in quarrels or contention.

257. *arms*] ensigns armorial, i.e. the white rose. Shakespeare "needed the word 'arms' to play on the idea of grappling in the next line" (Scott-Giles, 140).

259. *force perforce*] by violent constraint. The doubling is emphatic; cf. *Sp. Tr.*, 3. 9. 12.

Scene II

Shakespeare chose for his dramatic purpose the legend of the "good duke Humphrey", and used his wife's ambitions as part explanation of his fall. See also Appendix 1, and note to I. i. 157–8.

The disgrace of the Duchess took place in 1441, four years before the arrival of Margaret.

2. *Ceres*] goddess of agriculture; cf. Ovid, *Metam.*, 5. 340–1: "Prima Ceres unco glaebam dimovit aratro, / prima dedit fruges alimentaque mitia terris . . ." and Virgil, *Georgics*, I. 1.

5. *sullen*] dull, gloomy; cf. *Sonn.*, 29. 12, "the lark . . . arising / From the sullen earth". Here, transferred epi-

Gazing on that which seems to dim thy sight?
What seest thou there? King Henry's diadem,
Enchas'd with all the honours of the world?
If so, gaze on, and grovel on thy face,
Until thy head be circled with the same.
Put forth thy hand, reach at the glorious gold.
What, is 't too short? I'll lengthen it with mine;
And, having both together heav'd it up,
We'll both together lift our heads to heaven,
And never more abase our sight so low
As to vouchsafe one glance unto the ground.

Glou. O Nell, sweet Nell, if thou dost love thy lord,
Banish the canker of ambitious thoughts!
And may that hour, when I imagine ill
Against my king and nephew, virtuous Henry,
Be my last breathing in this mortal world!
My troublous dreams this night doth make me sad.

Duch. What dream'd my lord? Tell me, and I'll requite it
With sweet rehearsal of my morning's dream.

Glou. Methought this staff, mine office-badge in court,
Was broke in twain; by whom I have forgot,
But, as I think, it was by th' Cardinal;
And on the pieces of the broken wand
Were plac'd the heads of Edmund Duke of Somerset,
And William de la Pole, first Duke of Suffolk.

17. Glou.] *edd.; Hum. Q, F (and throughout the scene).* 19. hour] *ASC, Vaughan conj.*; thought *F.*

thet. Cf. *Arden*, 3. I. 45, "Then fix his sad eis on the sollen earth".

8. *Enchas'd*] studded, adorned; cf. *I Tamb.*, 292, "Thy Garments . . . / Enchast with precious iuelles of mine owne".

9. *grovel on thy face*] to solicit supernatural aid; cf. I. iv. 11 (Brooke); Hall, 454, "grovelynge on the grounde".

17 ff.] With Humphrey on his wife's ambition, compare Gaunt on his wife's passion for revenge, *R2*, I. ii.

18. *canker*] spreading sore, ulcer.

19. *hour*] see collation; "thought", as Vaughan suggested, probably derived from its occurrence in the previous line, and the *t hour* of *that hour*.

19–22.] Note the irony of this and the following speech, in view of Humphrey's fate.

21. *my last breathing*] my last, or latest, gasp; cf. "Forsake me not . . . in my *last breathing*" (Hieron, *Works*, I. 736 (1608)—*OED.*).

22. *this night*] last night.

24. *morning's dream*] true dream; an ancient superstition; cf. Jonson, *Love Restored*: "morning hastes to come in view / And all the morning dreams are true" (Hart.)

25. *Methought*] it seemed to me.

This was my dream; what it doth bode, God knows.
Duch. Tut! this was nothing but an argument,
That he that breaks a stick of Gloucester's grove
Shall lose his head for his presumption.
But list to me, my Humphrey, my sweet duke:
Methought I sat in seat of majesty
In the cathedral church of Westminster,
And in that chair where kings and queens are crown'd;
Where Henry and Dame Margaret kneel'd to me,
And on my head did set the diadem.
Glou. Nay, Eleanor, then must I chide outright:
Presumptuous dame! ill-nurtur'd Eleanor!
Art thou not second woman in the realm,
And the Protector's wife, belov'd of him?
Hast thou not worldly pleasure at command,
Above the reach or compass of thy thought?
And wilt thou still be hammering treachery,
To tumble down thy husband and thyself
From top of Honour to Disgrace's feet?
Away from me, and let me hear no more!
Duch. What, what, my lord! Are you so choleric
With Eleanor, for telling but her dream?
Next time I'll keep my dreams unto myself,
And not be check'd.
Glou. Nay, be not angry; I am pleas'd again.

Enter a Messenger.

Mess. My Lord Protector, 'tis his Highness' pleasure
You do prepare to ride unto Saint Albans,
Where as the King and Queen do mean to hawk.

38. are] *Q; wer F.* 42. nurtur'd] *F* (nurter'd). 55. S.D. *a*] *Q; om. F.*

32. *argument*] proof, evidence; cf. *Ado*, II. iii. 254, "no great argument of her folly".

38. *chair*] the Coronation chair in Westminster Abbey.

42. *ill-nurtur'd*] ill-bred, ill-educated; cf. *AYL.*, II. vii. 97; *Ven.*, 134; *Ecclesiasticus*, 22. 3, "evil-nurtured".

43. *second woman*] since Gloucester was heir presumptive or "next of blood" (I. i. 150; I. ii. 63).

47. *hammering*] devising, designing; cf. *Tit.*, II. iii. 39.

49. From . . . Honour] *Mirror* (Suffolk), p. 162, l. 4, "From top of honors hye".

54. *check'd*] rebuked, chidden; still so used in Scotland.

58. *Where as*] cf. n. to I. i. 226.

Glou. I go. Come, Nell, thou 'lt ride with us, I'm sure?
Duch. Yes, my good lord, I'll follow presently.
[*Exeunt Gloucester and Messenger.*
Follow I must; I cannot go before,
While Gloucester bears this base and humble mind.
Were I a man, a duke, and next of blood,
I would remove these tedious stumbling-blocks
And smooth my way upon their headless necks;
And, being a woman, I will not be slack
To play my part in Fortune's pageant.
Where are you there, Sir John? nay, fear not, man,
We are alone; here's none but thee and I.

Enter HUME.

Hume. Jesu preserve your royal Majesty!
Duch. What say'st thou? Majesty! I am but Grace.
Hume. But, by the grace of God, and Hume's advice,
Your Grace's title shall be multiplied.
Duch. What say'st thou, man? Hast thou as yet conferr'd
With Margery Jourdain, the witch of Eie,
With Bolingbroke, the cunning conjurer,

59. thou 'lt . . . us, I'm sure] *Dyce, from Q;* thou wilt . . . us? *F. See n.* 60. S.D. *Exeunt . . .*] *Capell; Ex. Hum* (59) *F;* Exet Humphrey. (59) *Q.* 68. there, Sir John?] *F* (there? Sir *Iohn;*). 70. Jesu] *ASC;* Iesus *Q, F. See n.* 75. witch] *ASC;* cunning witch *Q, F. See n.* of Eie] *Alexander;* of *Ely Q1, 2;* of *Rye Q3; om. F. See n.* 76. With] *ASC;* With *Roger Q, F. See n.*

59.] see collation. Possibly F omits the Q "I am sure".

64. *stumbling-blocks*] Biblical.

67. *pageant*] scene or act in a mystery-play; hence show, spectacle, procession.

68. *Sir John*] a common early designation for clerks in holy orders. Hume is *Thomas* in the Chronicles.

70. *Hume*] the spelling is peculiar to Fox; the other sources have "Hum" or "Hun".

Jesu] see collation. The form "Jesus" occurs only here, at *3 H 6*, v. vi. 75, and *1 H 4*, II. ii. 86, all plays derived from Q copy. The other 17 examples read "Iesu", which was almost certainly Shakespeare's consistent usage; cf. v. i. 215 below.

71–3. *Grace . . . multiplied*] = your Grace; a play on *1 Peter*, I. 2, "Grace and peace be multiplied unto you."

75, 76] see collation. F has been corrupted by the use of Q copy, and imperfect amendment. Q3 reads, as three lines of prose: "*Elnor* . . . with *Margery Iourdain*, the / cunning witch of *Rye*, with *Roger Bullenbrooke* and the rest? and / will they vndertake to do me good?" The corrector, it may be supposed, failed to delete "*Roger*"; deleted 'and the rest? and"; wrote "And" before "will" at the beginning of the third line; and inserted the words "the Coniurer?", one below the other, in the left margin opposite

And will they undertake to do me good?
Hume. This they have promis'd me, to show your Highness
A spirit rais'd from depth of under ground,
That shall make answer to such questions
As by your Grace shall be propounded him.
Duch. It is enough: I'll think upon the questions.
When from Saint Albans we do make return
We'll see these things effected to the full.
Here, Hume, take this reward; make merry, man,
With thy confederates in this weighty cause. [*Exit.*
Hume. Hume must make merry with the Duchess' gold;
Marry and shall. But how now, Sir John Hume!
Seal up your lips and give no words but mum:
The business asketh silent secrecy.
Dame Eleanor gives gold to bring the witch:
Gold cannot come amiss, were she a devil.
Yet have I gold flies from another coast:
I dare not say from the rich Cardinal
And from the great and new-made Duke of Suffolk;
Yet I do find it so: for, to be plain,
They, knowing Dame Eleanor's aspiring humour,

78. me] *Q; om. F.*

"cunning" to form the phrase "the cunning Coniurer?", with a sign directing the phrase to be placed between the second and third lines to follow "Bullenbrooke". The compositor must have misunderstood, or the sign been inadequate, so that "cunning" was allowed to remain where it was. The F omission of "*Rye*" may be either an erroneous deletion instead of "*Roger*"; a typical compositor's omission through confusion with "*Roger*"; or an attempt to normalize the metre.

"of Eie" and "cunning coniurer" are in Hall, 202 (Appendix I)

75. *Eie*] near Winchester (Fox, 3. 708).

77. *do me good*] enable me to succeed; cf. IV. iii. 14; *Wiv.*, I. iv. 152; *Genesis*, 32. 12.

79. *depth of under ground*] cf. II. i. 166; *Sp. Tr.*, I. 6. 1–2, "Come we for thee from depth of under ground." and Ovid, *Metam.*, 5. 507, "opaci mundi inferni".

88. *Hume . . .*] Brooke suggests that the statement, in Hall, that Hume "had his pardon" may have prompted this betrayal scene. It may be; but that did not affect his fate in I. iv.

89. *no words but mum*] proverbial; cf. Heywood, *Proverbs*, 162.

90. *asketh*] requires; cf. *Sp. Tr.*, 2. 4. 23, "for pleasure asketh ease".

silent secrecy] again at II. ii. 67.

93. *coast*] quarter, direction.

94. *the rich Cardinal*] note the emphasis on the cardinal's hatred for Gloucester; for "rich", see Appendix I (Hall, 210).

97. *aspiring humour*] ambitious nature.

Have hired me to undermine the Duchess,
And buz these conjurations in her brain.
They say "A crafty knave does need no broker";
Yet am I Suffolk and the Cardinal's broker.
Hume, if you take not heed, you shall go near
To call them both a pair of crafty knaves.
Well, so it stands; and thus, I fear, at last
Hume's knavery will be the Duchess' wrack,
And her attainture will be Humphrey's fall.
Sort how it will, I shall have gold for all. [*Exit.*

SCENE III.—*The palace.*

Enter three or four Petitioners, PETER, *the Armourer's man, being one.*

1 Pet. My masters, let's stand close: my Lord Protector will come this way by and by, and then we may deliver our supplications in the quill.

2 Pet. Marry, the Lord protect him, for he's a good man, Jesu bless him!

Scene III

Locality.] *Hanmer.* Entry.] *F* (*om. Peter*)*;* Enter two Petitioners, and *Peter* the Armourers man. *Q.* 3. in the quill] *F;* in sequel *Collier. See n.*

99. *buz*] whisper (infectious tales or ideas); cf. *Ham.*, IV. v. 90.

conjurations] incantations, charms.

100. *A crafty knave . . . broker*] cf. *A Knacke* (1594): "Some will say / A crafty knave needs no broker / But here is a craftie knave and a broker too." Marlowe, *Jew,* 956–7: "And with extorting, cozening, forfeiting, / And tricks belonging unto Brokery."

broker] agent, go-between, middleman; generally with a suggestion of dishonesty.

105. *wrack*] ruin; cf. *1 H 6*, IV. i. 56, "my country's wrack".

106. *attainture*] attainder, conviction; cf. "tainture", II. i. 180.

107. *Sort how it will*] "let the issue be what it will" (Singer).

Scene III

The armourer incident, independent in the Chronicles, is linked by Shakespeare with the fate of York, and the suspicion of treason used as a reason for not appointing York as regent of France (l. 206, and cf. l. 97).

1. *close*] quiet and unobserved; still (Schmidt); or, in close order or rank (*OED.:* close: a. and adj. A14a, b; B1a). See n. to 3 below.

3. *in the quill*] in a body (*OED.*). We should probably read "in sequel" = in order, in succession; cf. *H 5*, v. ii. 361. Peter's "I'll be the first" may corroborate. See also n. to 1 above.

4. *protect*] another pun; cf. 37, below.

Enter SUFFOLK *and* QUEEN.

Peter. Here a comes, methinks, and the Queen with him. I'll be the first, sure.

2 Pet. Come back, fool! this is the Duke of Suffolk, and not my Lord Protector.

Suf. How now, fellow! would'st any thing with me?

1 Pet. I pray, my lord, pardon me: I took ye for my Lord Protector.

Queen. [*Reads*.] "To my Lord Protector!" Are your supplications to his lordship? Let me see them: what is thine?

1 Pet. Mine is, and 't please your Grace, against John Goodman, my Lord Cardinal's man, for keeping my house, and lands, and wife, and all, from me.

Suf. Thy wife too! that's some wrong indeed. What's yours? What's here! [*Reads*.] "Against the Duke of Suffolk, for enclosing the commons of Long Melford." How now, sir knave!

2 Pet. Alas! sir, I am but a poor petitioner of our whole township.

Peter. Against my master, Thomas Horner, for saying that the Duke of York was rightful heir to the crown.

Queen. What say'st thou? Did the Duke of York say he was rightful heir to the crown?

Peter. That my master was? No, forsooth: my master said

5. S.D.] *F;* Enter the Duke of *Suffolke* with the Queene, and they take him for Duke *Humphrey*, and giues him their writings. *Q*. 6 ff.] *F; for Q, see App. 4.* 13, 20. *Reads.*] *after Rowe; om. Q, F.* 21. Long] *Theobald, from Q.* 29. master] *Warburton;* Mistresse *F.*

13. *Queen*] Margaret, after her formal entry in Scene i, becomes at once the dominant character of the remaining plays of the series. Note that she enters with Suffolk.

17. *Cardinal*] another causal link in the structure of the play; cf. headnote.

21. *enclosing the commons*] the appropriation, by fencing, of common ground. Shakespeare was involved in such a matter in Stratford (Chambers, *W.S.*, I. 141 ff.). Long Melford, in Suffolk, had for its chief family, in the time of Henry VI, de Clopton. The name reinforces the possibility of a connection with Stratford, where Clopton House was familiar.

22. *sir knave*] "sir" was often prefixed to a designation of rank, status, or occupation; cf. "sir page" *Tit.*, IV. iii. 2; it was sometimes used, as here, ironically.

26. *York . . . heir*] Shakespeare's invention, to link this incident (as formerly Suffolk, the queen, and the cardinal) with York's claim to the crown, and the main plot generally; cf. 97 below.

29. *master*] the F "mistress" may, of

that he was, and that the King was an usurer.
Queen. An usurper, thou wouldst say.
Peter. Ay, forsooth, an usurper.
Suf. Who is there?

Enter Servant.

Take this fellow in, and send for his master with a
pursuivant presently. We'll hear more of your matter
before the King. [*Exit with Peter.*
Queen. And as for you, that love to be protected
Under the wings of our Protector's grace,
Begin your suits anew, and sue to him.
[*Tear the supplication.*
Away, base cullions! Suffolk, let them go.
All. Come, let's be gone. [*Exeunt.*
Queen. My Lord of Suffolk, say, is this the guise,
Is this the fashions in the court of England?
Is this the government of Britain's isle,
And this the royalty of Albion's king?
What! shall King Henry be a pupil still
Under the surly Gloucester's governance?
Am I a queen in title and in style,
And must be made a subject to a duke?
I tell thee, Pole, when in the city Tours

30–2. usurer . . . forsooth an] *Q; om. F.* 33. S.D. *Servant*] *F;* one or two *Q.* 36. S.D. *Exit with Peter.*] *Exit. F; Exet* with the Armourers man. *Q.* 37–41.] *F; for Q, see App. 4.* 39. S.D.] *F;* He teares the papers. *Q. See n.* 43. fashions] *F;* fashion *Rowe + edd.*

course, be an intentional error, like "usurer".

31–2. *An usurper . . . usurper.*] added from Q. The F compositor's eye may have jumped these lines.

35. *pursuivant*] a junior officer attendant on the heralds; an officer at arms.

37, 38. *protected . . . Protector's*] the pun continued from 4.

39. S.D.] see collation. Q is quite definite that the "writings" are given to Suffolk, and that he tears them. The F S.D., though placed opposite the queen's speech, does not exclude the Q version. There need, therefore, be no inconsistency.

40. *base cullions*] low-born wretches; from It. *coglioni*.

42. *is this . . .*] Margaret maintains the impression of strangeness, but passes to her later rôle; cf. 13, above.

guise] recognized custom or fashion; cf. *Cym.*, v. i. 32; often used of the custom of a country, e.g. Kendall, *Flowers of Epigrams* (1577), 54, "all disordered lye my looks, after the Spanish *guise*".

46–7. *pupil . . . governance*] see Appendix 1 (Hall, 208; Fox, 712).

48. *style*] title; cf. 1. i. 110; *1 H 6*, iv. vii. 72.

50–1. *Tours . . . a tilt*] at the "triumphant Justes" held there when Suf-

Thou ran'st a tilt in honour of my love,
And stol'st away the ladies' hearts of France,
I thought King Henry had resembled thee
In courage, courtship, and proportion:
But all his mind is bent to holiness,
To number Ave-Maries on his beads;
His champions are the prophets and apostles,
His weapons holy saws of sacred writ,
His study is his tilt-yard, and his loves
Are brazen images of canoniz'd saints.
I would the college of the Cardinals
Would choose him Pope, and carry him to Rome,
And set the triple crown upon his head:
That were a state fit for his Holiness.

Suf. Madam, be patient; as I was cause
Your Highness came to England, so will I
In England work your Grace's full content.

Queen. Beside the haught Protector, have we Beaufort
The imperious churchman; Somerset, Buckingham,
And grumbling York; and not the least of these
But can do more in England than the King.

Suf. And he of these that can do most of all
Cannot do more in England than the Nevils:
Salisbury and Warwick are no simple peers.

68. haught] *F2–4;* haughtie *F1. See n.*

folk went to fetch the queen as procurator. Imitated by Marlowe, *Ed. 2*, 2475–7: "Tell Isabell the Queene, I lookt not thus, / When for her sake I ran at tilt in Fraunce, / And there unhorste the duke of Cleremont."

54. *courtship*] courtliness of manners, with a possible pun on the sense of "wooing".

proportion] (comely) form.

55–64.] For the character of Henry, see Appendix I (Hall, 208, 212), and below, IV. iv; *3 H 6*, V. vi; II. i. 156. Note Margaret's attitude, in contrast to her first meeting in I. i.

57. *His champions . . .*] *Ephesians*, 2. 20, "ye are . . . built upon the foundation of the apostles and prophets". For the general metaphor, cf. *Ephesians*, 6. 11–17.

58. *saws*] sayings, texts.

60. *canoniz'd*] accented on the second syllable; cf. *Ham.*, I. iv. 47.

61. *college of the Cardinals*] the 70 cardinals of the Roman Church, who constitute the Pope's council. and elect to the papacy from their own number (*OED.*).

63. *triple crown*] of the Pope; cf. Appendix I (Hall, 211).

68. *haught*] a regular form in Shakespeare and the Chronicles, probably modernized by the F editor e.g. *3 H 6*, II. i. 169.

73. *do more . . . Nevils*] see Appendix I (Hall, 232).

Queen. Not all these lords do vex me half so much
As that proud dame, the Lord Protector's wife:
She sweeps it through the court with troops of ladies,
More like an empress than Duke Humphrey's wife.
Strangers in court do take her for the queen:
She bears a duke's revenues on her back,
And in her heart she scorns our poverty.
Shall I not live to be aveng'd on her?
Contemptuous base-born callet as she is,
She vaunted 'mongst her minions t'other day,
The very train of her worst wearing gown
Was better worth than all my father's lands,
Till Suffolk gave two dukedoms for his daughter.
Suf. Madam, myself have lim'd a bush for her,
And plac'd a quire of such enticing birds
That she will light to listen to their lays,
And never mount to trouble you again.
So, let her rest: and, madam, list to me;
For I am bold to counsel you in this:
Although we fancy not the Cardinal,
Yet must we join with him and with the lords
Till we have brought Duke Humphrey in disgrace.
As for the Duke of York, this late complaint
Will make but little for his benefit:
So, one by one, we'll weed them all at last,

80.] *F; om. Q1, 2;* She . . . Dukes whole reuennewes . . . backe. *Q3.* 89. plac'd] *F* (plac't). 90. their] *Rowe;* the *F.*

75–86. *Not all . . . lands*] The duchess was disgraced three years before Margaret's arrival in England; but is introduced here for contrast, and in order to point her fall, and—through her—her husband's. For her pride, cf. *Mirror*, 433, ll. 29–49.

80. *She bears . . .*] This line, accidentally dropped out of Q1, was restored in Q3; cf. Marlowe, *Ed. 2*, 704, "He weares a lords revenewe on his back". Q3 may derive from a corrected sheet of Q1.

83. *Contemptuous*] contemptible; cf. *John*, II. i. 384.

callet] trull; cf. *Oth.*, IV. ii. 122.

88. *lim'd a bush*] smeared the twigs with bird-lime.

89. *quire*] choir, company, group.

enticing birds] decoys. Shakespeare uses these images (from fowling) frequently, e.g. below, II. iv. 54; III. iii. 16; *3 H 6*, V. vi. 13; and *Ham.*, III. iii. 68, "O limed soul that struggling to be free . . ." His sympathies were all for the victim.

90. *light*] alight.

92. *let her rest*] think no more about her; so much for her.

97. *this late complaint*] *scil.* of Peter the armourer against his master. See head-note to this scene.

And you yourself shall steer the happy helm.

Sound a sennet. Enter the KING, *Duke* HUMPHREY *of* GLOUCESTER, *Cardinal* BEAUFORT, BUCKINGHAM, YORK, SOMERSET, SALISBURY, WARWICK, *and the Duchess of* GLOUCESTER.

King. For my part, noble lords, I care not which;
Or Somerset or York, all's one to me.
York. If York have ill demean'd himself in France,
Then let him be denay'd the regentship.
Som. If Somerset be unworthy of the place,
Let York be regent; I will yield to him.
War. Whether your Grace be worthy, yea or no,
Dispute not that: York is the worthier.
Car. Ambitious Warwick, let thy betters speak.
War. The Cardinal's not my better in the field.
Buck. All in this presence are thy betters, Warwick.
War. Warwick may live to be the best of all.
Sal. Peace, son! and show some reason, Buckingham,
Why Somerset should be preferr'd in this.
Queen. Because the king, forsooth, will have it so.
Glou. Madam, the king is old enough himself
To give his censure. These are no women's matters.
Queen. If he be old enough, what needs your Grace
To be Protector of his Excellence?
Glou. Madam, I am Protector of the realm,

100. S.D. *Sound*] *Theobald, Q; Exit.* / Sound *F.* *Sound . . . Gloucester*] *F* (*subst., om. Somerset*); Enter King *Henry* and the Duke of *Yorke* and the Duke of *Somerset* on both sides of the King, whispering with him, and enter Duke *Humphrey*, Dame *Elnor*, the Duke of *Buckingham*, the Earle of *Salsbury*, the Earle of *Warwicke*, and the Cardinall of *Winchester*. *Q.* 116. *Glou.*] *Humf. F; Hum. Q; and throughout the scene.*

100. *steer . . . helm*] of state. Cf. *Ed. 3*, III. i. 120, "Steer, angry Nemesis, the happy helm".

100. S.D. sennet] a set of notes on the trumpet or cornet, used as a signal for the ceremonial entrance or exit of a body of players (*OED.*).

102.] Shakespeare makes a feature throughout of the rivalry of York and Somerset, suggested by Hall, 215–16; and develops it at III. i. 290 ff. and V. i. 87 ff. The Q S.D. is illuminating.

104. *denay'd*] an old form of "denied"; L. *denegare;* cf. *Tw.N.*, II. iv. 127; *Alphonsus*, 1066.

regentship] see Appendix I (Hall, 206).

116. *old enough*] on the king's age see n. at I. i. 163–4.

117. *censure*] L. sense = opinion judgement.

118–19.] For the queen's policy, see Appendix I (Hall, 208). She opens the concerted attack on Gloucester.

And at his pleasure will resign my place.
Suf. Resign it then, and leave thine insolence.
Since thou wert king—as who is king but thou?—
The commonwealth hath daily run to wrack;
The Dauphin hath prevail'd beyond the seas;
And all the peers and nobles of the realm
Have been as bondmen to thy sovereignty.
Car. The commons hast thou rack'd; the clergy's bags
Are lank and lean with thy extortions.
Som. Thy sumptuous buildings and thy wife's attire
Have cost a mass of public treasury.
Buck. Thy cruelty in execution
Upon offenders hath exceeded law,
And left thee to the mercy of the law.
Queen. Thy sale of offices and towns in France,
If they were known, as the suspect is great,
Would make thee quickly hop without thy head.
[*Exit Gloucester. The Queen drops her fan.*
Give me my fan: what, minion! can ye not?
[*She gives the Duchess a box on the ear.*
I cry you mercy, madam; was it you?
Duch. Was't I! yea, I it was, proud Frenchwoman:
Could I come near your beauty with my nails
I 'd set my ten commandments in your face.

128. rack'd] *F* (rackt). 130. wife's] *F* (Wiues). 137. S.D. *Gloucester*] *Humfrey F.* *The Queen . . . fan.*] *Johnson; om. F;* The Queene lets fall her gloue, and hits the Duches of *Gloster*, a boxe on the eare. *Q.* 138. S.D. *She gives . . . ear.*] *F;* She strikes her. *Q.* 142. I'd] *Pope + edd.* (I'ld)*;* I could *F;* Ide *Q.*

122–7.] Suffolk's charges, and Margaret's concerning France, 135–6, are those "put up to the King and the Lordes" by the Commons against Suffolk himself. The Cardinal's charge comes under the same heading (Hart).

123 ff.] Briggs compares the attack on the King and Gaveston in *Ed. 2*, 953 ff.

125. *Dauphin*] the title of the French king's eldest son and heir apparent. Here = the French king, Charles VII, whose title was not acknowledged by the English (Brooke).

128. *rack'd . . .*] the charge is repeated below, III. i. 61–2.

130. *sumptuous buildings*] The Duke occupied Greenwich palace, which was greatly enlarged by his Renascence taste. In Shakespeare's time it was a favourite residence of Queen Elizabeth and King James (Brooke). Cf. above, 80, on his wife's expenses.

137. *hop without thy head*] a stock Elizabethan expression.

138. *minion*] hussy. Originally a dependent, or favourite.

can ye not?] our "can't you?"

139. *I cry you mercy*] I beg your pardon (here ironical).

142. *ten commandments*] finger-nails;

King. Sweet aunt, be quiet; 'twas against her will.
Duch. Against her will, good King? Look to 't in time;
She'll hamper thee and dandle thee like a baby:
Though in this place most master wear no breeches,
She shall not strike Dame Eleanor unreveng'd. [*Exit*.
Buck. Lord Cardinal, I will follow Eleanor,
And listen after Humphrey, how he proceeds:
She's tickled now; her fury needs no spurs,
She'll gallop far enough to her destruction. [*Exit*.

Re-enter GLOUCESTER.

Glou. Now, lords, my choler being over-blown
With walking once about the quadrangle,
I come to talk of commonwealth affairs.
As for your spiteful false objections,
Prove them, and I lie open to the law:
But God in mercy so deal with my soul
As I in duty love my king and country!
But to the matter that we have in hand.
I say, my Sovereign, York is meetest man
To be your Regent in the realm of France.
Suf. Before we make election, give me leave
To show some reason, of no little force,
That York is most unmeet of any man.

144. will, good King?] *F;* will. Good King *Q*. 150. fury] *Grant White;* fume *F*. *See n.* needs] *F1;* can neede *F2–4;* needs now *Keightley*. 151. far] *F;* fast *Pope*. 151. S.D.] *edd.; Enter Humfrey. F; Enter Duke* Humfrey. *Q*.

cf. *Locrine*, 4. 2, "fearing she would set her ten commandments in my face"; *Deut.*, 9. 10; *Exod.*, 31. 18. "In allusion, it is thought, to the tradition that God scratched the Ten Commandments on the Tables with his nails" (Noble).

143. *be quiet*] a mild protest characteristic of the King.

145. *hamper*] fetter, clog, obstruct. Perhaps with a back-sense of the cradle (Hart).

146. *most master wear no breeches*] the wife (the greatest master) rules the house; cf. "his wife . . . taking up a cudgel (for the most maister went breechles)", Greene, *Pandosto*, 4. 276 (Wilson).

149. *listen after*] inquire about; take an interest in; keep a watch on.

150. *tickled*] irritated.

fury] see collation. "Fume" would be an easy mis-reading of "Furie". Cf. Marlowe, *Dido*, 813; *furie* Q; *Fame* edd.

150–1. *spurs . . . gallop*] a common proverb, modified. Cf. Jonson, *Tale of a Tub*, "spur a *free* horse, he'll run himself to death".

157. *But God . . .*] *Ps.*, 119, 124, "Deal with thy servant according unto thy mercy."

162. *election*] choice.

York. I'll tell thee, Suffolk, why I am unmeet:
First, for I cannot flatter thee in pride;
Next, if I be appointed for the place,
My Lord of Somerset will keep me here,
Without discharge, money, or furniture,
Till France be won into the Dauphin's hands.
Last time I danc'd attendance on his will
Till Paris was besieg'd, famish'd, and lost.
War. That can I witness; and a fouler fact
Did never traitor in the land commit.
Suf. Peace, headstrong Warwick!
War. Image of Pride, why should I hold my peace?

Enter HORNER *the Armourer, and his man* PETER, *guarded.*

Suf. Because here is a man accus'd of treason:
Pray God the Duke of York excuse himself!
York. Doth any one accuse York for a traitor?
King. What mean'st thou, Suffolk? Tell me, what are these?

171. danc'd] *F* (danc't). 172. famish'd] *F* (famisht). 176 S.D.] *Theobald;* Enter the Armorer and his Man. *Q*, *F* (the *om. F*).

166. *for*] because.

169. *discharge*] payment of what he owes; financial settlement. Still the legal sense.

furniture] equipment for war; cf. *1 Tamb.*, 1427; *Dido*, 1478.

171. *Last time*] Hart refers to *1 H 6*, IV. iii. 9–11—the siege of *Bordeaux*, in Talbot's last campaign in 1453 (i.e., *after* these events): "A plague upon that villain Somerset / That thus delays my promised supply / Of horsemen that were levied for this siege!" Paris had been lost in 1437; cf. Hall, 179, "the duke of Somerset . . . by all waies and meanes possible . . . bothe hindered and detracted [York] . . . causyng hym to linger in Englande, without dispatche, till Paris and the floure of Fraunce, were gotten by the Frenche kyng." Wilson points out that Holinshed, 3. 208, under 1446, refers back here to that "last time", "But the duke of Summerset still maligning the duke of Yorkes advancement, as he had sought to hinder his dispatch at the first when he was sent over to be regent, as before yee have heard:" and argues that there is no necessity to suppose a reference to Part I. Cf. above, I. i. 143.

173. *fact*] L. sense = deed, crime; cf. "apprehended in the fact", II. i. 165; "accessory before (after) the fact".

176. *Image*] embodiment, type; cf. *Lr.*, IV. vi. 162, "the great *image* of authority"; *Sp. Tr.*, I. 3. 12, "this earth, Image of mellancholly".

177.] As noted above, Shakespeare links this incident to the main plot by introducing the allegation of treason with the Duke of York's claim to the crown, and then uses the accusation to discredit York in the matter of the French regency, 206 below.

177, 178. *accus'd . . . excuse*] *Romans*, 2. 15, "while accusing or else excusing one another".

Suf. Please it your Majesty, this is the man
That doth accuse his master of high treason.
His words were these: that Richard Duke of York
Was rightful heir unto the English crown,
And that your Majesty was an usurper.

King. Say, man, were these thy words?

Hor. And 't shall please your Majesty, I never said nor thought any such matter: God is my witness, I am falsely accus'd by the villain.

Pet. By these ten bones, my lords, he did speak them to me in the garret one night, as we were scouring my Lord of York's armour.

York. Base dunghill villain, and mechanical,
I'll have thy head for this thy traitor's speech.
I do beseech your royal Majesty
Let him have all the rigour of the law.

Hor. Alas! my lord, hang me if ever I spake the words. My accuser is my prentice; and when I did correct him for his fault the other day, he did vow upon his knees he would be even with me: I have good witness of this: therefore, I beseech your Majesty, do not cast away an honest man for a villain's accusation.

King. Uncle, what shall we say to this in law?

Glou. This doom, my lord, if I may judge by case:
Let Somerset be Regent o'er the French,
Because in York this breeds suspicion;
And let these have a day appointed them
For single combat in convenient place;
For he hath witness of his servant's malice.

King. This is the law, and this Duke Humphrey's doom.

204. by case] *ASC, Q; om. F.* 210. *King.*] *ASC; om. F; see App. 4, and n.*

184. *rightful heir*] as he claims to be in II. ii. Cf. Appendix I (Hall, 219, 246), and *1 H 6*, II. iv, v.

188. *God is my witness*] *Romans*, I. 9.

190. *by these ten bones*] the fingers. Used by Lyly, *Woman in the Moone*, 5. I. 23; *Pappe*, vol. 3, 412. 12; both times in association with apes and mowes, or chattering.

193. *mechanical*] engaged in a manual occupation, and so, contemptuously, menial; cf. *Wiv.*, II. ii. 290; *MND.*, III. ii. 9.

201–2. *cast away*] ruin, destroy; cf. *LLL.*, v. ii. 682.

204. *by case*] from case-law, or precedent. A F omission, restored from Q. Not only does the phrase restore the metre; it is also the natural reply to the King's query as to "the law".

210.] Here Theobald inserted the lines, from Q, in which the king gives

Som. I humbly thank your royal Majesty.
Hor. And I accept the combat willingly.
Pet. Alas! my lord, I cannot fight; for God's sake, pity my case! The spite of man prevaileth against me. O Lord, have mercy upon me! I shall never be able to fight a blow. O Lord, my heart!
Glou. Sirrah, or you must fight or else be hang'd.
King. Away with them to prison; and the day
Of combat be the last of the next month.
Come, Somerset, we'll see thee sent away.
[*Flourish. Exeunt.*

SCENE IV.—GLOUCESTER'S *Garden.*

Enter MARGERY JOURDAIN, HUME, SOUTHWELL, *and* BOLINGBROKE.

Hume. Come, my masters; the Duchess, I tell you, expects performance of your promises.
Boling. Master Hume, we are therefore provided: will her ladyship behold and hear our exorcisms?

218-20.] *arranged Capell; as prose F.* 219. be] *ASC;* shall be *Q,F.* month.] *F;* month. / With *Eben* staues and *Standbags* combatting / In Smythfield, before your Royall Maiestie. *Q.*

Scene IV

Locality.] *Capell, from Q.* Entry.] *Rowe, from Q, F.* Margery Jourdain] *the Witch F.* Hume, Southwell] *the two Priests F;* sir *Iohn Hum Q.* 1–22.] *F; for Q, see App. 4.*

Somerset the appointment. The king was obviously meant to give his approval here of Gloucester's "doom". See Appendix 4. The passage may have been affected in the recasting of the next scene: and if it has been shortened, the King must have been meant to speak l. 210. See collation.

214. *prevaileth*] *Ps.* 6. 2; 9. 13; 13. 4.

Scene IV

Locality.] Q specifies an orchard and a tower to which Elianor "goes up". F omits mention of these, but "aloft", 8, shows that the business remains the same in the revised opening. Wilson thinks that "breake in" (S.D., 39) indicates a room, but it is surely possible to "break in" to an orchard, especially a stage one.

The beginning of the scene, with the end of the last, was rewritten, possibly to remove the direct part taken by the Duchess in a treasonable proceeding. For the earlier version, as reported, see App. 4; and Intro. p. xxvii.

An alternative explanation might be that the passage in Q was vamped by the reporters from recollections of Marlowe and Kyd.

4. *exorcisms*] the calling up of spirits; conjurations.

Hume. Ay, what else? Fear you not her courage.

Boling. I have heard her reported to be a woman of an invincible spirit: but it shall be convenient, Master Hume, that you be by her aloft, while we be busy below; and so, I pray you, go, in God's name, and leave us. [*Exit Hume*.] Mother Jourdain, be you prostrate, and grovel on the earth; John Southwell, read you; and let us to our work.

Enter DUCHESS *aloft*, HUME *following*.

Duch. Well said, my masters; and welcome all. To this gear, the sooner the better.

Boling. Patience, good lady; wizards know their times:
Deep night, dark night, the silent of the night,
The time of night when Troy was set on fire,
The time when screech-owls cry, and ban-dogs howl,
And spirits walk, and ghosts break up their graves;
That time best fits the work we have in hand.

12. *Enter . . . following.*] *Dyce* (*subst.*); *Enter Elianor aloft. F;* She goes vp to the Tower. *Q*. 16. silent] *F;* silence *Collier* (*Q*), *Wilson*.

5. *what else?*] a strong affirmation—certainly; cf. *Sp. Tr.*, 3. 14. 164.

7. *invincible spirit*] a phrase applied to Talbot, *1 H 6*, IV. ii. 32.

8. *aloft*] i.e. on the upper stage, or even on the "top" or turret, representing a tower, as in Q. Cf. 12 S.D.

9. *below*] a pun?

11. *Southwell*] not in Q. His "part" has obviously been given to Bolingbroke, as shown by the F S.D., "Bolingbroke or Southwell reads", 22 below. See n. to 22 below.

13. *Well said*] well done; cf. *Tit.*, IV. iii. 63, "now, masters, draw. (*They shoot.*) O well said, Lucius!"; *2 Tamb.*, 4289.

13–14. *To this gear*] on with the business.

16. *silent of the night*] cf. *2 H 4*, V. iii. 49–50, "The sweet o' the night"; *Tp.*, I. ii. 327, "that vast of night"; Ovid, *Amores*, 2. 9. 40.

17. *The time . . . Troy . . .*] cf. *Æneid*, 4. 462–3; and Book 2 as a whole.

18–19. *screech-owls cry, and ban-dogs howl, And spirits walk*] A reflection of the passage in Ovid, *Metam.*, 15. 745 ff, describing the murder and deification of Julius Caesar, in close association with his descent from Aeneas—the passage from which Shakespeare (*Cæs.*) derived the descriptions of the omens preceding Caesar's death: "tristia mille locis Stygius dedit omina bubo . . . / inque foro circumque domos et templa deorum / nocturnos ululasse canes umbrasque silentum / erravisse ferunt . . ." (781, 796–8). Shakespeare probably had also in mind Ovid, *Amores*, 2. 19 and Marlowe's translation (39–40): "Search at the dore, who knocks oft in the darke, / *In nights deepe silence* why the *ban-dogges* barke." which is nearer than Golding's version.

18. *ban-dogs*] or band-dogs; dogs tied up on account of their ferocity.

Madam, sit you, and fear not: whom we raise
We will make fast within a hallow'd verge.

[*Here do the ceremonies belonging, and make the circle; Bolingbroke or Southwell reads*, Conjuro te, *&c. It thunders and lightens terribly; then the Spirit riseth.*

Spir. Adsum.
M. Jourd. Asnath!
By the eternal God, whose name and power
Thou tremblest at, answer that I shall ask;
For till thou speak thou shalt not pass from hence.
Spir. Ask what thou wilt. That I had said and done!

22. S.D.] *F; for Q, see App. 4.* 23. *M. Jourd.*] *edd.; Witch. F.* Asnath!] *ASC; Asmath, F. See n.* 23–6.] *arranged Capell; Asnath,* . . . God, / . . . at, / . . . speake, / . . . hence. *F; om. Q.*

22. *hallow'd verge*] charmed circle.

22. S.D.] Typical supernatural machinery; cf. Peele, *Old Wives' Tale*, "Re-enter Sacrapant; *It lightens and thunders*: the Second Brother falls down . . . Sacrapant . . . Adeste daemones! Enter Two Furies."; and *Dr Faustus*, 235 ff.

Bolingbroke or] probably inserted in the prompt-book early (i.e. before the text reported in Q was given out to the actors) in order to cut out Southwell. If the S.D. is permissive and authorial, its presence strengthens the argument that the author's MS. became the prompt-book. See e.g. Greg, *Ed. Prob.*, ch. II, and *The Shakespeare First Folio*, p. 183. The Q lines (Appendix 4) beginning "Send vp I charge you" are probably an English version of the L. conjuration, which was presumably read from a scroll.

23. *Asnath*] see collation. Hart's "Probably 'Asmenoth, guider of the North' in Greene's *Frier Bacon*", and Professor Dover Wilson's suggestion of Asmodeus (*Tobit*, 3. 8–17), are equally unconvincing.

The context, however, with its reference to *James*, III. 19, "the devils also believe and tremble", suggests that we have here a devil, if not *the* devil, who trembled at, and could be compelled by, the name of God. This is confirmed by the further reference implicit in "False Fiend auoide." at l. 39. *Err.*, IV. iii. 43, "Sathan, auoid", points in the same direction. The phrase, and the spelling "Sathan", occurred in the *Gospel for the First Sunday in Lent* both in the First Prayer Book of Edward VI, and the First of Elizabeth (Noble, 280).

I suggest, therefore, that the name is simply a minim misprint for *Asnath*, an anagram of *Sathan*, as *Caliban* derives from "cannibal". This device was commonly associated with conjuring; "dog" for "God" is well known; and Marlowe's reference is specific (*Dr Faustus*, 242–3):

Within this circle is *Iehouahs* name,
Forward and backward anagrammatiz'd . . .

"The Deuils writ", at l. 56, is a natural sequel.

24. *eternal God*] *James*, 2. 19, "the devils also believe and tremble".

27. *That*] would that. Steevens says here that spirits who remained above ground answered questions with reluctance. Malone refers to *Mac.*, IV. i. 72, "Dismiss me, enough!" Cf. 37, below.

Boling. [*Reads.*] "First, of the King, what shall of him
become?"
Spir. The duke yet lives that Henry shall depose;
But him outlive, and die a violent death.
[*As the Spirit speaks, Southwell writes the answer.*
Boling. "Tell me what fate awaits the Duke of Suffolk."
Spir. By water shall he die and take his end.
Boling. "What shall betide the Duke of Somerset?"
Spir. Let him shun castles:
Safer shall he be upon the sandy plains
Than where castles mounted stand.
Have done, for more I hardly can endure.
Boling. Descend to darkness and the burning lake:
False fiend, avoid!
[*Thunder and lightning. Exit Spirit.*

Enter YORK *and* BUCKINGHAM, *with their guard, and break in.*

York. Lay hands upon these traitors and their trash.
Beldam, I think we watch'd you at an inch.
What! madam, are you there? The king and
commonweal

28. S.D. *Reads.*] *Reading out of a paper. Capell, marginally; om. Q, F.* 30. S.D. *As . . . answer.*] *Capell; om. F.* 31. Tell me] *Pope; om. Q, F. Seen.* fate awaits] *Q 2, 3, Capell;* fate awayt *Q 1;* fates await *F.* 33. betide] *Q;* befall *F. See n.* 34–6.] *F; as prose Q.* 38–9.] *F; for Q, see App. 4.* 39. S.D. *Exit Spirit.*] *F;* He sinkes down againe. *Q.* *Enter . . . in.*] *edd.; Enter the Duke of Yorke and the Duke of Buckingham . . . in. F.* 41. watch'd] *Q, F* (watcht).

28 ff.] The prophecies are invented to draw together the fall of the Duchess (and Humphrey) and the subsequent tragedies throughout the play (and beyond), and are re-introduced, with the fall of Somerset, to round off and add a sense of unity. They act also in the manner of omens in Greek tragedy to throw the shadow of fate forward on events to come.

31. *Tell me*] omitted in F through use of uncorrected Q copy: cf. 62.

33. *betide*] F "befall" is possibly an error due to "shall" (32, 33).

38. *the burning lake*] *Rev.*, 16. 10; 19. 20; Seneca (Tudor Trans., 1. 107), *Thebais*, "I will Descend to darke infernall Lake".

39. *avoid*] *Matt.*, 4. 10 (Geneva), as in *Err.*, "Sathan, auoid".

break in] see head-note to this scene.

41. *at an inch*] at close quarters; in immediate readiness. Cf. Seneca, *Thebais* (Tudor Trans., 1. 103), "through rough and smoth I wil be *at an ynch*"; Greene, *Frier Bacon*, 501, "we are all ready *at an inch*"; *Third Part of Conny Catching* (Grosart, 10. 180) "The rest following the gentlemen *at an inch*".

42.] "What! . . . there?" is from Q, and should be a foot shorter.

Are deeply indebted for this piece of pains:
My Lord Protector will, I doubt it not,
See you well guerdon'd for these good deserts.

Duch. Not half so bad as thine to England's king,
Injurious Duke, that threatest where's no cause.

Buck. True, madam, none at all. What call you this?
Away with them! let them be clapp'd up close,
And kept asunder. You, madam, shall with us:
Stafford, take her to thee.

[*Exeunt above Duchess and Hume, guarded.*

We'll see your trinkets here all forthcoming.
All, away!

[*Exeunt guard, with Southwell, Bolingbroke, etc.*

York. Lord Buckingham, methinks you watch'd her well:
A pretty plot, well chosen to build upon!
Now, pray, my lord, let's see the Devil's writ.
What have we here? [*Reads.*
"The duke yet lives that Henry shall depose;
But him outlive, and die a violent death."
Why, this is just "Aio te, Æacida,
Romanos vincere posse." Well, to the rest:

49. clapp'd] *F* (clapt). 51. S.D.] *Dyce; Exet Elnor aboue. Q.; om. F.* 53. S.D.] *Rowe; Exit. F; Exet with them. Q.* 54. watch'd] *F* (watcht). 60–1.] *arranged ASC;* Why . . . *posso.* / . . . rest: *F.* 60. te] *Warburton; om. F.* 61. posse] *edd.; posso F.*

47. *Injurious*] insulting, abusive—the L. sense.

49. *clapp'd up close*] imprisoned closely.

51–3.] mislined, and probably incorrect.

52. *trinkets*] = trash (above); their conjuring adjuncts.

see . . . forthcoming] a proper legal term used of any person or thing given into one's charge; cf. II. i. 171; Strype, *Whitgift*, 2. 2. "committed to the custody of his father, upon sufficient bonds . . . that he shall be *forthcoming*."

55. *plot . . . build upon*] a pun on "plot".

56. *Devil's writ*] as opposed to Holy Writ. or "sacred Writ" at I. iii. 58.

60. *just*] precisely; exactly.

60–1. *Aio te . . . posse*] The ambiguous answer the Pythian Apollo gave Pyrrhus (according to the *Annals* of Ennius) when he inquired whether he would vanquish Rome (Cicero, *De Divin.*, 2. 56). It may mean either "I affirm that thou, descendant of Æacus, canst conquer the Romans", or "I affirm that the Romans can vanquish thee, descendant of Æacus" (Craig). Puttenham deals with this subject (*Arte of English Poesie*, Arber, 267, 1586–9) under the heading of *Amphibologia*, or the Ambiguous: "these *doubtful* speaches were used much in the old times by their false Prophets" (Hart). Cf. the same device in *Ed. 2*, 2340, 2343.

"Tell me what fate awaits the Duke of Suffolk."
"By water shall he die and take his end."
"What shall betide the Duke of Somerset?"
"Let him shun castles:
Safer shall he be upon the sandy plains
Than where castles mounted stand."
Come, come, my lords, these oracles
Are hardly attain'd, and hardly understood.
The King is now in progress towards Saint Albans;
With him the husband of this lovely lady:
Thither goes these news as fast as horse can carry them:
A sorry breakfast for my Lord Protector.

Buck. Your Grace shall give me leave, my Lord of York,
To be the post, in hope of his reward.

York. At your pleasure, my good lord. Within there, ho!

Enter a Servingman.

Invite my Lords of Salisbury and Warwick
To sup with me to-morrow night. Away! [*Exeunt.*

68–9.] *arranged Capell;* Lords, / . . . attain'd, / . . . vnderstood. *F.* 72.] *arranged Pope;* thither . . . Newes, / . . . them: *F.* goes] *F; go Rowe + edd.* 76.] *arranged ASC;* At . . . Lord. / . . . hoe? *F.* Within there, ho!] *ASC;* Whose within there? *Q* (Who's *Q3*); Who's within there, hoe? *F. See n.*

68, 69 ff.] note mislineation due to use of Q copy. See Introduction, p. xxxvi. An adjective is obviously missing before "oracles".

69. *hardly attain'd*] obtained with difficulty.

72. *goes*] common Elizabethan usage where the verb precedes the subject; cf. v. i. 60, "What intends these forces".

76. *Within . . .*] The text has been corrupted by the use of Q "copy". "Who's" was left undeleted; and the phrase remains in a separate line in F.

78. *sup*] The supper is described in II. ii.

ACT II

SCENE I.—*Saint Albans.*

Enter the KING, QUEEN, GLOUCESTER, *Cardinal, and* SUFFOLK, *with Falconers hallooing.*

Queen. Believe me, lords, for flying at the brook,
I saw not better sport these seven years' day:
Yet, by your leave, the wind was very high,
And, ten to one, old Joan had not gone out.
King. But what a point, my lord, your falcon made,
And what a pitch she flew above the rest!

ACT II

Scene I

Locality.] *Pope.* Entry.] *F* (*subst., reading Protector for Gloucester*); Enter the King and Queene with her Hawke on her fist, and Duke *Humphrey* and *Suffolke,* and the *Cardinall,* as if they came from hawking. *Q.*

The scene follows from I. ii. 56 ff, and is based on Hall, 236 (Appendix I), though the hawking is here adapted to a different end—the aggravation of the quarrels among the nobles, and especially of their animosity against Gloucester. The second part, 60 ff, is from Fox (Appendix I), with the addition of "the Mayor and his brethren"; but St Albans was not incorporated till 1552 (French, 172).

I. *at the brook*] i.e. at water-fowl. "Hawking at the river or brook was the true royal sport of falconry; mallards, herons, etc., being the quarry. James I delighted in it. 'The king looked abroad in his litter, to see some flights *at the brook*' (*Court and Times of James I*, Letter dated 8 Jan. 1624–5)." (Hart).

2. *these seven years' day*] for the last seven years — an approximation, however; cf. Lyly, *Gallathea*, I. I. 42, "at every five yeeres day".

4. *Joan . . . gone out*] the hawk . . . taken her flight at the game.

5. *point . . . falcon made*] "gained a secure position to windward, from which she could wait the fowl." "The Lanner never lieth upon the Wing after she hath flown to Mark, but after once stooping she maketh a *Point*, and then, like the Goshawk, waits the Fowl." (Nicholas Cox, *The Gentleman's Recreation*, pp. 180–1, ed., 1721) (Hart).

falcon] Gloucester's badge was a falcon with a maiden's head—which gives point to the gibes of Suffolk and the Cardinal.

6. *pitch*] the falcon's height, especially extreme height, of flight.

6, 12, 14. *flew . . . pitch . . . soar*] cf. *Caes.*, I. i. 78; *R 2*, I. i. 109; *Ed. 3*, II. i. 86–7: "And every ornament that thou wouldst praise, / Fly it a pitch above the soare of praise."

To see how God in all his creatures works!
Yea, man and birds are fain of climbing high.
Suf. No marvel, and it like your Majesty,
My Lord Protector's hawks do tower so well;
They know their master loves to be aloft,
And bears his thoughts above his falcon's pitch.
Glou. My lord, 'tis but a base ignoble mind
That mounts no higher than a bird can soar.
Car. I thought as much; he'd be above the clouds.
Glou. Ay, my lord Cardinal, how think you by that?
Were it not good your Grace could fly to heaven?
King. The treasury of everlasting joy.
Car. Thy heaven is on earth; thine eyes and thoughts
Beat on a crown, the treasure of thy heart;
Pernicious Protector, dangerous peer,
That smooth'st it so with king and commonweal!
Glou. What, Cardinal, is your Priesthood grown peremptory?
Tantæne animis cœlestibus iræ?
Churchmen so hot? Good uncle, can you dote,

13. *Glou.*] *F* (*Glost.*); *Humphrey* (*Humph.*, *Hum.*) *Q*. 15. he'd] *Pope* + *edd;* he would *F;* your grace would *Q*. 23–4.] *F;* How now my Lord, why this is more then needs, *Q*. 25–6.] *ASC;* Church-men so hote. Good Vnckle can you doate. (dote? *Q2;* do't. *Q3*) *Q;* Good Vncle hide such mallice: / With such Holynesse can you doe it? *F. See n.*

7. *God . . . works*] The religious attitude and allusions throughout the scene are typical of Henry.

8. *fain*] fond.

10. *tower*] soar, rise in circles of flight till she reaches her "place".

15–150.] F has here been largely set up from Q3, and is consequently defective; see Introduction, pp. xxiii–xxxv; note the mislineation in F.

15. *he'd*] F retains "would" from Q.

16–17. *how think you by that? . . .*] the emphasis is on *you* and *your*. "How do *you* come to think about that?" i.e. to think as much, being yourself so ambitious.

17 ff. *heaven . . . treasury . . . earth . . . treasure . . . heart*] an echo of *Matt.*, 6. 19–21, "Lay not up for yourselves treasures upon earth . . . but lay up for yourselves treasures in heaven . . . For where your treasure is, there will your heart be also."

18. *treasury of everlasting joy*] cf. Spenser, *Astrophel*, 161–2: "And her faire brest, the threasury of ioy, / She spoyld thereof, and filled with annoy." Though not published until 1595, the poem may have circulated in manuscript earlier, as did many others of Spenser's.

20. *Beat on*] hammer, ponder upon; cf. *Tp.*, v. i. 246.

21. *Pernicious*] likely to cause destruction (L. *pernicies*).

dangerous] mischievous, harmful.

22. *smooth'st it*] adopts a flattering or humouring attitude. Cf. I. i. 155 above.

24. Tantæne . . .] Virgil, *Æneid*, I. 11.

25–6.] F makes nonsense here, ow-

To hide such malice with such holiness?
Suf. No malice, sir; no more than well becomes
So good a quarrel and so bad a peer.
Glou. As who, my lord?
Suf. Why, as yourself, my lord;
An 't like your lordly Lord-Protectorship.
Glou. Why, Suffolk, England knows thine insolence.
Queen. And thy ambition, Gloucester.
King. I prithee, peace,
Good queen, and whet not on these furious peers;
For blessed are the peacemakers on earth.
Car. Let me be blessed for the peace I make
Against this proud Protector with my sword!
Glou. [*Aside to Car.*] Faith, holy uncle, would 'twere come to that!
Car. [*Aside to Glou.*] Marry, when thou darest.
Glou. [*Aside to Car.*] Dare! I tell thee, priest,
Plantagenets could never brook the dare.
Car. [*Aside to Glou.*] I am Plantagenet as well as thou,
And son to John of Gaunt.
Glou. [*Aside to Car.*] In bastardy!
Car. [*Aside to Glou.*] I scorn thy words!
Glou. [*Aside to Car.*] Make up no factious numbers for the matter;
In thine own person answer thy abuse.

29. yourself] *Pope;* you *Q, F.* 30. Lord-Protectorship] *Capell;* Lords Protectorship *Q, F.* 32–3.] *arranged Malone;* I . . . Queene, / . . . Peeres. *F.* 37 ff. *Aside.*] *Rowe; om. F.* 38. darest] *Q1, 2;* dar'st *Q3, F.* 38–42. *Glou.* Dare . . . words.] *ASC, Q (subst.); om. F. See n.*

ing to the insertion from MS. of "[To] hide . . . holiness" in the wrong place in the exemplar of Q3 used for setting up; see Introduction, p. xxxv. The intention is obviously ironical—an expansion of the L. quotation. Note the progressive error in "do't", adopted by F as "doe it", from Q3 copy.

30. *Lord-Protectorship*] a retort to Gloucester's "your Priesthood", 23. The QF - *: s* misprint (cf. *mother-* in F, for *mother's*, at IV. i. 84) indicates Q copy for F.

34. *For blessed . . .*] *Matt.*, 5. 9.

35, 36. *peace . . . sword*] *Matt.*, 10. 34, "I came not to send peace, but a sword." The Cardinal's "peace" is probably a play on *piece* (Vaughan), or *pass*, or *pace*.

38 ff. Glou. . . . *words.*] Restored from Q. Probably censored: cf. the deletion of a similar passage in Fabyan, 533.

43. *Make up . . . matter*] bring no members of your faction into the quarrel.

Car. [*Aside to Glou.*] Ay, where thou dar'st not peep: and if thou dar'st,
This evening on the east side of the grove.
King How now, my lords!
Car. Believe me, cousin Gloucester,
Had not your man put up the fowl so suddenly,
We had had more sport. [*Aside to Glou.*] Come with thy two-hand sword.
Glou. True, uncle. [*Aside to Car.*] Are ye advis'd? the east side of the grove.
Car. [*Aside to Glou.*] I am with you.
King. Why, how now, uncle Gloucester!
Glou Talking of hawking; nothing else, my lord.
[*Aside to Car.*] Now, by God's mother, I'll shave your crown for this,
Or all my fence shall fail.
Car. [*Aside to Glou.*] *Medice, teipsum*—
Protector, see to't well, protect yourself.

45–6.] *arranged Theobald;* I, where . . . peepe: / . . . Euening, / Groue. *F.* 50. Are . . . grove.] *given to Car. by Theobald + edd. See n.* 51. *Car.* I . . . you.] *ASC;* Cardinall, I . . . you. *F; Glou.* Cardinal, I .. . you. *Theobald + edd.* 53. Now . . . mother] Now . . . Mother, Priest *F;* Faith Priest *Q1, 2;* Gods Mother Priest *Q3. See n.* 53–4.] *arranged Pope;* Now . . . Mother, Priest, / . . . this, / . . . fayle. *F.* 54–5.] *arranged Theobald; as prose F.*

48. *put up the fowl*] raised or started the game.

49. *two-hand sword*] long sword—an old-fashioned weapon by Shakespeare's time. Jonson, *Epicene* (1609), 4. 2, speaks of it as a curiosity: "He has got somebody's old *two-hand sword*, to mow you off at the knees . . . he is hung with pikes, halberds, petronels, calivers, and muskets, that he looks like a justice-of-peace's hall."

50. *Are ye advis'd?*] are you agreed, determined?

50–1.] see collation. Some emendation is obviously necessary. Theobald's is supported only by the fact that the King answers *Glou.* and not *Car.* But it assumes the omission of two speech-prefixes. The above reading assumes that one prefix has been incorporated in the dialogue (Cardinal). Gloucester's *aside* balances the Cardinal's, accepting the assignation in its own terms; and is supported by Q, where Gloucester names the time and place, and the Cardinal replies, "Here's my hand, I will." "Advis'd" will suit either reading.

53. *God's mother*] if correct, did Q3 derive from an uncensored or uncorrected sheet of Q1?

shave your crown] a reference, of course, to the tonsure.

54. *fence*] skill in fencing.

Medice, teipsum] *Luke*, 4. 23 (Vulgate), "Medice, cura teipsum". Probably proverbial and well-known. This is the only quotation from the Vulgate by Shakespeare. See *H 5*, IV. viii. 121, for his ignorance of the Vulgate (Noble, 81, 121).

King. The winds grow high; so do your stomachs, lords.
How irksome is this music to my heart!
When such strings jar, what hope of harmony?
I pray, my lords, let me compound this strife.

Enter One, crying "A miracle."

Glou. What means this noise? Fellow, what miracle
Dost thou proclaim?
One. A miracle! a miracle!
Suf. Come to the King and tell him what miracle.
One. Forsooth, a blind man at Saint Alban's shrine,
Within this half hour hath receiv'd his sight;
A man that ne'er saw in his life before.
King. Now, God be prais'd, that to believing souls
Gives light in darkness, comfort in despair!

Enter the Mayor of Saint Albans and his brethren, with music, bearing the man, SIMPCOX, *between two in a chair; his Wife and Townsmen following.*

Car. Here comes the townsmen, on procession,
To present your Highness with the man.

59. S.D.] *Q1, 3* (*repeating* "a miracle"); *Q2, F.* 60–1.] *arranged ASC;* What . . . noise? / . . . proclayme? / . . . Miracle. *F.* 62. him] *F; om. Seymour conj.* 67. S.D. *Enter . . . man*] *Q* (*subst.*); *F* (*subst., om. with music*). Simpcox] *edd.; om. Q, F.* *between . . . chair;*] *F;* that had bene blind betweene . . . chaire *Q.* *his Wife . . . following.*] *edd.; om. Q, F.* 69. To] *F;* For to *Keightley conj.*

56. *stomachs*] angry tempers; cf. Chronicles, *passim*.

57, 58. *music . . . jar . . . harmony*] another of Shakespeare's metaphors involving the current Elizabethan identification of the elements in the world, the state, and the soul, with musical notes and their concords—a body of imagery not sufficiently noticed.

59. *compound . . . strife*] to compose or settle a difference or dispute (L. *lites, discordias* and *componere*).

60. *miracle*] Probably derived from Fox, rather than from More's *Dialogue concerning heresies* or Grafton's *Chronicle*; see Appendix I, and Introduction, p. xl. The lameness is added by Shakespeare. The incident is used, as in Fox, 3. 712, to emphasize the "goodness" and judgement of Humphrey.

60–77. *miracle . . . receiv'd his sight . . . God be prais'd . . . sin . . . Born blind*] follows *John*, 9.

66–7. *to believing souls / Gives light in darkness*] from Morning Prayer, Benedictus (*Luke*, 1. 79), "To give light to them that sit in darkness"; cf. *Ps.*, 112. 4, "unto the Godly there ariseth up light in the darkness".

68. *on procession*] an obsolete use for "in procession"; cf. Jonson, *New Inn*, 3. 2. 218.

King. Great is his comfort in this earthly vale,
Although by sight his sin be multiplied.
Glou. Stand by, my masters; bring him near the King:
His Highness' pleasure is to talk with him.
King. Good fellow, tell us here the circumstance,
That we for thee may glorify the Lord.
What! hast thou been long blind, and now restor'd?
Simp. Born blind, and 't please your Grace.
Wife. Ay, indeed, was he.
Suf. What woman is this?
Wife. His wife, and 't like your worship.
Glou. Hadst thou been his mother, thou could'st have better told.
King. Where wert thou born?
Simp. At Berwick in the north, and 't like your Grace.
King. Poor soul! God's goodness hath been great to thee:
Let never day nor night unhallow'd pass,
But still remember what the Lord hath done.
Queen. Tell me, good fellow, cam'st thou here by chance,
Or of devotion, to this holy shrine?
Simp. God knows, of pure devotion; being call'd
A hundred times and oft'ner, in my sleep,
By good Saint Alban; who said, "Simon, come;
Come, offer at my shrine, and I will help thee."
Wife. Most true, forsooth; and many time and oft

71. by] *Lloyd conj., Wilson;* by his *F.* 83. Berwick] Barwick(e) *Q, F.* 91 Simon] *F* (Symon)*;* Simpcox *Pope, Theobald + edd.;* Saunder *Capell.*

70. *this earthly vale*] cf. *Ps.*, 84. 6 (*CP.*), "this vale of misery"; *Homily against Wilful Rebellion*, 490, "this wretched earth and vale of all misery".

71. *by sight . . . multiplied*] Noble compares *John*, 9. 41, "If ye were blind, ye would have no sinne, but now ye say, We see: therefore your sinne remaineth."

75. *glorify the Lord*] *Matt.*, 5. 16, "and glorify your Father which is in heaven". Noble points out that the sentence is most frequently read at the Communion Offertory.

77–80.] clearly verse, but impossible to restore; cf. 108–23 below.

86. *still*] always.

91. *Simon*] Brooke, defending this F reading (Symon) against Theobald's emendation to "Simpcox", says, "the latter is merely a derivative of Simon, through Sim-cock (Simon-boy). It is more in keeping with the saint's dignity to employ the Biblical name in its purity."

92. *offer*] make an offering (of money).

Myself have heard a voice to call him so.
Car. What! art thou lame?
Simp. Ay, God Almighty help me!
Suf. How cam'st thou so?
Simp. A fall off of a tree.
Wife. A plum-tree, master.
Glou. How long hast thou been blind?
Simp. O! born so, master.
Glou. What! and would'st climb a tree?
Simp. But that in all my life, when I was a youth.
Wife. Too true; and bought his climbing very dear.
Glou. 'Mass, thou lov'd'st plums well, that would'st venture so.
Simp. Alas! good master, my wife desir'd some damsons,
And made me climb with danger of my life.
Glou. A subtle knave! But yet it shall not serve.—
Let me see thine eyes: wink now: now open them.
In my opinion yet thou see'st not well.
Simp. Yes, master, clear as day, I thank God and Saint Alban.
Glou. Say'st thou me so? What colour is this cloak of?
Simp. Red, master; red as blood.
Glou. Why, that's well said. What colour is my gown of?
Simp. Black, forsooth; coal-black as jet.
King. Why then, thou know'st what colour jet is of?
Suf. And yet, I think, jet did he never see.
Glou. But cloaks and gowns before this day a many.
Wife. Never, before this day, in all his life.
Glou. Tell me, sirrah, what's my name?
Simp. Alas! master, I know not.
Glou. What's his name?
Simp. I know not.
Glou. Nor his?
Simp. No, indeed, master.
Glou. What's thine own name?
Simp. Saunder Simpcox, and if it please you, master.

109. Red *Q3, F;* Why red *Q1, 2.*

108–23.] The dialogue should be in verse, but is corrupt beyond the possibility of restoration. Contrast 124–32 and see n.

Glou. Then Saunder, sit thou there, the lying'st knave
In Christendom. If thou hadst been born blind,
Thou might'st as well have known our names, as thus
To name the several colours we do wear.
Sight may distinguish of colours; but suddenly
To nominate them all, it is impossible.
Saint Alban here hath done a miracle;
And would ye not think his cunning to be great,
That could restore this cripple to his legs?
Simp. O master, that you could!
Glou. My masters of Saint Albans, have you not
A beadle in your town, and things call'd whips?
Mayor. Yes, my lord.

124–32.] *arranged ASC* (*partly after Pope, Hanmer*) ; *as prose Q; as verse F, divided* . . . there, / . . . Christendome. / . . . blinde, / . . . Names, / . . . weare. / . . . Colours: / . . . all, / . . . impossible. / . . . Miracle: / . . . great, / . . . againe. *See n.* 124. thou] *ASC; om. Q, F;* thee *Keightley.* 126. our] *ASC;* all our *Q, F.* 128. of] *Q, F; om. ASC conj.* 130. Saint] *ASC;* My Lords, Saint *Q, F.* 131. And] *Q, F; om. ASC conj.* his] *Q;* it, *F;* that *Rowe.* 132. legs] *Pope;* legs againe *Q, F.* 134–5.] *arranged ASC; Q, F, as verse, divided* . . . *Albones,* / . . . Towne, / . . . Whippes? 135. A beadle] *ASC;* Beadles *Q, F.* 136. Yes, my lord. *Glou.* Send . . . presently.] *ASC;* Yes, my Lord, if it please your Grace. *Glost.* Then send . . . presently. *Q, F.*

124–32.] original verse, set up practically unchanged from Q; printed as prose, and divided in F by phrasing or punctuation. The metre is easily restored by the omission of recognized memorial particles and phrases, and allowance for possible printer's errors or omissions. Further improvements could be made, as suggested in collation above.

124. *sit thou there*] there you are; you are proclaimed (Hart).

124–5. *the lying'st knave / In Christendom*] again in *Shr.*, Ind., II. 26. A common Elizabethan idiom or construction.

125–8. *blind . . . colours*] cf. Kyd, *Soliman and Perseda*, 2. 1. 45, "blinde can judge no colours".

129. *nominate*] give them their true names, implying recognition (Hart).

130.] see collation. QF *My Lords* is memorial, as at e.g. III. i. 84–6 (twice).

135. *beadle*] An inferior parish officer appointed by the vestry to keep order in church, punish petty offenders . . . a parish constable; "Let the Bedle . . . with . . . his owne whypp medle, And lashe theym soundlye." (*OED*).

things call'd whips] Armin, *Nest of Ninnies* (1608) inaccurately refers this phrase to *Hamlet*, "There are as Hamlet says, *things called whips* in store". The words occur also in Jonson's (?) additions to Kyd's *Spanish Tragedy*, 3. 10.

The origin of the phrase may have been Deloney's "A New Ballet of the strange and most cruel whips, which the Spaniards had prepared to whip and torment English men and women: which were found and taken at the overthrow of certain of the Spanish ships, in July last past, 1588." This contains the lines, "And for that purpose had prepared / of *whips* such wondrous *store*."

Glou. Send for one presently.
Mayor. Sirrah, go fetch the beadle hither straight.
[*Exit an Attendant.*
Glou. Now fetch me a stool hither by and by.
Now, sirrah, if you mean to save yourself
From whipping, leap me over this stool and run.
Simp. Alas! master, I am not able to stand alone:
You go about to torture me in vain.

Enter a Beadle with whips.

Glou. Well, sirrah, we must have you find your legs.
Whip him till he leap over that same stool.
Beadle. Come on, sirrah, off with your doublet, quickly.
Simp. Alas! master, what shall I do? I am not able to stand.

[*After the Beadle hath hit him once, he leaps over the stool and runs away; and they follow and cry, "A miracle!"*

King. O God! seest Thou this, and bearest so long?
Queen. It made me laugh to see the villain run.
Glou. Follow the knave; and take this drab away.
Wife. Alas! sir, we did it for pure need.
Glou. Let them be whipp'd through every market-town,
Till they come to Berwick, from whence they came.
[*Exeunt Mayor, Beadle, Wife, etc.*
Car. Duke Humphrey has done a miracle to-day.
Suf. True; made the lame to leap and fly away.
Glou. But you have done more miracles than I;
You made in a day, my lord, whole towns to fly.

137. S.D.] *Capell; Exet* one. *Q; Exit. F.* 139–40.] *arranged ASC; as verse in Q, divided after* whipping; *as prose F.* 140. run.] *ASC;* runne away. *Q, F.* 141. am not able to] *Q, F;* cannot *ASC conj.* 142. S.D.] *F;* Enter Beadle. *Q1, 2; Enter a Beadle. Q3.* 143. sirrah] *ASC;* sir *Q, F.* 144. Whip] *ASC;* Sirrah Beadle, whip *Q, F.* 145. Come] *ASC;* I will, my Lord. Come *Q* (*subst.*), *F.* 146. am not able to] *Q, F;* cannot *ASC conj.* 146. S.D.] *Q, F* (one girke *Q; once F*). 151. whipp'd] *Q, F* (whipt). 152. Till . . . from whence] *F;* Until . . . whence *Keightley.* 152. S.D.] *Capell; Exit. F; Exet* Mayor *Q.*

136. *presently*] immediately.

140. *leap . . . stool*] This seems to have been an indoor sport; see Jonson, 10. 42.

me] ethic dative.

150. *pure need*] absolute necessity.

154. *the lame to leap*] cf. *Isaiah*, 35. 6, "Then shall the lame man leape as an hart" (Noble).

156. *whole towns*] referring to the queen's dowry. Cf. *2 Tamb.*, 3251 "make whole cyties caper in the aire.',

Enter BUCKINGHAM.

King. What tidings with our cousin Buckingham?
Buck. Such as my heart doth tremble to unfold:
A sort of naughty persons, lewdly bent,
Under the countenance and confederacy
Of Lady Eleanor, the Protector's wife,
The ringleader and head of all this rout,
Have practis'd dangerously against your state,
Dealing with witches and with conjurers:
Whom we have apprehended in the fact;
Raising up wicked spirits from under ground,
Demanding of King Henry's life and death,
And other of your Highness' Privy Council,
As more at large your Grace shall understand.
Car. And so, my Lord Protector, by this means
Your lady is forthcoming yet at London.
This news, I think, hath turn'd your weapon's edge;
'Tis like, my lord, you will not keep your hour.
Glou. Ambitious churchman, leave to afflict my heart:
Sorrow and grief have vanquish'd all my powers;
And, vanquish'd as I am, I yield to thee,
Or to the meanest groom.
King. O God! what mischiefs work the wicked ones,

175, 176. vanquish'd] *F* (vanquisht).

157. *tidings*] just when Gloucester has achieved a triumph of administration, the news of his wife's "confederacy" arrives to mark the turn of the wheel of fortune and the beginning of his decline.

159. *A sort . . . lewdly bent*] a set of worthless persons, inclined to wickedness. "Lewdly" is used in the wide Elizabethan sense of "wickedly"; cf. Deloney's poem on the Queen at Tilbury (1588) in A. F. Pollard, *Tudor Tracts*, 492, "For the punishment of persons that are *lewd* or badly *bent*."

160. *confederacy*] alliance in conspiracy.

162. *ringleader*] Hall, 242 (App. 1).
head] leader.
rout] disorderly company.

165. *in the fact*] at the deed; red-handed.

166. *Raising spirits . . . under ground*] cf. above, I. ii. 79.

167. *Demanding*] asking (questions).

169. *at large*] at length; in full detail.

171. *forthcoming*] arrested and due to be brought forth for trial; cf. I. iv. 52.

173. *hour*] appointment, for the duel, arranged at 49, above.

178–9. *what mischiefs . . .*] *Ps.*, 7. 15–17 (Sternhold and Hopkins): "And all the mischief that he wrought / shall fall upon his head." *Ps.*, 14. 4 (ibid.): "Is all their judgement so farre lost, / that all work mischief still?" (Baldwin).

178. *wicked ones*] *Matt.*, 13. 38.

Heaping confusion on their own heads thereby!
Queen. Gloucester, see here the tainture of thy nest,
And look thyself be faultless, thou wert best.
Glou. Madam, for myself, to heaven I do appeal,
How I have lov'd my King and commonweal;
And, for my wife, I know not how it stands.
Sorry I am to hear what I have heard:
Noble she is, but if she have forgot
Honour and virtue, and convers'd with such
As, like to pitch, defile nobility,
I banish her my bed and company,
And give her as a prey to law and shame,
That hath dishonour'd Gloucester's honest name.
King. Well, for this night we will repose us here:
To-morrow toward London back again,
To look into this business thoroughly,
And call these foul offenders to their answers,
And poise the cause in Justice' equal scales,
Whose beam stands sure, whose rightful cause prevails.
[*Flourish. Exeunt.*

187. convers'd] *F* (conuers't).

180. *tainture*] defilement. An echo of the proverb, "It is a foule byrd that fyleth his own nest." Cf. *AYL*., IV. i. 207, "show the world what the bird hath done to her own nest"; *Jack Straw* (Dodsley, 5. 390), "So true a bird would file so fair a nest"; and *Mirror*, p. 220, l. 1. The sequence of metaphor is continued in 188 below.

188. *pitch, defile*] from *Ecclus*., 13.1, "Who so toucheth pitche, shall be defiled withall"; cf. *Ado*, III. iii. 60; Lyly, *Euphues*, I. 250. 23; etc.

196–7. *And poise the cause . . . Whose beam . . . whose . . . cause*] "and determine in the scales of justice which of the two offenders has right on his side." For this Latinism, cf. IV. x. 52–3; and for the metaphor, *All's W*., II. iii. 161; *Oth*., I. iii. 331; *Ham*., IV. v. 157.

The beam is the transverse bar from which the scales are suspended, in a balance.

Idea and construction are a close parallel to Virgil, *Æneid*, 12. 725 ff: "Iuppiter ipse duas aequato examine lances / sustinet et fata imponit diversa duorum, / *quem* damnet labor et *quo* vergat pondere letum." ("Jupiter himself upholds two scales in even balance, and lays therein the destinies of both, whom the strife dooms, and with whose weight death sinks down." Loeb.)

SCENE II.—*London. The Duke of* YORK's *Garden.*

Enter YORK, SALISBURY, *and* WARWICK.

York. Now, my good Lords of Salisbury and Warwick,
Our simple supper ended, give me leave,
In this close walk, to satisfy myself,
In craving your opinion of my title,
Which is infallible, to England's crown.
Sal. My lord, I long to hear it at full.
War. Sweet York, begin; and if thy claim be good,
The Nevils are thy subjects to command.
York. Edward the Third, my lords, had seven sons:
The first, Edward the Black Prince, Prince of Wales;
The second, William of Hatfield; and the third,
Lionel Duke of Clarence; next to whom
Was John of Gaunt, the Duke of Lancaster;
The fifth was Edmund Langley, Duke of York;
The sixth was Thomas of Woodstock, Duke of
Gloucester;
William of Windsor was the seventh and last.
Edward the Black Prince died before his father,
And left behind him Richard, his only son,
Who, after Edward the Third's death, reign'd as king;
Till Henry Bolingbroke, Duke of Lancaster,

Scene II

Locality.] *Capell.* Entry.] *F, Q (subst.).* 6. at full] *F;* at the full *Capell;* all at full *Wilson conj.* 9. Edward the Third, my lords, had] *ASC;* Then thus: / Edward the third, my Lords, had *F;* Then thus my Lords. / Edward the third had *Q*. *See n.*

Source: Hall, 2, 23, 27, 246 (Appendix 1), and not Holinshed; see Introduction, p. xl. The text of the whole scene is affected by the intermittent use of Q copy; see Introduction, p. xxxvi.

2. *supper*] to which Salisbury and Warwick were invited by York at I. iv. 77–8.

3. *close walk*] retired or private path or space; cf. "plot", 59.

4–5.] The genealogy, from Hall, is presented in a slighter form in *1 H 6*, II. iv, v. For genealogical tables, see Appendix 2.

6. *hear*] probably disyllabic; cf. "Henry", 22, below.

9.] see collation. The amender, when transferring "my Lords" to its F position, omitted to delete "Then thus". The whole expression is also used, memorially, in *Tr. Tr.*, but not in *3 H 6*, at I. ii. 22; similarly in *Wiv.*, (Q), 1405.

20 ff.] The original sin of the house of Lancaster—the crime from which,

The eldest son and heir of John of Gaunt,
Crown'd by the name of Henry the Fourth,
Seiz'd on the realm, depos'd the rightful king,
Sent his poor Queen to France, from whence she came,
And him to Pomfret; where, as all you know,
Harmless Richard was murder'd traitorously.

War. Father, the duke of York hath told the truth;
Thus got the house of Lancaster the crown.

York. Which now they hold by force, and not by right;
For Richard, the first son's heir, being dead,
The issue of the next son should have reign'd.

Sal. But William of Hatfield died without an heir.

York. The third son, Duke of Clarence, from whose line
I claim the crown, had issue Philippe, a daughter,
Who married Edmund Mortimer, Earl of March;
Edmund had issue, Roger, Earl of March;
Roger had issue, Edmund, Anne, and Eleanor.

Sal. This Edmund, in the reign of Bolingbroke,

27. duke of York] *ASC; Duke F.* told the truth] *F;* told the very truth *Hanmer;* surely told the truth *Capell;* told the truth in this *Keightley.* 33–4.] *arranged Pope;* . . . Clarence, / . . . Crowne, / . . . Daughter. *F.* 34, 48. Philippe] *Hanmer;* Phillip *F;* Philippa *Collier, Wilson.*

according to the chroniclers and Shakespeare, all the subsequent ills of England resulted.

25. *as all you know*] cf. Hall, 14, 246, etc.; *2 H 4*, III. i. 35; *F.Q.*, 2. 1. 61, as addressed to two people.

27. *duke of York*] the printer's eye has jumped from du*ke* to Yor*ke*: see collation.

33 ff.] note the F mislineation in the rest of the scene, due to use of Q copy. See Introduction, p. xxxvi.

37. *Edmund, Anne, and Eleanor*] Hall, 2. Holinshed, 3. 657, gives a fourth child, Roger; Grafton adds a fifth, Alice.

38. *Edmund*] Here, as in *1 H 4*, I. iii. 80 ff, Shakespeare follows Hall (and the other chroniclers) in fusing Edmund Mortimer, the 5th Earl, and his uncle, Sir Edmund. It was Sir Edmund who was captured by Glendower, thrown into prison, and married to Glendower's daughter. After his release by the Percies, he appears in *1 H 6*, II. v, as the heir apparent to the crown, a prisoner in the Tower, where he dies, after passing on his claim to Richard Plantagenet, Duke of York. This agrees with Hall, 28, "For the earle of Marche was euver kepte in the courte under suche a keper that he could nether doo or attempte any thyng againste the kyng without his knowledge, and died without issue, levying his right title and interest to Anne his sister and heire, married to Rycharde erle of Cambridge father to the duke of Yorke." In fact, as Malone points out, "he appears to have been at liberty during the whole reign of King Henry V—and there is no proof that he ever was confined, as a state-prisoner, by King Henry IV."

Here, however, Shakespeare, from an imperfect reading or recollection of Hall, 23, confused him with another

As I have read, laid claim unto the crown;
And, but for Owen Glendower, had been king,
Who kept him in captivity till he died.
But to the rest.

York. His eldest sister, Anne,
My mother, being heir unto the crown,
Married Richard, Earl of Cambridge, who was son
To Edmund Langley, Edward the Third's fifth son.
By her I claim the kingdom: she was heir
To Roger, Earl of March, who was the son
Of Edmund Mortimer, who married Philippe,
Sole daughter unto Lionel Duke of Clarence:
So, if the issue of the elder son
Succeed before the younger, I am king.

War. What plain proceedings is more plain than this?
Henry doth claim the crown from John of Gaunt,
The fourth son; York claims it from the third.
Till Lionel's issue fails, his should not reign:
It fails not yet, but flourishes in thee,
And in thy sons, fair slips of such a stock.
Then, father Salisbury, kneel we together,
And in this private plot be we the first
That shall salute our rightful sovereign
With honour of his birthright to the crown.

Both. Long live our sovereign Richard, England's king!

York. We thank you, lords. But I am not your king
Till I be crown'd and that my sword be stain'd
With heart-blood of the house of Lancaster;
And that's not suddenly to be perform'd

44–9.] *arranged Theobald* (*subst.*), *Capell;* Marryed . . . Cambridge, / . . . *Langley*, / . . . fift Sonnes Sonne; / . . . Kingdome: / . . . March, / . . . *Mortimer*, / . . . Daughter / . . . Clarence. *F.* 52. proceedings] *F, Alexander;* proceeding *Camb.* + *edd.* 63–5.] *arranged Pope;* We . . . Lords: / . . . Crown'd, / . . . stayn'd / . . . Lancaster: *F.*

son-in-law of Glendower, Lord Gray of Ruthvin, who is mentioned in the same paragraph, and to whom is applied the phrase—peculiar to Hall —"kept hym . . . in captivitee till he died".

52. *proceedings*] the process of events on the pedigree, not the narration of them. Cf. *Mer.*, III. i. 354.

56, 57. *flourishes . . . slips . . .*] a gardening metaphor, suggested by the genealogical tree, and possibly the "private plot".

57. *slips*] cuttings.

59. *private plot*] piece of ground, affording privacy; cf. 3 above.

But with advice and silent secrecy.
Do you as I do in these dangerous days,
Wink at the Duke of Suffolk's insolence,
At Beaufort's pride, at Somerset's ambition,
At Buckingham, and all the crew of them,
Till they have snar'd the shepherd of the flock,
That virtuous prince, the good Duke Humphrey:
'Tis that they seek; and they, in seeking that,
Shall find their deaths, if York can prophesy.

Sal. My lord, break off; we know your mind at full.

War. My heart assures me that the Earl of Warwick
Shall one day make the Duke of York a king.

York. And, Nevil, this I do assure myself:
Richard shall live to make the Earl of Warwick
The greatest man in England but the king. [*Exeunt.*

SCENE III.—*A hall of justice.*

Sound trumpets. Enter the KING, *the* QUEEN, GLOUCESTER, YORK, SUFFOLK, *and* SALISBURY; *the Duchess of* GLOUCESTER, MARGERY JOURDAIN, SOUTHWELL, HUME, *and* BOLINGBROKE, *under guard.*

King. Stand forth, Dame Eleanor Cobham, Gloucester's wife.
In sight of God and us, your guilt is great;

68–75.] *F; for Q, see App. 4.* 76. break] *Capell;* break we *F.*

Scene III

Locality.] *Capell.* Entry.] *after Theobald and Capell; Enter the King and State, with Guard, to banish the Duchesse. F; Enter King Henry, and the Queene, Duke Humphrey, the Duke of Suffolke, and the Duke of Buckingham, the Cardinall, and Dame Elnor Cobham, led with the Officers, and then enter to them the Duke of Yorke, and the Earles of Salsbury and Warwicke. Q.*

67. *advice*] deliberate consideration; cf. *H 5*, II. ii. 43, "on his more advice" = maturer reflection (Onions).

70. *pride . . . ambition*] referring back to I. i. 179.

72. *shepherd . . . flock*] the first of a series of animal metaphors, on beasts of prey and their victims, suggested by the "intestine divisions" in the state, and partly by the language of Hall, 112, "a shepherde whom his flocke loued"; and a tribute, by his enemies, to the character of Humphrey.

74, 75. *seeking . . . Shall find*] Luke, II. 9.

75. *prophesy*] a typical Shakespearean foreshadowing of events by prophecies, omens, etc.; already exemplified in Eleanor's conjuring in I. iv; cf. II. iv. 48; III. i. 189.

77.] For a censored speech of Warwick here, see Appendix 4.

Receive the sentence of the law for sins
Such as by God's book are adjudg'd to death.
You four, from hence to prison back again;
From thence unto the place of execution:
The witch in Smithfield shall be burn'd to ashes,
And you three shall be strangled on the gallows.
You, madam, for you are more nobly born,
Despoiled of your honour in your life,
Shall, after three days' open penance done,
Live in your country here in banishment,
With Sir John Stanley, in the Isle of Man.

Duch. Welcome is banishment; welcome were my death.

Glou. Eleanor, the law, thou seest, hath judged thee:
I cannot justify whom the law condemns.
[*Exeunt Duchess and other Prisoners, guarded.*
Mine eyes are full of tears, my heart of grief.
Ah! Humphrey, this dishonour in thine age
Will bring thy head with sorrow to the grave.
I beseech your Majesty, give me leave to go;
Sorrow would solace and mine age would ease.

King. Stay, Humphrey, Duke of Gloucester: ere thou go,
Give up thy staff: Henry will to himself
Protector be; and God shall be my hope,
My stay, my guide, and lantern to my feet.

3. sins] *Theobald;* sinne *F.* 16. S.D. *Exeunt . . . guarded.*] *Theobald; Exit some with Elnor. Q; om. F.* 19. grave] *ASC;* ground *F. See n.* 22–5.] *arranged Pope;* Stay . . . Gloster, / . . . Staffe, / . . . be, / . . . guide, / . . . feete: *F.*

4. *God's book . . . death*] cf. *Exodus*, 22. 18; *Lev.*, 20. 6; *Deut.*, 18. 10–12, "Thou shalt not suffer a witch to live", "And the soul that turneth after such as have familiar spirits . . . I shall . . . cut him off." (Noble.)

adjudg'd to death] Hall, 202, "adiudged to die".

11. *three days' . . . penance done*] *Homilies*, 154, "done open penance". Note the L. construction.

13. *John*] Hall, Holinshed. Fabyan and Stow read correctly "Thomas". (Boswell-Stone, 259, is misleading here, on Holinshed.) He is the Lord Stanley of *R 3*, and elder brother of Sir William Stanley in *3 H 6*, IV. v.

18–19. *age . . . grave*] cf. *Genesis*, 42. 38, "ye shall bring my gray head with sorowe to the grave" (Noble). Cf. *Gent.*, III. i. 19–21; and V. i. 162 ff below. The series of associations at V. i. 162 ff and the graphical similarity, combine to support the amendment of F "ground" to "grave". For the same error, see *Ham.*, IV. v. 37 (Q1F grave; Q2 ground).

21. *would*] would have; cf. "I would no other company", *H 5*, IV. i. 32.

25. *stay*] cf. *Ps.*, 71. 5; 18. 1 (Bishop's); 42. 9 (Sternhold and Hopkins), "my guide and stay";

And go in peace, Humphrey, no less belov'd
Than when thou wert Protector to thy King.
Queen. I see no reason why a king of years
Should be to be protected like a child.
God and King Henry govern England's helm!
Give up your staff, sir, and the King his realm.
Glou. My staff? here, noble Henry, is my staff:
As willingly do I the same resign
As erst thy father Henry made it mine;
And even as willing at thy feet I leave it
As others would ambitiously receive it.
Farewell, good king! when I am dead and gone,
May honourable peace attend thy throne. [*Exit.*
Queen. Why, now is Henry King, and Margaret Queen;
And Humphrey Duke of Gloucester scarce himself,
That bears so shrewd a maim: two pulls at once;
His lady banish'd, and a limb lopp'd off;
This staff of honour raught: there let it stand,
Where it best fits to be, in Henry's hand.

30. helm] *Steevens* (*Johnson conj.*); realme *F. See n.* 34. erst] *Q1, 2*; ere *Q3, F.* 35. willing] *Q, Pope*; willingly *F. See n.* 38. S.D. *Exit*] Exit *Gloster. Q, F.* 42. banish'd] *F* (banisht). lopp'd] *F* (lopt).

or *2 Sam.*, 22. 1 (Geneva) (Noble).

lantern] *Ps.*, 119. 105, "Thy word is a lantern to my feete" (*CP.*, and Geneva; "lamp" *A.V.*).

28, 39, 52] note the Queen's animosity against Gloucester, in keeping with her masculine character in the Chronicles.

28. *a king of years*] "beyng of perfect age & mans estate" Hall, 208 (Appendix 1). Cf 1. i. 164–5; and *Mirror* (Humphrey), p. 455, "A king of yeares, stil governed to bee Lyke a Pupil . . ."

29. *child*] cf. *1 H 6*, 1. i. 35–6: "None do you like but an effeminate prince, / Whom, like a school-boy, you may over-awe." and Marlowe, *Ed. 2*, 1336–7: "As though your highness were a schoolboy still, / And must be awed and governed like a child."

30. *helm*] see collation; "govern" carries its L. sense of "steer" (*gubernare*); cf. 1 iii. 100, "steer the happy helm."

31. *Give up your staff*] There is no historical authority for Gloucester's dismissal from office consequent upon his wife's disgrace. It was probably suggested by the passage in Hall, 208, referred to above, n. to 28.

staff] as Lord Protector (Rothery, 115).

35. *willing*] see collation; the F "willingly" is probably due to the influence of 33; cf. v. i. 51.

37. *dead and gone*] cf. *1 H 6*, 1. iv. 93 *Ham.*, IV. v. 29.

41. *bears so shrewd a maim*] endures so sharp or grievous a mutilation.

pulls] that which is pulled or torn off. A pull, or plucking, of fruit, is still common provincially. The metaphor is continued in "limb lopped off . . . pine . . . sprays".

43. *raught*] reached, attained.

Suf. Thus droops this lofty pine and hangs his sprays;
Thus Eleanor's pride dies in her youngest days.
York. Lords, let him go. Please it your Majesty
This is the day appointed for the combat;
And ready are the appellant and defendant,
The armourer and his man, to enter the lists,
So please your Highness to behold the fight.
Queen. Ay, good my lord; for purposely therefore
Left I the court to see this quarrel tried.
King. A God's name, see the lists and all things fit:
Here let them end it; and God defend the right!
York. I never saw a fellow worse bested,
Or more afraid to fight, than is the appellant,
The servant of this armourer, my lords.

Enter, at one door, the Armourer, and his Neighbours drinking to him so much that he is drunk; and he enters bearing his staff with a sand-bag

46. youngest] *F;* haughtiest *Staunton conj.;* highest *Kinnear conj.* 58. S.D.] *Q, F (subst.).*

45. *this lofty pine*] an "allusion to the stock of a tree, certainly borne as a badge by the Duke's father, Henry IV, and derived from Thomas of Woodstock, Duke of Gloucester, who adopted it in allusion to his place of birth and his political condition" (Rothery, 47).

The whole idea, or background, is from Whitney's *Emblems*, 1586 (used for some of the devices in *Pericles*), 59: "The *loftie Pine*, that one the mountaine growes, / And spreades her armes, with branches freshe, & greene, / The raginge windes, on sodaine overthrowes, / And makes her *stoope*, that longe a farre was seene: / So they, that truste to muche in fortunes smiles, / Thoughe worlde do laughe, and wealthe do most abounde, / When leste they thinke, are often snar'de with wyles, / And from alofte, doo hedlonge fall to grounde: . . ." "Saepius ventis agitatur ingens / Pinus, & celsae graviore casu / Decidunt turres, feriuntque summos / Fulmina montes." (Hor. *Carm.*, 2. Od. 10). For "worlde . . . laughe", cf. below II. iv. 82; and *Sonn.*, 64 for "celsae turres".

46. *youngest*] Eleanor is the shoot or "spray" of the pine (Gloucester), and, in her pride, is still young. Brooke suggests novissimi = latest. Kinnear, *Cruces*, 257–8, conjectures "highest", founding on the collocation of "pride" and "height" at I. ii. 42; *R 3*, v. iii. 175; *Per.*, II. iv. 6. Mason, *Comments*, suggests *her* = *its*: cf. Abbott, 229, which makes it possible that Shakespeare was influenced by the Latin feminine.

47. *let him go*] think no more about him.

49. *appellant and defendant*] challenger and challenged in single combat.

52. *therefore*] therefor, for that purpose.

53. *quarrel*] difference.

56. *bested*] in a (worse) plight.

58. sand-bag] bag of sand attached to the end of a stick. Hart casts doubt on this practice, but Singer quotes Butler, *Hudibras*: "Engag'd with

fastened to it; a drum before him: and at the other door, his man with a drum and sand-bag, and Prentices drinking to him.

1 Neigh. Here, neighbour Horner, I drink to you in a cup of sack: and fear not, neighbour, you shall do well enough.

2 Neigh. And here, neighbour, here's a cup of charneco.

3 Neigh. And here's a pot of good double beer, neighbour: drink, and fear not your man.

Hor. Let it come, i' faith, and I'll pledge you all; and a fig for Peter!

1 Pren. Here, Peter, I drink to thee; and be not afeard.

2 Pren. Be merry, Peter, and fear not thy master: fight for credit of the prentices.

Peter. I thank you all: drink, and pray for me, I pray you; for I think I have taken my last draught in this world. Here, Robin, and if I die, I give thee my apron; and, Will, thou shalt have my hammer: and here, Tom, take all the money that I have. O Lord bless me, I pray God, for I am never able to deal with my master, he hath learnt so much fence already.

Sal. Come, leave your drinking, and fall to blows. Sirrah, what's thy name?

Peter. Peter, forsooth.

Sal. Peter! what more?

Peter. Thump.

Sal. Thump! Then see thou thump thy master well.

67. afeard] *Q1, 2;* afraid *Q3, F.*

money bags, as bold / As men with sand bags did of old", and gives a reference to St Chrysostom.

59.] The rest of the scene, including the S.DD. here and at II. iv. 1, was set up mainly from Q3; see Introduction, pp. xxxiii ff.

62. *charneco*] a kind of sweet wine. Origin doubtful, but perhaps from the name of a village in Portugal; see Sugden, 111.

63. *double*] extra strong.

65. *Let it come*] Let the glass go round. A drinking expression; cf. *2 H 4*, v. iii. 52 (Hart).

65–6. *a fig for . . .*] a contemptuous gesture consisting in thrusting the thumb between the first and second fingers (Onions).

67 ff. *I drink . . . Be merry . . . I die*] Possibly a recollection of "Eat, drink, and be merry for tomorrow you die." Cf. also Froissart (Globe, 258), "The same proper morning Wat Tyler, Jack Straw, and John Ball had assembled their company . . . and there were together all of affinity more than twenty thousand, and yet there were many still in the town, *drinking and making merry* in the taverns."

Hor. Masters, I am come hither, as it were, upon my man's instigation, to prove him a knave, and myself an honest man: and touching the Duke of York, I will take my death I never meant him any ill, nor the King, nor the Queen: and therefore, Peter, have at thee with a downright blow.

York. Dispatch: this knave's tongue begins to double.
Sound, trumpets, alarum to the combatants.

[*Alarum. They fight, and Peter strikes him down.*

Hor. Hold, Peter, hold! I confess, I confess treason. [*Dies.*

York. Take away his weapon. Fellow, thank God, and the good wine in thy master's way.

Peter. [*kneeling.*] O God! have I overcome mine enemies in this presence? O Peter! thou hast prevail'd in right.

King. Go, take hence that traitor from our sight;
For by his death we do perceive his guilt:
And God in justice hath reveal'd to us
The truth and innocence of this poor fellow,
Which he had thought to have murder'd wrongfully.
Come, fellow, follow us for thy reward.

[*Sound a flourish. Exeunt.*

88. with a . . . blow] *F;* with . . . blowes, as Beuys of Southampton fell vpon Askapart. *Q.* 90. Sound, trumpets] *Collier;* Sound Trumpets *F.* 90. S.D. *Alarum.*] *Capell; om. F.* 91. S.D. *Dies.*] *Theobald;* He dies. *Q; om. F.* 94. *kneeling*] He kneeles down. *Q; om. F.* 97. Go, take] *Q, F;* Go, and take *Hanmer.*

86. *take my death*] stake my life on it (*OED.*, 40b); cf. Marston, *The Insatiate Countess* (ed. Wood), 3. 75, "They take't upon their death, they slew your Nephew"; Hall, 202; Fox, 3. 707; *Tudor Tracts* (Pollard), 347; Hol., 4. 893.

88. *downright*] perpendicular; cf. *3 H 6,* I. i. 12. Cotgrave has "*aplomb:* m. A perpendicular, or *downe-right* fall; a plumpe descent" (Hart).

88.] see collation: Bevis may have been one of the original actors (cf. S.D., IV. ii. 1), and this phrase a personal allusion.

89. *double*] like a hare (Madden) = stutter.

91.] note the use of Hall's armourer to emphasize and anticipate York's treason.

93. *in thy master's way*] in the way of your master's power to fight.

SCENE IV.—*A street.*

Enter GLOUCESTER *and his men, in mourning cloaks.*

Glou. Thus sometimes hath the brightest day a cloud;
And after summer evermore succeeds
Barren winter, with his wrathful nipping cold:
So cares and joys abound, as seasons fleet.
Sirs, what's o'clock?
Serv. Ten, my lord.
Glou. Ten is the hour that was appointed me
To watch the coming of my punish'd duchess:
Uneath may she endure the flinty streets,
To tread them with her tender-feeling feet.
Sweet Nell, ill can thy noble mind abrook
The abject people gazing on thy face
With envious looks, laughing at thy shame,
That erst did follow thy proud chariot wheels
When thou didst ride in triumph through the streets.
But soft! I think she comes; and I'll prepare
My tear-stain'd eyes to see her miseries.

Scene IV

Locality.] *Theobald.* Entry.] *Q, F* (*reading Duke Humfrey*). 3. Barren] *F;* Bare *Capell.* 5. Ten] *F;* Almost ten *Q;* 'Tis almost ten *Lettsom conj.* 7. punish'd] *F* (punisht).

For the sentence and punishment of the Duchess, see Appendix I (Hall, 202). The taper, 16 S.D. (not in Hall), is in Fox, 3. 711, and Holinshed (1587), 3. 623. The sheet, taper, "bare foot", are in *Mirror*, pp. 436, 455.

1. *brightest day . . . cloud*] cf. *All's W.*, v. iii. 35; *Sonn.*, 33; *2 Tamb.*, 2969 ff, "Black is the beauty of the brightest day . . . / He bindes his temples with a frowning cloude."

2–4. *summer . . . winter . . . nipping . . . joys*] cf. *Sp. Tr.*, I. I. 12, 13, "But in the harvest of my summer joys / Death's winter nipped the blossoms of my bliss."

8. *Uneath*] not easily; with difficulty; cf. Whitney, *Emblems* (ed. Green), 263; *Mirror*, p. 220, l. 10.

10. *abrook*] brook, endure.

12. *envious*] malicious, spiteful; cf. 23, 35 below. Possibly accentuated on the second syllable, as in *Locrine*, I. I. 229, "Hard-herted gods, and too envious fates."

13. *erst*] formerly.

13–14. *proud chariot wheels . . . streets*] from Marlowe, *2 Tamb.*, 2532–3: "And as thou rid'st in triumph through the streets, / The pavement underneath thy chariot wheels . . . /" Cf. *Massacre*, 991, "And he shall follow my proud chariot wheeles."

Enter the Duchess of GLOUCESTER, *barefoot in a white sheet, and a taper burning in her hand; with Sir* JOHN STANLEY, *the Sheriff, and Officers.*

Serv. So please your Grace, we'll take her from the sheriff.
Glou. No, stir not, for your lives; let her pass by.
Duch. Come you, my lord, to see my open shame?
Now thou dost penance too. Look how they gaze!
See how the giddy multitude do point,
And nod their heads, and throw their eyes on thee!
Ah! Gloucester, hide thee from their hateful looks,
And, in thy closet pent up, rue my shame,
And ban thine enemies, both mine and thine.
Glou. Be patient, gentle Nell; forget this grief.
Duch. Ah! Gloucester, teach me to forget myself;
For whilst I think I am thy married wife,
And thou a prince, Protector of this land,
Methinks I should not thus be led along,
Mail'd up in shame, with papers on my back,
And follow'd with a rabble that rejoice
To see my tears and hear my deep-fet groans.
The ruthless flint doth cut my tender feet,
And when I start, the envious people laugh,
And bid me be advised how I tread.
Ah! Humphrey, can I bear this shameful yoke?
Trowest thou that e'er I'll look upon the world,

16. S.D.] *edd.;* Enter Dame Elnor Cobham bare-foote, and a white sheet about her, with a waxe candle in her hand, and verses written on her backe and pind on, and accompanied with the Sheriffes of London, and Sir *Iohn Standly*, and Officers with billes and holbards. *Q; Enter the Duchesse in a white Sheet, and a Taper burning in her hand, with the Sherife and Officers. F.*

19. *open shame*] *Hebrews*, 6. 6; *Ps.*, 79. 4 (*CP.*); *Mirror* (Eleanor), l. 133; (Humphrey), l. 299, both times in conjunction with "penance".

23. *hateful*] full of hate.

24. *closet*] private apartment, study. *rue*] pity.

25. *ban*] curse; cf. III. ii. 332.

31. *Mail'd up*] wrapped up, enveloped—a term in falconry. "Mail a hawk" is to wrap her up in a handkerchief or other cloth, that she may not be able to stir her wings or to struggle (Holmes, *Academy of Armory*). The line was used by Drayton, *Heroical Epistles*, 1598 (Hart).

with papers . . .] cf. S.D. in Q "and verses written on her backe and pind on".

35. *start*] twitch with pain.

36. *be advised*] take care, be careful; cf. *R 3*, II. i. 107.

Or count them happy that enjoys the sun?
No; dark shall be my light, and night my day;
To think upon my pomp shall be my hell.
Sometime I'll say, I am Duke Humphrey's wife,
And he a prince and ruler of the land:
Yet so he rul'd, and such a prince he was,
As he stood by whilst I, his forlorn duchess,
Was made a wonder and a pointing-stock
To every idle rascal follower.
But be thou mild, and blush not at my shame,
Nor stir at nothing till the axe of death
Hang over thee, as sure it shortly will;
For Suffolk, he that can do all in all
With her that hateth thee, and hates us all,
And York, and impious Beaufort, that false priest,
Have all lim'd bushes to betray thy wings;
And, fly thou how thou canst, they'll tangle thee:
But fear not thou, until thy foot be snar'd,
Nor never seek prevention of thy foes.

Glou. Ah! Nell, forbear: thou aimest all awry;
I must offend before I be attainted;
And had I twenty times so many foes,
And each of them had twenty times their power,
All these could not procure me any scathe,
So long as I am loyal, true, and crimeless.

39. enjoys] *F; enjoy Rowe + edd.*

39. *enjoys*] For the agreement, see Abbott, 247.

45. *As*] that; Abbott, 109.

46. *wonder*] cf. "a nine days' wonder", and "These few days' wonder", at 69; *3 H 6,* III. ii. 112–13; *AYL.,* III. ii. 185.

pointing-stock] butt; cf. laughing-stock; gazing-stock (Sidney); mocking-stock (Gascoigne).

47. *rascal*] base, good-for-nothing.

49. ff *the axe . . .*] another foreboding of Gloucester's fate; cf. II. ii. 75.

54. *lim'd*] smeared with bird-lime; cf. I. iii. 88.

56. *fear not thou*] Eleanor knows her husband's simplicity (cf. Lady Macbeth) and treats it ironically.

snar'd] a continuation of the metaphorical sequence begun at II. ii. 72.

57. *prevention*] in the L. sense of "anticipation" = action taken beforehand to foil their schemes.

59 ff. *I must offend*] note the irony of false security, the breach of which begins at 70. Compare the false security of Hastings in *R 3*.

59. *attainted*] condemned for treason or felony.

62. *scathe*] injury, damage, as in "unscathed".

Would'st have me rescue thee from this reproach?
Why, yet thy scandal were not wip'd away,
But I in danger for the breach of law.
Thy greatest help is quiet, gentle Nell:
I pray thee, sort thy heart to patience;
These few days' wonder will be quickly worn.

Enter a Herald.

Her. I summon your Grace to his Majesty's Parliament,
Holden at Bury the first of this next month.
Glou. And my consent ne'er ask'd herein before!
This is close dealing. Well, I will be there. [*Exit Herald.*
My Nell, I take my leave: and, Master sheriff,
Let not her penance exceed the King's commission.
Sher. And 't please your grace, here my commission stays,
And Sir John Stanley is appointed now
To take her with him to the Isle of Man.
Glou. Must you, Sir John, protect my lady here?
Stan. So am I given in charge, may 't please your Grace.
Glou. Entreat her not the worse in that I pray
You use her well. The world may laugh again;
And I may live to do you kindness if
You do it her: and so, Sir John, farewell.
Duch. What! gone, my lord, and bid me not farewell.
Glou. Witness my tears, I cannot stay to speak.
[*Exeunt Gloucester and his men.*
Duch. Art thou gone too? All comfort go with thee!
For none abides with me: my joy is death;
Death, at whose name I oft have been afeard,

65. wip'd] *F* (wipt). 73. S.D.] *Q; om. F.* 79. here] *F;* there *S. Walker conj.* 83–4.] *arranged Pope; Q, F, divided after* her. 86. S.D. *and his men.*] *Q; om. F.*

67. *Thy greatest help . . .*] Hart quotes Johnson, "The poet has not endeavoured to raise much compassion for the duchess, who indeed suffers but what she had deserved. Shakespeare's two earliest women, if these be they, are not attractive."

68. *sort*] adapt, fit.

70. *Parliament*] Hall, 209 (Appendix I).

73. *close dealing*] secret contriving or plotting. The first blow falls quickly.

75. *King's commission*] royal or state warrant, or instrument.

82. *The world may laugh again*] better times may be in store. An example of Gloucester's simple optimism, on the eve of his murder. Cf. *Homily against the Fear of Death*, 81, "men, whom this world doth not so greatly laugh upon"; and Whitney, *Emblems*, quoted above at II. iii. 45.

Because I wish'd this world's eternity.
Stanley, I prithee, go, and take me hence;
I care not whither, for I beg no favour,
Only convey me where thou art commanded.

Stan. Why, madam, that is to the Isle of Man;
There to be us'd according to your state.

Duch. That's bad enough, for I am but reproach:
And shall I then be us'd reproachfully?

Stan. Like to a duchess, and Duke Humphrey's lady:
According to that state you shall be us'd.

Duch. Sheriff, farewell, and better than I fare,
Although thou hast been conduct of my shame.

Sher. It is my office; and, madam, pardon me.

Duch. Ay, ay, farewell; thy office is discharg'd.
Come, Stanley, shall we go?

Stan. Madam, your penance done, throw off this sheet,
And go we to attire you for our journey.

Duch. My shame will not be shifted with my sheet:
No; it will hang upon my richest robes,
And show itself, attire me how I can.
Go, lead the way; I long to see my prison.

[*Exeunt.*

105.] *arranged Pope; Stanley.* Madame, . . . done, / Throw . . . Sheet, *F.*

101. *conduct*] conductor, guide; cf. *Rom.*, III. i. 129; V. iii. 116.

107. *shifted*] changed, in a double sense.

ACT III

SCENE I.—*The Abbey at Bury St. Edmunds.*

Sound a sennet. Enter KING, QUEEN, CARDINAL, SUFFOLK, YORK, BUCKINGHAM, SALISBURY, *and* WARWICK, *to the Parliament.*

King. I muse my Lord of Gloucester is not come:
'Tis not his wont to be the hindmost man,
Whate'er occasion keeps him from us now.

Queen. Can you not see, or will ye not observe
The strangeness of his alter'd countenance?
With what a majesty he bears himself,
How insolent of late he is become,
How proud, how peremptory, and unlike himself?
We know the time since he was mild and affable,
And if we did but glance a far-off look,
Immediately he was upon his knee,
That all the court admir'd him for submission:
But meet him now, and be it in the morn,
When every one will give the time of day,
He knits his brow and shows an angry eye,
And passeth by with stiff unbowed knee,

ACT III

Scene I

Locality.] *edd.* Entry.] *F;* Enter to the Parlament. Enter two Heralds before, then the Duke of *Buckingham*, and the Duke of *Suffolke*, and then the Duke of *Yorke*, and the *Cardinall* of *Winchester*, and then the King and the Queene, and then the Earle of *Salisbury*, and the Earle of *Warwicke*. *Q.* 4. see,] *Q1, 2;* see? *Q3, F.* 8. proud, how] *F;* proud, *Steevens.*

The holocaust begins. The imagery develops from the "snare" for the shepherd Gloucester to the jungle and the slaughter-house. A long list of the animal metaphors and allusions was collected by Furnivall in *Trans N.S.S.*, 1875–6, pp. 280 ff.

1. *I muse*] I wonder. A common Shakespearean opening (Hart).

4.] Note Margaret's apparent concern for the King, covering her real attack on Gloucester. Cf. II. iii. 28.

9. *since*] when; cf. *2 H 4*, III. ii. 189; *Wint.*, V. i. 219.

14. *give the time of day*] the day's greeting; good-morrow.

Disdaining duty that to us belongs.
Small curs are not regarded when they grin,
But great men tremble when the lion roars;
And Humphrey is no little man in England.
First note that he is near you in descent,
And should you fall, he is the next will mount.
Me seemeth then it is no policy,
Respecting what a rancorous mind he bears,
And his advantage following your decease,
That he should come about your royal person
Or be admitted to your Highness' Council.
By flattery hath he won the commons' hearts,
And when he please to make commotion,
'Tis to be fear'd they all will follow him.
Now 'tis the spring, and weeds are shallow-rooted;
Suffer them now, and they'll o'ergrow the garden,
And choke the herbs for want of husbandry.
The reverent care I bear unto my lord
Made me collect these dangers in the Duke.
If it be fond, call it a woman's fear;
Which fear if better reasons can supplant,
I will subscribe, and say I wrong'd the Duke.
My Lord of Suffolk, Buckingham, and York,
Reprove my allegation if you can;
Or else conclude my words effectual.

Suf. Well hath your Highness seen into this duke;
And had I first been put to speak my mind,
I think I should have told your Grace's tale.
The Duchess by his subornation,
Upon my life, began her devilish practices:

18. *grin*] show the teeth.

19. *lion*] the armorial symbol of England and the King.

23–4. *no policy, / Respecting*] not wise, considering . . .

29. *make commotion*] raise an insurrection; cf. n. to 358; Hall, 219, "to cause some great commocion".

31–7. *weeds . . . garden . . . herbs . . . husbandry . . . collect . . . supplant*] A sequence of gardening images (cf. 89–90 below) with a suggestion of the parable of the Sower.

36. *fond*] foolish.

38. *subscribe*] agree, from the sense of signing at the foot of an agreement; cf. *1 H 6*, II. iv. 44; *Lr.*, III. vii. 64.

40. *Reprove*] disprove; cf. *Ado*, II. iii. 210, "'tis a truth . . . I cannot reprove it".

41. *effectual*] to the point, pertinent, conclusive.

45. *subornation*] instigation to crime —a transferred use from the proper sense of procurement for perjury, or perjury itself; cf. 145.

Or if he were not privy to those faults,
Yet, by reputing of his high descent,
As next the King he was successive heir,
And such high vaunts of his nobility,
Did instigate the bedlam brain-sick Duchess
By wicked means to frame our sovereign's fall.
Smooth runs the water where the brook is deep,
And in his simple show he harbours treason.
The fox barks not when he would steal the lamb:
No, no, my sovereign; Gloucester is a man
Unsounded yet, and full of deep deceit.

Car. Did he not, contrary to form of law,
Devise strange deaths for small offences done?

York. And did he not, in his Protectorship,
Levy great sums of money through the realm
For soldiers' pay in France, and never sent it?
By means whereof the towns each day revolted.

Buck. Tut! these are petty faults to faults unknown,

48. *reputing of*] thinking highly of; priding himself on; cf. 50.

51. *bedlam*] frantic.

53–7. *Smooth . . . deep . . . Unsounded*] from Camerarius's version of Aesop (*Fabellae Aesopicae*, a standard grammar-school text-book of the 16th century) (cf. Baldwin, *Small Latine*, I. 620):

"Amnium silentia.

"Rusticus transiturus flumen vadum vestigabat. Ac primum quadam parte se reperturum sperabat, qua defluebat illud placide, & cum silentio, sed a tentante reperitur magna ibi profunditas. Facit igitur alibi periculum ubi quidem reperit vadum, aqua vero cum strepitu & impetu decurrebat. Tum ille haec secum: Non, video, inquit, amnium murmura & fremitus, sed silentium & leves sibili metuendi sunt.

"Non esse periculum fabula docet, a clamatoribus & minacibus, sed a mussitantibus & taciturnis. Caesarem etiam dicere solitum accepimus, non metui a se Antonium & Dolabellam corpulentos & rubicundos, sed Cassii & Bruti maciem & pallorem."

Cf. Lyly, *Euphues*, 2. 65, "where the streame runneth smoothest, the water is deepest", and *Sappho and Phao*, 2. 4. 24.

For a series of borrowings from Aesop see 75, 77, and 343 below, and notes.

54. *simple show*] appearance of innocence or artlessness.

55. *fox . . . lamb*] These occur together in a variety of adages and fables; in Shakespeare in *Meas.*, V. i. 300; *Troil.*, III. ii. 200; *Tim.*, IV. iii. 331; etc.

58–9. *contrary to . . . law . . . small offences*] This is a repetition of Buckingham's charge (I. iii. 132–4). And yet once more by York below, 121–3 (Hart).

61–2. *money . . . pay in France*] The Queen broached these French accusations already, I. iii. 135–7. And see the charges collected again in Gloucester's reply below, 107–18, where the taxing of the Commons is mentioned again from I. iii. 138–9, the Cardinal's accusation.

64. *to*] compared to.

Which time will bring to light in smooth Duke
Humphrey.
King. My lords, at once: the care you have of us,
To mow down thorns that would annoy our foot,
Is worthy praise; but, shall I speak my conscience,
Our kinsman Gloucester is as innocent
From meaning treason to our royal person,
As is the sucking lamb or harmless dove.
The duke is virtuous, mild, and too well given
To dream on evil, or to work my downfall.
Queen. Ah! what's more dangerous than this fond affiance?
Seems he a dove? His feathers are but borrow'd,
For he's disposed as the hateful raven:
Is he a lamb? His skin is surely lent him,
For he's inclin'd as is the ravenous wolves.
Who cannot steal a shape that means deceit?

78. wolves] *F; wolf Rowe + edd.*

66. *at once*] let us proceed without more ado (Onions).

67. *annoy*] injure; cf. *H 5*, II. ii. 102.

68. *shall I speak my conscience*] if I am to tell my sincere belief in what is true.

71. *sucking lamb*] *1 Samuel*, 7. 9.

harmless dove] *Matt.*, 10, 16, "harmlesse as the . . . Doves", Bishops' Bible (Noble).

72. *well given*] well disposed; cf. *Caes.*, I. ii. 197, "He is a noble Roman and well given".

74. *fond affiance*] foolish trust; cf. Hall, 209 (Appendix I).

75–6. *dove . . . raven*] Shakespeare's mind now runs on Aesop (cf. 11, 77, 343) and his characters are identified with the animals (cf. Introduction, pp. liii–liv). This is from Camerarius,

"De Cornice superbiente aliarum avium pennis.

"Cornicula collectas pennas de reliquis avibus sibi accommodaverat, & superba varietate illa, reliquas omnes prae se aviculas contemnebat. Cum forte hirundo notata sua penna, advolans illam aufert, quo facto & reliquae postea aves quaeq: suam ademere cornici, ita illa risum movit omnibus, furtivis nudata coloribus, ut ait Horatius.

"Significat fabula, commendicatam speciem neq: diu durare, & perlevi momento dissolvi."

Query: Was Greene referring to this passage, i.e. to *2 H 6* as well as to *3 H 6*, in his attack (Introduction, pp. xlii ff)?

77–9. *lamb . . . wolves*] One fable suggests another:

"Lupus.

"Induerat pellem ovis lupus, atque cum ita ignoraretur, aliquantisper impune in gregem fuit grassatus. Sed pastor mox animadversa fraude, necatum hunc de arbore suspendit. Hoc qui pelle decipiebantur admirantibus: Pellis quidem est, pastor inquit, ovis, sed sub hac lupus latebat.

"Habitus & vultus indicia non habenda pro certis fabula docet, ideoq: facta & rem spectare oportere." But the verbal reference is to *Matt.*, 7. 15, "Beware of the false prophets which come to you in sheep's clothing, but inwardly they are ravening wolves".

Take heed, my lord; the welfare of us all
Hangs on the cutting short that fraudful man.

Enter SOMERSET.

Som. All health unto my gracious sovereign!
King. Welcome, Lord Somerset. What news from France?
Som. That all your interest in those territories
Is utterly bereft you: all is lost.
King. Cold news, Lord Somerset: but God's will be done!
York. [*Aside.*] Cold news for me; for I had hope of France
As firmly as I hope for fertile England.
Thus are my blossoms blasted in the bud,
And caterpillars eat my leaves away;
But I will remedy this gear ere long,
Or sell my title for a glorious grave.

Enter GLOUCESTER.

Glou. All happiness unto my lord the King!
Pardon, my liege, that I have stay'd so long.
Suf. Nay, Gloucester, know that thou art come too soon,
Unless thou wert more loyal than thou art.
I do arrest thee of high treason here.
Glou. Well, Suffolk's Duke, thou shalt not see me blush,
Nor change my countenance for this arrest:
A heart unspotted is not easily daunted.
The purest spring is not so free from mud
As I am clear from treason to my sovereign.
Who can accuse me? Wherein am I guilty?

87. *Aside.*] *Rowe + edd.* 98. Suffolk's duke] *Malone, from Q; Suffolke F.*

81. *cutting short*] "Craig thinks a reference to shortening by the head (as in *R 2*, III. iii. 12) is intended" (Hart). Cf. Hall, 275, "brought to Bridgwater, and ther cut shorter by the hedde".

fraudful] "full of deep deceit" (57); treacherous.

83. *Somerset*] appointed regent of France, I. iii. 205. For the losses, and their effect on the relations of Somerset and York, see Hall, 215, 216 (Appendix I).

87. *Cold news*] a repetition of York's hopes at I. i. 238.

89. *blossoms*] the garden imagery resumed from 31.

98. *Suffolk's Duke*] see collation: a F printer's omission by jumping from "Suffol*kes*" to "Du*ke*": cf. II. ii. 27.

100. *heart unspotted*] cf. *1 H 6*, V. iii. 182; *James*, I. 27, "to keep himself unspotted from the world"; and Peele, *Polyhymnia* (1590): "But though from court to cottage he depart, / His saint is sure of his unspotted heart."

York. 'Tis thought, my lord, that you took bribes of France,
And, being Protector, stay'd the soldiers' pay;
By means whereof his Highness hath lost France.
Glou. Is it but thought so? What are they that think it?
I never robb'd the soldiers of their pay,
Nor ever had one penny bribe from France.
So help me God, as I have watch'd the night,
Ay, night by night, in studying good for England!
That doit that e'er I wrested from the King,
Or any groat I hoarded to my use,
Be brought against me at my trial-day!
No; many a pound of mine own proper store,
Because I would not tax the needy commons,
Have I dispursed to the garrisons,
And never ask'd for restitution.
Car. It serves you well, my lord, to say so much.
Glou. I say no more than truth, so help me God!
York. In your Protectorship you did devise
Strange tortures for offenders, never heard of,
That England was defam'd by tyranny.
Glou. Why, 'tis well known that, whiles I was Protector,
Pity was all the fault that was in me;
For I should melt at an offender's tears,
And lowly words were ransom for their fault.
Unless it were a bloody murderer,
Or foul felonious thief that fleec'd poor passengers,
I never gave them condign punishment:
Murder indeed, that bloody sin, I tortur'd

110. watch'd] *Q*, *F* (watcht).

108. *robb'd . . . soldiers of . . . pay*] This was expressly charged against Somerset; see Appendix I (Hall, 216).

110.] cf. Lord Say, at IV. vii. 80.

115. *proper store*] personal property or possessions.

117. *dispursed*] disbursed.

121–3. *devise . . . tortures . . . tyranny*] cf. 58, 59 above, and I. iii. 132–4.

123. *That . . . defam'd by tyranny*] With the result that . . . gained a bad reputation (L. fama) for . . .

129. *felonious*] wicked, criminal, "pillaging with violence" (Schmidt); the legal sense is later.

fleec'd] plundered.

passengers] wayfarers, travellers on foot.

130. *condign*] well deserved. From Fox, 3. 717, "And thus have you heard the full story and discourse of duke Humphrey, and of all his adversaries: also of God's *condign punishment* upon them for their *bloody* cruelty". Hall, 209, and Hol., 3. 211, have "condigne reward".

Above the felon or what trespass else.
Suf. My lord, these faults are easy, quickly answer'd;
But mightier crimes are laid unto your charge,
Whereof you cannot easily purge yourself.
I do arrest you in his Highness' name;
And here commit to my Lord Cardinal
To keep, until your further time of trial.
King. My Lord of Gloucester, 'tis my special hope
That you will clear yourself from all suspense:
My conscience tells me you are innocent.
Glou. Ah! gracious lord, these days are dangerous.
Virtue is chok'd with foul Ambition,
And Charity chas'd hence by Rancour's hand;
Foul Subornation is predominant,
And Equity exil'd your Highness' land.
I know their complot is to have my life;
And if my death might make this island happy,
And prove the period of their tyranny,
I would expend it with all willingness.
But mine is made the prologue to their play;
For thousands more, that yet suspect no peril,
Will not conclude their plotted tragedy.
Beaufort's red sparkling eyes blab his heart's malice,
And Suffolk's cloudy brow his stormy hate;
Sharp Buckingham unburthens with his tongue

137. to] *Capell;* you to *F. See n.* 140. suspense] *F;* suspect *Capell, Camb.:* suspects *Malone.* 143. chok'd] *F* (choakt).

132. *Above the felon . . . else*] more severely than the "felonious thief" or any other criminal. Cf. "What ceremony else?" *Ham.*, v. i. 248; "With promise of his sister, and what else", *3 H 6*, III. i. 51.

133. *easy*] insignificant, slight, unimportant.

137.] note the joint responsibility of Suffolk and the Cardinal, which continues down to Gloucester's murder. Cf. III. i. 187, 276; III. ii. 2, 123, 179.

to] see collation. The F *you* was probably caught from 136.

140. *suspense*] doubt. Hart compares Gabriel Harvey, *A New Letter*, 1593, "They that know the danger of Truces . . . must begge leave to ground their repose upon more cautels, then one: and to proceede in termes of *suspence*; or Pause, till they may be resolued with infallible assurance".

145. *Subornation*] see above, 45.

146. *exil'd*] with the normal Elizabethan stress on the second syllable.

147. *complot*] plot; stressed on the first syllable.

149. *period*] end.

The envious load that lies upon his heart;
And dogged York, that reaches at the moon,
Whose overweening arm I have pluck'd back,
By false accuse doth level at my life.
And you, my sovereign lady, with the rest,
Causeless have laid disgraces on my head,
And with your best endeavour have stirr'd up
My liefest liege to be mine enemy.
Ay, all of you have laid your heads together—
Myself had notice of your conventicles—
And all to make away my guiltless life.
I shall not want false witness to condemn me,
Nor store of treasons to augment my guilt;
The ancient proverb will be well effected:
A staff is quickly found to beat a dog!

Car. My liege, his railing is intolerable.
If those that care to keep your royal person
From Treason's secret knife and traitors' rage
Be thus upbraided, chid, and rated at,
And the offender granted scope of speech,
'Twill make them cool in zeal unto your Grace.

Suf. Hath he not twit our sovereign lady here
With ignominious words, though clerkly couch'd,
As if she had suborned some to swear

159. pluck'd] *F* (pluckt). 179. couch'd] *F* (coucht).

158. *dogged . . . moon*] one of Whitney's *Emblems*, 213, illustrates the dog baying the moon; cf. *Caes.*, IV. iii. 27, "I'd rather be a dog, and bay the moon".

160. *accuse*] accusation. Verb for noun, as at I. i. 2, "depart". Abbott, 451, gives a list of verbs, mainly of French origin, used in this way.

level at] aim (of a missile weapon) at.

162. *Causeless*] adj. for adv.—causelessly, without cause.

164. *liefest*] dearest.

166. *conventicles*] "irregular or clandestine meetings of a supposed sinister character" (*OED.*). Cf. Hall, 242, "The Erles of Marche and Warwicke, and other beyng at Calice, *had knowledge of* all these doynges, and secrete *conventicles*". Accented *conventicles.*

167. *make away*] destroy. Cf. *Ed. 2*, 1037, "Why then weele have him privilie made away."

170. *effected*] given effect to.

178. *twit*] twitted. A normal Elizabethan omission of *ed* after *t* or *d*; cf. "acquit", *R 3*, v. v. 3.

179. *clerkly couch'd*] adroitly, cleverly phrased, as by a scholar or man of learning (L. *clericus*; F. *clerc*).

180–1. *suborned . . . False*] *Acts*, 6. 11, 13, "Then they suborned men . . . And set up false witnesses."

False allegations to o'erthrow his state?
Queen. But I can give the loser leave to chide.
Glou. Far truer spoke than meant: I lose, indeed;
Beshrew the winners, for they play'd me false!
And well such losers may have leave to speak.
Buck. He'll wrest the sense and hold us here all day.
Lord Cardinal, he is your prisoner.
Car. Sirs, take away the Duke, and guard him sure.
Glou. Ah! thus King Henry throws away his crutch
Before his legs be firm to bear his body.
Thus is the shepherd beaten from thy side,
And wolves are gnarling who shall gnaw thee first.
Ah! that my fear were false; ah! that it were;
For, good King Henry, thy decay I fear. [*Exit, guarded.*
King. My lords, what to your wisdoms seemeth best,
Do, or undo, as if ourself were here.
Queen. What! will your Highness leave the Parliament?
King. Ay, Margaret; my heart is drown'd with grief,
Whose flood begins to flow within mine eyes,
My body round engirt with misery,
For what's more miserable than discontent?
Ah! uncle Humphrey, in thy face I see
The map of Honour, Truth, and Loyalty;
And yet, good Humphrey, is the hour to come
That e'er I prov'd thee false, or fear'd thy faith.
What low'ring star now envies thy estate,
That these great lords, and Margaret our Queen,
Do seek subversion of thy harmless life?

194. S.D.] *Theobald; Exit Gloster. F; Exet Humphrey,* with the *Cardinals* men *Q.*

182. *give the loser leave to chide*] cf. Heywood, *Proverbs*, 31, "Alway to let the losers have their words"; and Jonson, 10. 19, "Give losers leave to speak."

187. *your prisoner*] cf. 137 above, and 276 below. These divide the responsibility between Suffolk and the Cardinal, and locate III. ii.

189 ff.] another typical foreboding; cf. II. ii. 75; II. iv. 49.

191–2. *shepherd . . . wolves*] cf. *Ezekiel*, 34. 8; *Matt.*, 26. 31. A continuation of the metaphor from II. ii. 72–3; cf. also 252–3 below.

192. *gnarling*] snarling. Craig quotes Nashe, *Have With You* (1596), "What will not a dogge doe that is angered? bite and gnarle at anie bone."

203. *map*] a common metaphor, 1580–90, especially as applied to the face; and much used by Greene.

Loyalty] "an echo (probably unintentional) of Gloucester's motto *Loyalle et belle*" (Scott-Giles, 131).

208. *subversion*] overthrow.

Thou never didst them wrong, nor no man wrong;
And as the butcher takes away the calf,
And binds the wretch, and beats it when it strains,
Bearing it to the bloody slaughter-house;
Even so, remorseless, have they borne him hence;
And as the dam runs lowing up and down,
Looking the way her harmless young one went,
And can do nought but wail her darling's loss;
Even so myself bewails good Gloucester's case
With sad unhelpful tears, and with dimm'd eyes
Look after him, and cannot do him good;
So mighty are his vowed enemies.
His fortunes I will weep; and 'twixt each groan
Say "Who's a traitor? Gloucester he is none." [*Exit.*

Queen. Free lords, cold snow melts with the sun's hot beams.
Henry my lord is cold in great affairs,
Too full of foolish pity; and Gloucester's show
Beguiles him as the mournful crocodile
With sorrow snares relenting passengers;

211. strains] *ASC; Vaughan conj.;* strayes *F;* strives *Theobald. See n.* 218. eyes] *Camb.;* eyes, *Rowe;* eyes; *F.* 222. S.D. *Exit.*] *F; Exet King, Salsbury,* and *Warwicke. Q.*

211. *strains*] see collation: "strayes" is, of course, absurd in the context. The same F compositor, A, makes exactly the same error in *H 5*, III. i. 32—produced as corroborative evidence of the amendment by Vaughan—"like grey-hounds / *Straying* vpon the Start," where the MS. possibly read "strayīng". Cf. also *Lr.*, I. i. 69, Q straied; F strain'd; and *Err.*, IV. iv. 103 S.D. "*offer to bind him. He strives.*" Theobald's "strives" covers the sense, but is graphically less likely than "strains".

212. *slaughter-house*] the first of a series of related metaphors and images suggested by the deaths and murders now in prospect.

217, 219. *myself bewails . . . Look*] implied change of subject to the first person.

219. *do him good*] profit him, be of use to him.

223. *Free*] of noble or honourable character, magnaminous; cf. *Oth.*, III. iii. 199, "your free and noble nature".

224. *cold*] not zealous or interested.

225. *show*] outward appearance (of innocence); cf. above, 54.

226–8. *crocodile . . . snake*] Hart notes that Hall, 239, has these two metaphors coupled, "This cancard *crocodryle* and subtile *serpent*, could not long lurke in malicious hartes, nor venomous stomackes." Perhaps a subconscious reminiscence.

The best account of the crocodile myth came home with Hawkins's *Second Voyage*, 1565. See Sparke's narrative in Hakluyt, "His nature is ever when he would have his prey, to cry and sob like a christian body, to provoke them to come to him, and then he snatcheth at them." Cf. *FQ.*, I. 5. 18.

Or as the snake, roll'd in a flow'ring bank,
With shining checker'd slough, doth sting a child
That for the beauty thinks it excellent.
Believe me, lords, were none more wise than I,
And yet herein I judge mine own wit good,
This Gloucester should be quickly rid the world,
To rid us from the fear we have of him.

Car. That he should die is worthy policy;
But yet we want a colour for his death.
'Tis meet he be condemn'd by course of law.

Suf. But in my mind that were no policy:
The King will labour still to save his life;
The commons haply rise to save his life;
And yet we have but trivial argument,
More than mistrust, that shows him worthy death.

York. So that, by this, you would not have him die.

Suf. Ah! York, no man alive so fain as I.

York. 'Tis York that hath more reason for his death.
But, my Lord Cardinal, and you, my Lord of Suffolk,
Say as you think, and speak it from your souls,
Were 't not all one an empty eagle were set
To guard the chicken from a hungry kite,

229. *shining . . . slough*] Ovid, *Metam.*, 9. 266–7: "utque novus serpens posita cum pelle senecta / luxuriare solet, squamaque nitere recenti".

233. *rid the world*] clear the world, with a suggestion of the sense "kill, destroy", as in Hardyng, 519, "He thought therefore without delaye to ryd them, as though the kyllyng of his kynsmen might ende his cause."

235, 236. *die . . . colour*] a very unseemly pun (Hart). "Colour" is the legal term—"pretext, justification"; cf. *Caes.*, II. i. 29.

239. *still*] always.

240. *commons haply rise*] see Hall, 209 (Appendix 1), for the decision to undo Gloucester otherwise than "by course of law", and his arrest at Bury.

241. *trivial*] unimportant, of small worth.

argument] proof, evidence; cf. *Ado*, II. iii. 243, "no great argument of her folly"; *Tw.N.*, III. ii. 12; *H5*, IV. iii. 113.

242. *worthy death*] *Acts*, 25. 25.

245. *York . . . hath more reason*] explained by the last two lines in this scene (Hart).

248–9. *empty eagle . . . To guard . . .*] cf. Ovid, *Ars Am.*, 2. 363–4: "Accipitri timidas credis, furiose, columbas? / Plenum montano credis ovile lupo?" Cf. 253 below, and *3 H 6*, I. i. 268.

249. *chicken . . . kite*] The kite, now comparatively rare in England, was the common scavenger of Elizabethan London (cf. V. ii. 11). It would snatch linen (*Wint.*, IV. iii. 23), and preyed on partridges (below III. ii. 190, *q.v.*) as well as chickens; cf. Nashe, *Christes Teares*, "The Henne clocketh her Chickens . . . The Henne shieldeth them and fighteth for them against the Puttocke."

Shakespeare regularly associates

As place Duke Humphrey for the king's Protector?
Queen. So the poor chicken should be sure of death.
Suf. Madam, 'tis true; and were 't not madness then
To make the fox surveyor of the fold?
Who, being accus'd a crafty murderer,
His guilt should be but idly posted over
Because his purpose is not executed.
No; let him die, in that he is a fox,
By nature prov'd an enemy to the flock,
Before his chaps be stain'd with crimson blood,
As Humphrey, prov'd by treasons, to my liege.
And do not stand on quillets how to slay him:
Be it by gins, by snares, by subtlety,
Sleeping or waking, 'tis no matter how,
So he be dead; for that is good deceit
Which mates him first that first intends deceit.
Queen. Thrice-noble Suffolk, 'tis resolutely spoke.
Suf. Not resolute, except so much were done;

260. Humphrey] *F; Humphrey's Hanmer.* treasons] *Hudson;* reasons *F. See n.*

kite — death — death-bed — sheets; death—soul—ghost; see Armstrong, *Shakespeare's Imagination*, chap. I.

252–3. *madness . . . fold*] cf. Ovid, *Ars Am.*, 3. 5, "And why deliver the sheep-fold to the ravening wolf?"; and n. to 248 above.

253. *surveyor*] overseer of a household, estate, etc.

254–5. *Who, being . . . / His . . .*] a case of the supplementary pronoun, (Abbott, 249) = whose, complicated by a participial phrase = Whose guilt, he being . . . murderer, should be . . .

255. *posted over*] hurried over; gone through with haste and negligence. From the sense of post-haste (Hart).

258–60. *By nature prov'd . . .*] As the fox (eagle, kite) is proved by nature to be an enemy to the flock (chicken), so Humphrey is proved by treason to be an enemy to the king, and there is no need to wait for them to show themselves in action, as they are bound to do, before dealing with them.

260. *treasons*] see collation. Hudson's amendment is supported by the whole tenor of the scene, and its insistence on Gloucester's "treason", especially 45–6, 54, 64–5, 70, 97, 102, 169, 174, 222. He has been arrested for treason, including incitement of the Duchess. He is "the false duke" (205, 322). Thus "we have but trivial argument" (241), and "want a colour for his death" (236). He cannot therefore be proved an enemy to the king by "*reasons*"; he can by *treasons*. For the misprint, cf. *R 2*, v. iii. 50—Q treason; F reason—made, like this one, by compositor B; and for the idea and the misprint, *1 H 4*, v. ii. 9, "For treason (Q8 reason) is but trusted like the fox".

261. *stand on quillets*] be particular about fine distinctions; cf. *1 H 6*, II. iv. 17, "these nice quillets of the law".

265. *mates*] checkmates, subdues, confounds; cf. *Dr Faustus*, Cho. 2, "Mars did mate the Carthaginians".

For things are often spoke and seldom meant:
But that my heart accordeth with my tongue,
Seeing the deed is meritorious,
And to preserve my sovereign from his foe,
Say but the word and I will be his priest.

Car. But I would have him dead, my Lord of Suffolk,
Ere you can take due orders for a priest:
Say you consent and censure well the deed,
And I'll provide his executioner;
I tender so the safety of my liege.

Suf. Here is my hand, the deed is worthy doing.

Queen. And so say I.

York. And I: and now we three have spoken it,
It skills not greatly who impugns our doom.

Enter a Post.

Post. Great lords, from Ireland am I come amain,

280. spoken] *Hanmer;* spoke *F. See n.* 282 ff.] *F; for Q, see App. 4.*

270. *the deed is meritorious*] cf. Marlowe, *Massacre*, 1147; used especially in a religious sense, of good works, as entitling to reward from God.

272. *be his priest*] kill him; in allusion to the priest's performing the last offices of the dying (Onions); cf. Kyd, *Sp. Tr.*, 3. 3. 38, "Who first laies hand on me, ile be his Priest"; Lyly, 2. 102. 4.

274. *take . . . orders*] arrange.

275. *censure*] give an opinion on; consider.

276. *I'll provide his executioner*] At III. ii. 2, it is Suffolk who seems responsible for this. The responsibility seems originally to have been intended to be joint, as in the Chronicles, and according to the Q version: "*Suffol.* Let that be my Lord Cardinals charge & mine. / *Car.* Agreed, for hee's already kept within my house." This agrees with III. ii. 123 and 179. The association of Suffolk and the Cardinal goes back to I. i. 167–8. Suffolk arrests Humphrey (III. i. 136) and commits him to the care of the Cardinal (137; cf. 187). The Cardinal indeed suggests providing the executioner (276), which seems to conflict with Suffolk's commands to the murderers (III. ii. 2). The contradiction, however, disappears on the assumption that the Cardinal did provide them, for Suffolk to instruct in detail. In addition, the opening of the murder scene was recast (Introduction, p. xxvii), and in Q Suffolk does not give orders to the murderers. The passage following, with its reference to Ireland, was probably recast under censorship, and the alterations may have extended back to these lines.

277. *tender so*] am so solicitous and careful of.

280. *spoken*] possibly written *spokē*; or influenced by 266 and 268 above.

281. *It skills not greatly*] makes little difference, matters little The root meaning is "discern, separate" (Skeat).

doom] judgement, decision.

282. *Ireland*] Hall, 213 (Appendix 1). Probably rewritten at the censor's instigation; see Introduction, p. xxvii.

amain] with all speed; cf. v. i. 114.

To signify that rebels there are up,
And put the Englishmen unto the sword.
Send succours, lords, and stop the rage betime,
Before the wound do grow uncurable;
For, being green, there is great hope of help.
Car. A breach that craves a quick expedient stop!
What counsel give you in this weighty cause?
York. That Somerset be sent as Regent thither.
'Tis meet that lucky ruler be employ'd;
Witness the fortune he hath had in France.
Som. If York, with all his far-fet policy,
Had been the Regent there instead of me,
He never would have stay'd in France so long.
York. No, not to lose it all, as thou hast done.
I rather would have lost my life betimes
Than bring a burden of dishonour home,
By staying there so long till all were lost.
Show me one scar character'd on thy skin:
Men's flesh preserv'd so whole do seldom win.
Queen. Nay then, this spark will prove a raging fire
If wind and fuel be brought to feed it with.
No more, good York; sweet Somerset, be still:
Thy fortune, York, hadst thou been Regent there,
Might happily have prov'd far worse than his.
York. What! worse than nought? Nay, then a shame take all!
Som. And in the number thee, that wishest shame.
Car. My Lord of York, try what your fortune is.

283. *signify*] announce, indicate.

285. *betime*] in time; by timely action.

288. *expedient*] expeditious; cf. *John*, II. i. 60.

290 ff. *That Somerset* . . .] For York's animosity against Somerset, see Appendix I (Hall, 215–16). His ironical proposal to appoint Somerset (with a glance at their earlier rivalry for the regency of France, I. iii. 102 ff) is thrown in by Shakespeare to fan the flames, which duly burst out in v. i. 87 ff, and provide a main grievance to justify York's rebellion.

293. *far-fet*] lit. far-fetched; deep, cunning. "Fetch" was a trick; cf *Ham.*, II. i. 38; *Lr.*, II. iv. 90.

297. *betimes*] early, earlier in life.

300. *character'd*] written; inscribed. Stressed on the second syllable.

301. *Men's flesh . . . do*] men, whose flesh is preserved . . . , do . . . Note the L. construction.

302. *Nay then* . . .] The queen, for once, seeks unity among the nobles.

306. *happily*] haply, perhaps.

308. *And in the number thee . . . shame*] in accordance with the motto of the Garter, "Honi soit qui mal y pense", quoted in *Wiv.*, v. v. 75.

309–10. *York . . . Ireland*] York's Irish

The uncivil kerns of Ireland are in arms
And temper clay with blood of Englishmen:
To Ireland will you lead a band of men,
Collected choicely, from each county some,
And try your hap against the Irishmen?

York. I will, my lord, so please his Majesty.

Suf. Why, our authority is his consent,
And what we do establish he confirms:
Then, noble York, take thou this task in hand.

York. I am content: provide me soldiers, lords,
Whiles I take order for mine own affairs.

Suf. A charge, Lord York, that I will see perform'd.
But now return we to the false Duke Humphrey.

Car. No more of him; for I will deal with him
That henceforth he shall trouble us no more.
And so break off; the day is almost spent.

Suf. Lord, you and I must talk of that event.

York. My Lord of Suffolk, within fourteen days
At Bristow I expect my soldiers;
For there I'll ship them all for Ireland.

Suf. I'll see it truly done, my Lord of York.

[*Exeunt all but York.*

York. Now, York, or never, steel thy fearful thoughts,
And change misdoubt to resolution:

322–6.] *F; for Q, see App. 4.* 326. *Suf.* Lord,] *ASC;* Lord *Suffolke, F. See n.* 330. S.D. *Exeunt . . .*] *edd.; Exit omnes, Manet Yorke. Q; Exeunt. Manet Yorke. F.*

expedition has been anticipated at I. i. 193–4, for another, local, purpose; as again at 360 below.

310. *uncivil*] disorderly, uncivilized.

kerns] "are nakid, but only their shertes and small coates; and many tymes when they come to the bycker, but bare nakid . . . and these have dartes, and short bowes" *Ulster Journal*, 6. 198–9; cf. *Mac.*, I. ii. 13 (Hart).

311. *temper*] moisten, as of mortar.

320. *take order for*] arrange; cf. 274.

322. *return we to . . .*] let us come back to the subject of.

325. *break off*] enough talk. Cf. *Sp. Tr.*, 4. 4. 74, 75: "Heere breake we off our sundrie languages / And thus conclude I in our vulgar tung."

326. Suf. *Lord*] see collation. F contradicts 323, as well as the regular association of Suffolk and the Cardinal in the affair; see n. to III. ii. 2, and references. There has been an error of inversion, or of duplication from 327. The amendment restores the metre, and removes the contradiction. I admit, however, that "Lord" is an exceptional usage, and probably wrong.

331. *steel*] harden; cf. *3 H 6*, II. ii. 41, "steel thy melting heart".

fearful] full of fear.

332. *misdoubt*] suspicion, mistrust.

Be that thou hop'st to be, or what thou art
Resign to death; it is not worth th' enjoying.
Let pale-fac'd fear keep with the mean-born man,
And find no harbour in a royal heart.
Faster than spring-time showers comes thought on
  thought,
And not a thought but thinks on dignity.
My brain, more busy than the labouring spider,
Weaves tedious snares to trap mine enemies.
Well, nobles, well; 'tis politicly done,
To send me packing with an host of men:
I fear me you but warm the starved snake,
Who, cherish'd in your breasts, will sting your hearts.
'Twas men I lack'd, and you will give them me:
I take it kindly; yet be well assur'd
You put sharp weapons in a madman's hands.
Whiles I in Ireland nourish a mighty band,
I will stir up in England some black storm
Shall blow ten thousand souls to heaven, or hell;
And this fell tempest shall not cease to rage
Until the golden circuit on my head,
Like to the glorious sun's transparent beams,
Do calm the fury of this mad-bred flaw.
And, for a minister of my intent,

333–4.] art / Resign *edd.*; art; / Resigne *F*. 335. pale-fac'd] *F* (pale-fac't). 344. cherish'd] *F* (cherisht). 345. lack'd] *Q*, *F* (lackt). 348. nourish] *F*; raise *Vaughan conj.*

335. *keep with*] live, dwell, associate, with; cf. *Mer. V.*, III. iii. 19, "the most impenetrable cur / That ever kept with man".

336. *harbour . . . royal heart*] with a suggestion of "harbour" = covert, and "hart royal".

340. *tedious*] laborious, intricate.

341. *politicly*] see n. on "policy", I. i. 83.

342. *packing*] off, out of the way.

343. *the starved snake*] from Camerarius, *Fabulae Aesopicae* (cf. above, 53, 75, 77):

"Agricola & Anguis.

"Repertum anguem frigore pene mortuum, Agricola misericordia motus, fovere sinu, & subter alas recondere. Anguis recreatus calore, vires recepit, ac confirmatus, agricolae, pro merito ipsius summo, letale vulnus inflixit.

"Fabula demonstrat eam mercedem, quam rependere beneficiis mali consuevere."

starved] *scil.* with cold. Cf above, I. i. 230, and *Tit.*, III. i. 252. Still current in the north.

347. *weapons . . . hands*] proverbial.

352. *circuit*] the crown.

354. *flaw*] squall; cf. *Ham.*, v. i. 239.

I have seduc'd a headstrong Kentishman,
John Cade of Ashford,
To make commotion, as full well he can,
Under the title of John Mortimer.
In Ireland have I seen this stubborn Cade
Oppose himself against a troop of kerns,
And fought so long, till that his thighs with darts
Were almost like a sharp-quill'd porpentine:
And, in the end being rescu'd, I have seen
Him caper upright like a wild Morisco,
Shaking the bloody darts as he his bells.
Full often, like a shag-hair'd crafty kern,
Hath he conversed with the enemy,
And undiscover'd come to me again,
And given me notice of their villanies.
This devil here shall be my substitute;
For that John Mortimer, which now is dead,
In face, in gait, in speech, he doth resemble:
By this I shall perceive the commons' mind,
How they affect the house and claim of York.
Say he be taken, rack'd, and tortured,

359. Mortimer] *Q1, 2, F;* Mortimer (For he is like him euery kinde of way) *Q3*.
373. gait] *F* (gate). 376. rack'd] *F* (rackt).

357. *Cade*] Hall, 220 (Appendix 1). The connection of Cade with Ireland, if not fortuitous, may have been suggested by Holinshed, 3. 632, "an Irishman as Polychronicon saith". In Hall he is, as here, a Kentishman. Holinshed adds "John Mortimer, coosine to the duke of Yorke". The name was intended to suggest the claim associated with Edmund Mortimer; cf. IV. ii. 129 ff.

358. *make commotion*] cf. Hall, 219, quoted at 29; and *Jack Straw* (Dodsley, 5. 390): "a crew of rebels are in the field, / And they have made commotions late in Kent."

360–2. *seen . . . Oppose . . . fought*] note confusion of two constructions.

363, 365. *porpentine . . . caper*] porcupine; cf. *2 Tamb.*, 2594 f.: "Their hair . . . like the quilles of Porcupines, / As black as Ieat, and hard as Iron or steel, / Their legs to dance and caper in the aire:" and *Ham.*, I. v. 20.

365. *a wild Morisco*] Moorish, or morris-dancer. A grotesque dance performed by persons in fantastic costumes, with bells attached to the legs, and usually representing characters from the Robin Hood legend—a feature of popular festivities in the 16th century; cf. Holland's *Plinie* (1601), 7. 46. 189, "A common thing it was among them to fling weapons and darts in the aire . . . to flourish also beforehand, yea, and to encounter and meet together in fight like sword-fencers, and to make good sport in a kinde of *Moriske* daunce." See also Chambers, *Med. Stage*.

372. *For that*] because.

375. *affect*] are fond of, favour.

I know no pain they can inflict upon him
Will make him say I mov'd him to those arms.
Say that he thrive, as 'tis great like he will,
Why, then from Ireland come I with my strength,
And reap the harvest which that rascal sow'd;
For Humphrey being dead, as he shall be,
And Henry put apart, the next for me. [*Exit.*

SCENE II.—*Bury St. Edmunds. A Room of State.*

Enter two or three running over the stage, from the murder of Duke Humphrey.

1 Murderer. Run to my Lord of Suffolk; let him know
We have dispatch'd the Duke, as he commanded.
2 Mur. O, that it were to do! What have we done?
Didst ever hear a man so penitent?

Enter SUFFOLK.

1 Mur. Here comes my Lord.
Suf. Now, sirs, have you dispatch'd this thing?
1 Mur. Ay, my good lord, he's dead.
Suf. Why, that's well said. Go, get you to my house;

382. Humphrey] Humfrey; *F.* 383. apart,] apart: *F.*

Scene II

Locality.] *edd.* Entry.] *F;* Then the Curtaines being drawne, Duke *Humphrey* is discouered in his bed, and two men lying on his brest, and smothering him in his bed. And then enter the Duke of *Suffolke* to them. *Q. See App.* 4. 4. S.D.] *F* (*in margin*). 6. Now, sirs,] *F;* How now sirs, what *Q.* dispatch'd] *Q, F* (dispatcht). 7. dead.] *F;* dead, I warrant you. *Q.*

378. *mov'd . . . arms*] instigated . . . armed bands; cf. IV. ix. 29; V. i. 18, 39.

379. *great like*] very likely.

381. *reap . . . sow'd*] reaping where another sowed, or another's harvest; from *Luke*, 19. 22.

382–3. *as he shall be . . . apart*] more prophetic anticipations.

Scene II

The beginning of the scene was recast, probably by order of the censor; see Introduction, p. xxvii, and the earlier, Q, version in Appendix 4. The murder is now committed off stage. The room is in the Cardinal's house, where Humphrey is kept prisoner.

For the main source, see Appendix 1 (Hall, 209).

2. *as he commanded*] for the joint responsibility of Suffolk and the Cardinal, see III. i. 137, 187, 276, and III. ii. 123, 179.

I will reward you for this venturous deed.
The King and all the peers are here at hand.
Have you laid fair the bed? Is all things well,
According as I gave directions?

1 Mur. 'Tis handsome, my good lord.

Suf. Away! be gone.
[*Exeunt Murderers.*

Sound trumpets. Enter the KING, *the* QUEEN, *Cardinal* BEAUFORT, SOMERSET, *with Attendants.*

King. Go, call our uncle to our presence straight;
Say we intend to try his Grace to-day,
If he be guilty, as 'tis published.

Suf. I'll call him presently, my noble lord. [*Exit.*

King. Lords, take your places; and, I pray you all,
Proceed no straiter 'gainst our uncle Gloucester
Than from true evidence, of good esteem,
He be approv'd in practice culpable.

Queen. God forbid any malice should prevail
That faultless may condemn a nobleman!
Pray God he may acquit him of suspicion!

King. I thank thee, Meg; these words content me much.

Re-enter SUFFOLK.

How now! why look'st thou pale? Why tremblest thou?

13. 'Tis handsome] *ASC;* 'Tis *F;* All things is handsome now, *Q.* 13. S.D. *Exeunt . . .*] *Q; Exeunt. F.* Queen] *F;* Queene, the Duke of *Buckingham. Q. Cardinal* Beaufort] *edd.; Cardinall, Suffolke F.* 25. Meg] *Capell;* Nell *F; om. Q. See n.* 25. S.D. *Re-enter*] *Enter F.*

13. *handsome*] see collation. The word was possibly deleted along with the Q words immediately before and after, or overlooked from its position there in the amended Q "copy".

14 ff.] note the irony of the collocation of this passage with the murder; and of the speeches of Suffolk, the Queen, and the Cardinal.

16. *If*] whether.

published] asserted, publicly stated.

17. *presently*] immediately — the standard Elizabethan usage.

19. *straiter*] more rigorously.

21. *approv'd in*] proved guilty of; cf. *Oth.*, II. iii. 203, "he that is approv'd in this offence".

25. *Meg*] F *Nell*; cf. the error at 78, 99, 119. Possibly a slip, which must have been corrected on the stage, caused by the presence of Gloucester's name. For a similar error, cf. *Gent.*, note vii, in the Camb. edn. The error is no doubt Shakespeare's, and suggests that the MS. sent to the printers was in his autograph. See also Introduction, p. xxxii, and references in n. 1.

Where is our uncle? What's the matter, Suffolk?
Suf. Dead in his bed, my lord; Gloucester is dead.
Queen. Marry, God forfend!
Car. God's secret judgment: I did dream to-night
The Duke was dumb and could not speak a word.
[*The King swoons.*
Queen. How fares my lord? Help, lords! The King is dead.
Som. Rear up his body; wring him by the nose.
Queen. Run, go, help, help! O, Henry, ope thine eyes!
Suf. He doth revive again: madam, be patient.
King. O heavenly God!
Queen. How fares my gracious lord?
Suf. Comfort, my sovereign! Gracious Henry, comfort!
King. What, doth my Lord of Suffolk comfort me?
Came he right now to sing a raven's note,
Whose dismal tune bereft my vital powers,
And thinks he that the chirping of a wren,
By crying comfort from a hollow breast,
Can chase away the first-conceived sound?
Hide not thy poison with such sug'red words;
Lay not thy hands on me; forbear, I say:
Their touch affrights me as a serpent's sting.
Thou baleful messenger, out of my sight!
Upon thy eye-balls murderous Tyranny
Sits in grim majesty to fright the world.
Look not upon me, for thine eyes are wounding:
Yet do not go away; come, basilisk,

31. S.D.] *King sounds. F; The King falls in a sound.* (*swoone. Q2*) *Q.*

29. *forfend*] forbid.

30. *God's . . . judgment*] prophetic of his own fate in III. iii, as Wilson notes; Fox, 4. 515.

to-night] the night just ending; cf. Jonson, *Alchemist*, I. 2. 147. The scene takes place, presumably, in the early morning, but there is no attempt to indicate point or passage of time.

33. *Rear up*] support, raise.

wring . . .] to arouse circulation, and bring back to life or consciousness, as in *Ven.*, 475.

39. *right now*] exactly at this time or juncture. The phrase has survived in America (Hart).

raven's note] a common superstition.

40. *vital powers*] faculties necessary, or pertaining, to life.

43. *first-conceived*] first received into the mind; first perceived.

44–6. *poison . . . sug'red . . . serpent*] the association may have been suggested by Hall, 236 (Appendix I).

51. *basilisk*] a fabulous reptile, also called cockatrice, supposed to be hatched by a serpent from a cock's egg, and said to kill by its breath and look (Onions). Cf. *Wint.*, I. ii. 388;

And kill the innocent gazer with thy sight;
For in the shade of death I shall find joy,
In life but double death, now Gloucester's dead.

Queen. Why do you rate my Lord of Suffolk thus?
Although the Duke was enemy to him,
Yet he, most Christian-like, laments his death:
And for myself, foe as he was to me,
Might liquid tears or heart-offending groans
Or blood-consuming sighs recall his life,
I would be blind with weeping, sick with groans,
Look pale as primrose with blood-drinking sighs,
And all to have the noble Duke alive.
What know I how the world may deem of me?
For it is known we were but hollow friends:
It may be judg'd I made the Duke away:
So shall my name with Slander's tongue be wounded,
And princes' courts be fill'd with my reproach.
This get I by his death. Ay me, unhappy!
To be a queen, and crown'd with infamy!

King. Ah! woe is me for Gloucester, wretched man.

Queen. Be woe for me, more wretched than he is.
What, dost thou turn away and hide thy face?
I am no loathsome leper; look on me.

74. leper] leoper *Q1*; Leaper *Q2, 3, F.*

Cym., II. iv. 107; etc. Pliny, *Nat. Hist.*, 8. 33, after mentioning the fatal power of the glance of the "catoblepas", says, "Eadem et basilisci serpentis est vis".

The basilisk was the *royal* serpent; cf. Pliny, 8. 78; 24, 66.

56–7. *enemy . . . laments his death*] according to the injunction of *Matt.*, 5. 4, "Love your enemies . . ."

59. *liquid tears*] conveys the sense of quantities, floods of tears. Cf. Peele, *David and Bethsabe*, 475a: "O would our eyes were conduits to our hearts, / And that our hearts were seas of liquid blood." (Hart).

60, 62. *blood-consuming / -drinking sighs*] an old belief, that every sigh cost the heart a drop of blood; cf. *3 H 6*, IV. iv. 22.

62. *pale as primrose*] Shakespeare constantly associates the primrose, as here, with liquid tears, pearl, or dew (*MND.*, I. i. 211; *Ham.*, I. iii. 41) and death: see Armstrong, *Shakespeare's Imagination*, chap. 9.

Cf. "pale primroses" in *Wint.*, IV. iv. 122; and Virgil, *Ecl.*, 2. 45–50, for "pallentes violas".

68. *my reproach*] reproach of me.

72. *Be woe for me*] "Say 'Woe is me' for me (the Queen), rather than for Gloucester."

74. *leper*] *Lev.*, 13. 45–6, "And the leper . . . shall cry, Unclean, unclean . . . he shall dwell alone."

What! art thou, like the adder, waxen deaf?
Be poisonous too, and kill thy forlorn Queen.
Is all thy comfort shut in Gloucester's tomb?
Why, then, Dame Margaret was ne'er thy joy:
Erect his statuë and worship it,
And make my image but an alehouse sign.
Was I for this nigh wreck'd upon the sea,
And twice by awkward wind from England's bank
Drove back again unto my native clime?
What boded this, but well forewarning wind
Did seem to say "Seek not a scorpion's nest,
Nor set no footing on this unkind shore"?
What did I then, but curs'd the gentle gusts
And he that loos'd them forth their brazen caves;
And bid them blow towards England's blessed shore,
Or turn our stem upon a dreadful rock.
Yet Æolus would not be a murderer,
But left that hateful office unto thee:
The pretty vaulting sea refus'd to drown me,
Knowing that thou wouldst have me drown'd on shore
With tears as salt as sea through thy unkindness:

78. Margaret] *Rowe;* Elianor *F.* 82. wind] winde *F;* winds *Q.* 87. then, but] then? But *F.* curs'd] *F* (curst). 90. stem] *ASC; Vaughan conj.;* stern *F. See n.*

75. *adder . . . deaf*] *Ps.*, 58. 4–5, "even like the deaf adder that stoppeth her ears; Which refuseth to hear the voice of the charmer: charm he never so wisely." Steevens quotes Gower, *Confessio Amantis*, I, fol. x: "He leyeth downe his one eare all plat / Unto the grounde and halt it fast: / And eke that other eare als faste / He stoppeth with his taille." (Hart).

82. *awkward*] adverse, contrary.

bank] shore. Cf. "the banks of England", *1 H 4*, III. i. 46.

84 ff. *well forewarning . . .*] predicting truthfully. Note the pathetic fallacy. The speech is full of alliteration and onomatopoeia, with plosives for the wind, gutturals for the rocks, and sibilants for the winds and waves.

88. *he*] attracted into the nominative by the adj. clause following it.

brazen] extremely strong. Cf. *Odyssey*, 10. 3–4, "where the island is said to have a τεῖχος χάλκεον. There is no mention of brass in the Virgilian account (*Aeneid*, I. 52–4)." (R. K. Root, *Classical Mythology*, 34.) Cf. *Per.*, III. i. 2–3: "thou, that hast / Upon the winds command, bind them in brass." This is one of the few signs of Shakespeare's direct acquaintance with Greek; cf. Baldwin, *Shakespeare's Small Latine*, vol. 2, ch. 49, esp. pp. 659–61.

90. *stem*] see collation. Vaughan supports the argument from the sense, by noting the jingle of "turn our stern".

The splitting rocks cower'd in the sinking sands,
And would not dash me with their ragged sides,
Because thy flinty heart, more hard than they,
Might in thy palace perish Margaret.
As far as I could ken thy chalky cliffs,
When from thy shore the tempest beat us back,
I stood upon the hatches in the storm,
And when the dusky sky began to rob
My earnest-gaping sight of thy land's view,
I took a costly jewel from my neck—
A heart it was, bound in with diamonds—
And threw it towards thy land. The sea receiv'd it,
And so I wish'd thy body might my heart:
And even with this I lost fair England's view,
And bid mine eyes be packing with my heart,
And call'd them blind and dusky spectacles
For losing ken of Albion's wished coast.
How often have I tempted Suffolk's tongue—
The agent of thy foul inconstancy—
To sit and witch me, as Ascanius did
When he to madding Dido would unfold
His father's acts, commenc'd in burning Troy!
Am I not witch'd like her? thou false like him?

99. Margaret] *Rowe;* Elianor *F.* 115. witch] *Theobald;* watch *F.* 118. witch'd] *F* (witcht). thou] *ASC; Steevens conj.;* or thou not *F. See n.*

96. *splitting*] formed for the purpose of splitting (ships).

sinking] which sink (ships). (Vaughan.)

99. *perish*] used transitively = destroy.

100. *ken*] discern at sea. An old nautical use; cf. Golding, *Ovid*, 7. 627, "the Cretish fleet he *kend*, / Which hitherward . . . did tend."

110. *be packing*] get away (with the heart-ornament).

111. *spectacles*] instruments of vision. Chaucer used the word of a spyglass or telescope.

112. *wished*] longed for.

115–16. *Ascanius . . . Dido*] It was "Cupid in the semblance of Ascanius who bewitched Dido" (Theobald). Wilson, lii, finds the probable source in a "not unnatural misreading of the Dido story in Chaucer's *Legend of Good Women.*" The source seems to be Virgil, *Æneid*, I. 658 ff: ". . . faciem mutatus et ora Cupido / pro dulci Ascanio veniat, donisque *furentem* / incendat reginam atque ossibus implicet ignem".

115, 118. *witch*] bewitch.

116. *madding*] being or becoming mad; cf. Peele, *Old Wives Tale*, 447b: "See where Venelia, my betrothed love / Runs *madding*, all enrag'd, about the woods." (Hart).

118. *thou*] see collation: "not" may have been repeated by printer or editor, and *or* added to regularize language and metre.

Ay me! I can no more. Die, Margaret!
For Henry weeps that thou dost live so long.

Noise within. Enter WARWICK, SALISBURY, *and many Commons.*

War. It is reported, mighty sovereign,
That good Duke Humphrey traitorously is murder'd
By Suffolk and the Cardinal Beaufort's means.
The commons, like an angry hive of bees
That want their leader, scatter up and down,
And care not who they sting in his revenge.
Myself have calm'd their spleenful mutiny,
Until they hear the order of his death.
King. That he is dead, good Warwick, 'tis too true;
But how he died God knows, not Henry.
Enter his chamber, view his breathless corpse,
And comment then upon his sudden death.
War. That shall I do, my liege. Stay, Salisbury,
With the rude multitude till I return.
[*Exeunt Warwick, and Salisbury with the Commons.*
King. O Thou that judgest all things, stay my thoughts—
My thoughts that labour to persuade my soul
Some violent hands were laid on Humphrey's life.
If my suspect be false, forgive me, God,

119. Margaret] *Rowe;* Elinor *F.* 120. S.D.] *F* (*om. Salisbury*). 134. S.D.] *edd.; Exet Salsbury. Q; om. F.*

119. *I can no more*] my strength fails me (Schmidt).

123. *Suffolk . . . Beaufort*] another indication of their joint responsibility for Gloucester's death; cf. III. i. 137, 187, 276, 323–6; III. ii. 2.

126. *his revenge*] in revenge for him. The old natural history supposed that each hive had a *king*; cf. *H 5*, I. ii. 183 ff.

127. *spleenful*] hot, eager (Schmidt); cf. *Tit.*, II. iii. 191.

128. *order*] manner, details, way in which it took place; cf. *Caes.*, III. i. 231, "the order of his funeral"; I. ii. 25, "the order of the course".

131. *view*] the usual term in the direction to a coroner's jury.

breathless] without breath, lifeless; cf. *1 H 4*, V. iii. 16; *R 2*, V. vi. 31; *John*, IV. iii. 66.

132. *comment*] make remarks; pass opinions on, reason about; cf. *Gent.*, II. i. 42; *Ven.*, 714; *Sonn.*, 15, 89.

133–4.] cf. 241 ff below, for Salisbury's power with the commons.

134. *rude multitude*] *Homily against Rebellion*, "the *rude* ignorant common people, great *multitudes* of whom . . ." *rude* is unpolished, uncivilized.

135. *that judgest all things*] cf. *Genesis*, 18. 25, "the judge of all the earth".

138. *suspect*] suspicion. Verb for noun, as at I. i. 2.

For judgment only doth belong to Thee.
Fain would I go to chafe his paly lips
With twenty thousand kisses, and to drain
Upon his face an ocean of salt tears,
To tell my love unto his dumb deaf trunk,
And with my fingers feel his hand unfeeling:
But all in vain are these mean obsequies, [*Bed put forth.*
And to survey his dead and earthy image
What were it but to make my sorrow greater?

WARWICK *draws the curtains, and shows Duke* HUMPHREY *in his bed.*

War. Come hither, gracious sovereign, view this body.
King. That is to see how deep my grave is made;
For with his soul fled all my worldly solace,
For, seeing him, I see my life in death.
War. As surely as my soul intends to live
With that dread King that took our state upon Him
To free us from his Father's wrathful curse,
I do believe that violent hands were laid
Upon the life of this thrice-famed duke.
Suf. A dreadful oath, sworn with a solemn tongue!
What instance gives Lord Warwick for his vow?
War. See how the blood is settled in his face.
Oft have I seen a timely-parted ghost,

145. S.D.] *F (between 145 and 146); om. Q. See n.* 147. S.D.] *Q; om. F.*

139. *judgment*] cf. *Daniel*, 9. 7, "righteousness belongeth unto thee"; the form is from Sternhold and Hopkins *Ps.*, 3. 8, "Salvation onely doth belong / to thee O Lord aboue."

142. *ocean . . . tears*] cf. *Sp. Tr.*, 2. 5. 23, "To drowne thee with an *ocean of my teares*".

145. S.D. Bed put forth.] Since the bed exposed in the original version at III. ii. 1 (see Appendix 4) first appears here in F, this S.D. reads like a prompter's note just ahead of the drawing of the curtains at 148. The curtains are presumably closed by the Cardinal as he leaves the stage at 201 (see collation).

151. *my life in death*] my life in a condition like death; cf. *Burial Service*, "In the midst of life we are in death."

153. *took our state upon Him*] cf. *Collects*, Christmas Day, "to take our nature upon him"; and Sunday next before Easter, "to take upon him our flesh".

154. *free . . . curse*] cf. *Galatians*, 3. 13, "Christ hath redeemed us from the curse of the law".

158. *instance*] proof.

159. *settled*] congealed; cf. *Rom.*, IV. v. 26, "Her blood is *settled*, and her joints are stiff."

160. *timely-parted ghost*] a dead person departed in a timely or natural

Of ashy semblance, meagre, pale, and bloodless,
Being all descended to the labouring heart;
Who, in the conflict that it holds with death,
Attracts the same for aidance 'gainst the enemy;
Which with the heart there cools, and ne'er returneth
To blush and beautify the cheek again.
But see, his face is black and full of blood,
His eye-balls further out than when he liv'd,
Staring full ghastly like a strangled man;
His hair uprear'd, his nostrils stretch'd with struggling;
His hands abroad display'd, as one that grasp'd
And tugg'd for life, and was by strength subdu'd.
Look, on the sheets his hair, you see, is sticking;
His well-proportion'd beard made rough and rugged,
Like to the summer's corn by tempest lodg'd.
It cannot be but he was murder'd here;
The least of all these signs were probable.

Suf. Why, Warwick, who should do the Duke to death?
Myself and Beaufort had him in protection;
And we, I hope, sir, are no murderers.

War. But both of you were vow'd Duke Humphrey's foes,
And you, forsooth, had the good Duke to keep:
'Tis like you would not feast him like a friend,

170. stretch'd] *F* (stretcht). 171. grasp'd] *F* (graspt).

manner. Contrast "untimely", *3 H 6*, III. iii. 187, and "timeless" = premature, 186 below. For "ghost", cf. *Ham.*, I. iv. 85.

161–2. *bloodless, / Being all descended*] a condensed construction; the subject of "being" is "blood", contained in "bloodless"—because the blood is all descended.

164. *the same*] the blood.

aidance] assistance, aid.

171. *abroad display'd*] spread out widely; cf. Kyd, *Cornelia*, 3. 1. 102, "I flonge *abroade* mine armes / To entertaine him"; and *F.Q.*, 3. 2. 47: "And the old woman carefully *displayed* / The clothes about her round."

175. *corn . . . lodg'd*] cf. Holland's *Plinie* (1601), 18 ch. 17, p. 574, "the corne standeth not upright, but is lodged and lieth along;" *R 2*, III. iii. 162; *Mac.*, IV. i. 55.

177. *probable*] capable of affording proof, or supporting belief (L. *probare*).

179. *Myself and Beaufort*] cf. above, 123. Suffolk arrested him, and committed him to the Cardinal; see III. i. 136–7.

181. *vow'd . . . foes*] see e.g. I. i. 165–9.

183–4. *feast . . . enemy*] an almost certain reference to the story of David and Nabal, as at V. ii. 50. See *1 Sam.*, 25. 10–13, "And Nabal answered David's servants, Shall I then take my bread, and my water, and my flesh that I have killed for my shearers, and give it unto men, whom I know not whence they be? . . . So David's young

And 'tis well seen he found an enemy.
Queen. Then you, belike, suspect these noblemen
As guilty of Duke Humphrey's timeless death.
War. Who finds the heifer dead, and bleeding fresh,
And sees fast by a butcher with an axe,
But will suspect 'twas he that made the slaughter?
Who finds the partridge in the puttock's nest,
But may imagine how the bird was dead,
Although the kite soar with unbloodied beak?
Even so suspicious is this tragedy.
Queen. Are you the butcher, Suffolk? Where's your knife?
Is Beaufort termed a kite? Where are his talons?
Suf. I wear no knife to slaughter sleeping men;
But here's a vengeful sword, rusted with ease,
That shall be scoured in his rancorous heart
That slanders me with murder's crimson badge.
Say, if thou dar'st, proud Lord of Warwickshire,
That I am faulty in Duke Humphrey's death.
[*Exeunt Cardinal and others.*
War. What dares not Warwick, if false Suffolk dare him?
Queen. He dares not calm his contumelious spirit,
Nor cease to be an arrogant controller,
Though Suffolk dare him twenty thousand times.
War. Madam, be still, with reverence may I say;
For every word you speak in his behalf
Is slander to your royal dignity.
Suf. Blunt-witted lord, ignoble in demeanour!
If ever lady wrong'd her lord so much,
Thy mother took into her blameful bed

201. S.D.] *Q; om. F; the Cardinal closes the curtains ana goes out. Wilson; Exeunt Cardinal, Somerset and others. Capell + edd.* 211. into] *F;* vnto *Q.*

men turned their way, and . . . told him all those sayings. And David said unto his men, Gird ye on every man his sword . . . And David also girded on his sword."

186. *timeless*] untimely.

187.] The imagery of the slaughter-house and of beasts of prey thickens.

190. *puttock*] kite; cf. III. i. 251; v. ii. 11. The association with blood (168), sheets (174), and death is a common image-cluster in Shakespeare. See Armstrong, *Shakespeare's Imagination*, chap. I.

196. *slaughter sleeping men*] cf. 225 below.

201. *faulty*] guilty.

203. *contumelious*] slanderous.

204. *controller*] censorious critic, detractor.

Some stern untutor'd churl, and noble stock
Was graft with crab-tree slip, whose fruit thou art,
And never of the Nevils' noble race.

War. But that the guilt of murder bucklers thee,
And I should rob the deathsman of his fee,
Quitting thee thereby of ten thousand shames,
And that my sovereign's presence makes me mild,
I would, false murd'rous coward, on thy knee
Make thee beg pardon for thy passed speech,
And say it was thy mother that thou meant'st;
That thou thyself wast born in bastardy:
And after all this fearful homage done,
Give thee thy hire and send thy soul to hell,
Pernicious blood-sucker of sleeping men!

Suf. Thou shalt be waking while I shed thy blood,
If from this presence thou dar'st go with me.

War. Away even now, or I will drag thee hence:
Unworthy though thou art, I'll cope with thee,
And do some service to Duke Humphrey's ghost.

[*Exeunt Suffolk and Warwick.*

King. What stronger breastplate than a heart untainted!
Thrice is he arm'd that hath his quarrel just,
And he but naked, though lock'd up in steel,
Whose conscience with injustice is corrupted.

[*A noise within.*

230, 234, 235. S.DD.] *F;* Warwicke puls him out. Exet *Warwicke* and *Suffolke*, and then all the Commons within, cries, downe with *Suffolke*, downe with *Suffolk*. And then enter againe, the Duke of *Suffolke* and *Warwicke*, with their weapons drawne. *Q*. 233. lock'd] *F* (lockt).

212. *stern*] rough, rugged; used here in a general sense.

213. *slip*] sliver, cutting, with an equivoque on the sense apparent in Hardyng, 506, "bastarde *slyppes* shall never take depe rootes."

215. *the guilt of murder bucklers thee*] a reference to the story of Cain, *Genesis*, 4. 14–15.

bucklers] shields. Cf. *Ed. 2*, 585. Not commonly used as a verb.

216. *deathsman*] executioner.

217. *Quitting*] acquitting, ridding.

222. *bastardy*] cf. n. to 213 above. An interesting comment on the amenities of Elizabethan invective, and the finer points of aristocratic genealogy.

223. *fearful . . . done*] note the L. participial construction.

224. *Give . . . hire*] *Matt.*, 20. 8, the parable of the labourers in the vineyard.

225. *Pernicious*] in the L. sense—"causing destruction".

231. *breastplate . . .*] cf. *Eph.*, 6. 14, "Stand therefore, having your loins girt about with truth, and having on the breastplate of righteousness." (Noble).

Queen. What noise is this?

Re-enter SUFFOLK *and* WARWICK, *with their weapons drawn.*

King. Why, how now, lords! your wrathful weapons drawn
Here in our presence! Dare you be so bold?
Why, what tumultuous clamour have we here?
Suf. The trait'rous Warwick, with the men of Bury,
Set all upon me, mighty sovereign.

Enter SALISBURY.

Sal. [*to the Commons entering*]. Sirs, stand apart; the King shall know your mind.
Dread lord, the commons sends you word by me,
Unless false Suffolk straight be done to death,
Or banished fair England's territories,
They will by violence tear him from your palace
And torture him with grievous ling'ring death.
They say, by him the good Duke Humphrey died;
They say, in him they fear your Highness' death;
And mere instinct of love and loyalty,
Free from a stubborn opposite intent,
As being thought to contradict your liking,
Makes them thus forward in his banishment.
They say, in care of your most royal person,
That if your Highness should intend to sleep,
And charge that no man should disturb your rest,
In pain of your dislike or pain of death,
Yet, notwithstanding such a strait edict,
Were there a serpent seen, with forked tongue,

236.] Why how now Lords? *Q;* Why . . . Lords? / . . . drawne, *F.* 240. S.D.] *F;* The commons againe cries, downe with *Suffolke*, downe with *Suffolke*. And then enter from them, the Earle of Salbury. *Q.* 241. *to . . . entering.*] *Capell.* 242. sends] *Q;* send *F.* 243. false] *Malone, from Q;* Lord *F, Camb.*

243.] see collation. F misprinted from 242, according to Malone's reading. This is more in keeping with the tone of the argument, and occurs at 202 and 265. But "false" could equally well be a recollection of 202, which is in Q.

249. *mere*] pure (L. *merus*).

instinct] accented on the second syllable, as usual. Impulse.

250. *opposite intent*] hostile or antagonistic purpose.

251. *contradict*] oppose, thwart.

257. *strait*] strict.

edict] normal Elizabethan accent on the second syllable.

That slily glided towards your Majesty,
It were but necessary you were wak'd,
Lest, being suffer'd, in that harmful slumber,
The mortal worm might make the sleep eternal:
And therefore do they cry, though you forbid,
That they will guard you, whe'r you will or no,
From such fell serpents as false Suffolk is;
With whose envenomed and fatal sting,
Your loving uncle, twenty times his worth,
They say, is shamefully bereft of life.

Commons. [*Within.*] An answer from the King, my Lord of Salisbury!

Suf. 'Tis like the commons, rude unpolish'd hinds,
Could send such message to their sovereign;
But you, my lord, were glad to be employ'd,
To show how quaint an orator you are:
But all the honour Salisbury hath won
Is that he was the lord ambassador,
Sent from a sort of tinkers to the King.

Commons. [*Within.*] An answer from the King, or we will all break in!

King. Go, Salisbury, and tell them all from me,
I thank them for their tender loving care;
And had I not been cited so by them,
Yet did I purpose as they do entreat;
For sure, my thoughts do hourly prophesy
Mischance unto my state by Suffolk's means:
And therefore, by His Majesty I swear,
Whose far unworthy deputy I am,
He shall not breathe infection in this air

264. whe'r] *edd.*; where *F.* 270. unpolish'd] *Q*, *F* (vnpolisht). 277. *Commons*] *edd.*; *om. F.* 277.] *F*; *The Commons cryes, an answere from my Lord of Salisbury. Q* (*as S.D.*).

261. *suffer'd*] allowed, *scil.* to sting; cf. v. i. 153.

harmful] transferred epithet.

262. *mortal worm*] deadly or fatal snake; cf. *Ant.*, v. ii. 242.

267. *his worth*] as worthy as he.

270. *rude*] barbarous; the L. sense, ranging from "unlearned" to "brutal". Cf. IV. iv. 32; v. i. 64.

hinds] boors, peasants.

273. *quaint*] skilful, clever; cf. *1 H 6*, IV. i. 102.

276. *sort*] pack, crew.

280. *cited*] incited, urged.

283. *Mischance*] disaster, calamity. Cf. *1 H 6*, I. i. 89, "Lords, view these letters, full of bad mischance", and 299 below.

But three days longer, on the pain of death.
[*Exit Salisbury.*
Queen. O Henry, let me plead for gentle Suffolk!
King. Ungentle Queen, to call him gentle Suffolk!
No more, I say; if thou dost plead for him
Thou wilt but add increase unto my wrath.
Had I but said, I would have kept my word;
But when I swear, it is irrevocable.
If after three days' space thou here be'st found
On any ground that I am ruler of,
The world shall not be ransom for thy life.
Come, Warwick, come, good Warwick, go with me;
I have great matters to impart to thee.
[*Exeunt all but Queen and Suffolk.*
Queen. Mischance and Sorrow go along with you!
Heart's Discontent and sour Affliction
Be playfellows to keep you company!
There's two of you; the Devil make a third!
And threefold Vengeance tend upon your steps!
Suf. Cease, gentle queen, these execrations,
And let thy Suffolk take his heavy leave.
Queen. Fie, coward woman and soft-hearted wretch!
Hast thou not spirit to curse thine enemy?
Suf. A plague upon them! Wherefore should I curse them?
Would curses kill, as doth the mandrake's groan,

287. S.D. *Exit Salisbury.*] *Q; om. F.* 298. S.D. *Exeunt . . .*] *edd.; Exit. F; Exet* King and *Warwicke, Manet* Queene and *Suffolke. Q.* 307. enemy] *F;* enemies *Capell, from Q.*

288. *gentle*] the usual Elizabethan sense of "noble".

293. *irrevocable*] This is one of the few decisive actions taken by Henry, perhaps the only one; its character is typically religious. Cf. *Jack Straw* (Dodsley, 5. 392): "And when a king doth set down his decree, / His sentence should be irrevocable." Accented on the first and third syllables.

299 ff.] The love of Margaret and Suffolk is developed, unhistorically, from Hall's statements (218) that she "entirely loved the Duke", and that he was "the Quenes dearlynge" (219).

This scene is generally compared with the similar parting of Edward and Gaveston in *Ed. 2*, 409 ff; and of Richard II and his Queen, *R 2*, v. i. 81 ff. But see n. to 338 below, for a debt to Ovid. Margaret is fast developing into the vindictive woman of *R 3*.

302. *two . . . third*] cf. *Mer. V.*, III. i. 66–7.

305. *heavy*] mournful, sad (L. *gravis*).

309. *mandrake's groans*] The mandrake is a poisonous plant. "The fabulous accounts . . . give it an inferior degree of animal life, and relate, that when torn from the ground it groans;

I would invent as bitter searching terms,
As curst, as harsh, and horrible to hear,
Deliver'd strongly through my fixed teeth,
With full as many signs of deadly hate,
As lean-fac'd Envy in her loathsome cave.
My tongue should stumble in mine earnest words;
Mine eyes should sparkle like the beaten flint;
My hair be fix'd an end, as one distract;
Ay, every joint should seem to curse and ban:
And even now my burden'd heart would break
Should I not curse them. Poison be their drink!
Gall, worse than gall, the daintiest that they taste!
Their sweetest shade a grove of cypress trees!
Their chiefest prospect murd'ring basilisks!
Their softest touch as smart as lizards' stings!
Their music frightful as the serpent's hiss,
And boding screech-owls make the consort full!
All the foul terrors in dark-seated hell—

Queen. Enough, sweet Suffolk; thou torments thyself;

317. My] *Q*; Mine *F*. fix'd] *Q*, *F* (fixt). an] *F*; on *Q*. 328. torments] *Q1*, *3*; torment'st *Q2*, *F*.

and that this groan being certainly fatal to him that is offering such unwelcome violence, the practice of those who gathered mandrakes was to tie one end of a string to the plant, and the other to a dog, upon whom the fatal groan discharged its malignity." (Singer).

311. *curst*] malignant.

314. *lean-fac'd Envy*] Ovid, *Metam.*, 2. 760–75: "protinus Invidiae nigro squalentia tabo / tecta petit: domus est . . . quae / igne vacet semper, caligine semper abundet . . . / pallor in ore sedet, macies in corpore toto."

317. *an*] Elizabethan form of "on". *distract*] distracted, mad.

318. *curse and ban*] excommunicate, in the religious sense. Note the sibilants that dominate the curse.

322. *cypress*] associated with funerals and grave-yards.

323. *basilisks*] cf. n. to III. ii. 51, for (*a*) basilisk = the royal serpent; for (*b*) basilisk = the largest type of Elizabethan cannon, weighing 9,000 lb., and firing a shot of 60 lb. a distance of 21 score yards, see A. F. Pollard, *Tudor Tracts*, 1532–88, p. 399.

324. *lizards' stings*] cf. *3 H 6*, II. ii. 138. The erroneous idea that lizards had stings may be traced to the mediaeval use of "lizard" as equivalent to "anguis". Cf. Wyclif, *Lev.*, xi. 30, "A lacert, that is a serpent that is clepid a liserd."; Caxton, *Dialogues* (EETS.) viii. 28, "Men ete not . . . Of bestes venemous . . . Serpentes, lizarts, scorpions." (*OED.*). Skelton, in "Though ye suppose" (Dyce, I. 26–7; Henderson, 23) uses "lesard" as the equivalent of "anguis" in his own Latin version (J. C. Maxwell).

326. *consort*] company of musicians.

328. *torments*] see collation; and cf. V. i. 130 *mistakes*; Franz, 152 (*a*).

And these dread curses, like the sun 'gainst glass,
Or like an overcharged gun, recoil
And turn the force of them upon thyself.

Suf. You bade me ban, and will you bid me leave?
Now, by the ground that I am banish'd from,
Well could I curse away a winter's night,
Though standing naked on a mountain top,
Where biting cold would never let grass grow,
And think it but a minute spent in sport.

Queen. O! let me entreat thee cease. Give me thy hand,
That I may dew it with my mournful tears;
Nor let the rain of heaven wet this place,
To wash away my woeful monuments.
O! could this kiss be printed in thy hand,
That thou might'st think upon these by the seal,
Through whom a thousand sighs are breath'd
for thee.
So, get thee gone, that I may know my grief;
'Tis but surmis'd whiles thou art standing by,
As one that surfeits thinking on a want.
I will repeal thee, or, be well assur'd,
Adventure to be banished myself;
And banished I am, if but from thee.
Go; speak not to me; even now be gone.
O! go not yet. Even thus two friends condemn'd
Embrace and kiss and take ten thousand leaves,
Loather a hundred times to part than die.

331. turn] *Rowe;* turnes *F.*

329.] dramatic irony, in view of Margaret's own curse in *R 3*.

332. *leave*] leave off, cease.

332, 333. *ban . . . banish'd*] a pun?

338 ff. *Give me . . .*] The rest of this parting is built on a recollection of Ovid, *Tristia*, I. 3, in which Ovid describes his parting from his wife to go into exile. He has tears, rain, kisses, sighs, promise of repeal, repeated farewells, the wish for death. *Tristia*, 3. 3 is brought in at 387; see n.

339. *dew it with . . . tears*] a common phrase with Kyd and Marlowe, e.g. *Sp. Tr.*, I. 4. 36; *2 Tamb.*, 3889.

341. *woeful monuments*] marks of woe, i.e. tears.

343–4. *That . . . these . . . seal . . .*] Johnson paraphrases, "That by the impression (as of a seal on wax) of my kiss forever remaining on thy hand thou mightest think on those lips through which a thousand sighs will be breathed for thee." Brooke notes the preciosity of the style.

349. *Adventure*] venture; cf. *R 3*, I. iii. 116, "I dare adventure to be sent to the Tower".

Yet now farewell; and farewell life with thee.
Suf. Thus is poor Suffolk ten times banished,
Once by the King, and three times thrice by thee.
'Tis not the land I care for, wert thou thence;
A wilderness is populous enough,
So Suffolk had thy heavenly company:
For where thou art, there is the world itself,
With every several pleasure in the world,
And where thou art not, desolation.
I can no more. Live thou to joy thy life;
Myself to joy in nought but that thou liv'st.

Enter VAUX.

Queen. Whither goes Vaux so fast? What news, I prithee?
Vaux. To signify unto his Majesty
That Cardinal Beaufort is at point of death;
For suddenly a grievous sickness took him,
That makes him gasp, and stare, and catch the air,
Blaspheming God, and cursing men on earth.
Sometimes he talks as if Duke Humphrey's ghost
Were by his side; sometime he calls the King,
And whispers to his pillow, as to him,
The secrets of his overcharged soul:
And I am sent to tell his Majesty
That even now he cries aloud for him.
Queen. Go, tell this heavy message to the King. [*Exit Vaux.*
Ay me! What is this world! What news are these!

365. to] *Singer; no F.* 378. S.D. *Exit Vaux.*] *Q* (. . . *Vawse.*); *Exit F.*

355. *farewell* . . .] cf. *Ed. 2*, 1933–4, "Father, farewell; . . . life, farewell with my friends."

359, 360. *wilderness . . . heavenly company*] *Mark*, I. 12, "And he was there in the wilderness forty days . . . and the angels ministered into him."; *Heb.*, 12. 22, ". . . the heavenly Jerusalem, and . . . an innumerable company of angels"; *Everyman* (Dodsley, I. 100) "of angels the heavenly company".

361–3. *For where thou art* . . .] Singer quotes Lucretius, I. 22–3: "Nec sine te pulchrum dias in luminis auras / Exoritur, neque sit laetum nec amabile quicquam." Cf. Ovid, *Tristia*, 3. 3. 18, "nulla venit sine te nox mihi, nulla dies."

365.] see collation; "no" has been taken in error from 364.

368. *at point of death*] cf. *John*, 4. 47; *Mark*, 5. 23, "My little daughter lieth at the point of death"; Hall, 16; Hardyng, 400.

374–5. *whispers to his pillow* . . .] cf. *Mac.*, v. i. 81: "Infected minds / To their deaf pillows will discharge their secrets."

But wherefore grieve I at an hour's poor loss,
Omitting Suffolk's exile, my soul's treasure?
Why only, Suffolk, mourn I not for thee,
And with the southern clouds contend in tears,
Theirs for the earth's increase, mine for my sorrows?
Now get thee hence: the King, thou know'st, is coming;
If thou be found by me thou art but dead.

Suf. If I depart from thee I cannot live;
And in thy sight to die, what were it else
But like a pleasant slumber in thy lap?
Here could I breathe my soul into the air,
As mild and gentle as the cradle-babe
Dying with mother's dug between his lips;
Where, from thy sight, I should be raging mad,
And cry out for thee to close up mine eyes,
To have thee with thy lips to stop my mouth:
So should'st thou either turn my flying soul,
Or I should breathe it so into thy body,
And then it liv'd in sweet Elysium.
To die by thee were but to die in jest;
From thee to die were torture more than death.
O! let me stay, befall what may befall.

Queen. Though parting be a fretful corrosive,
It is applied to a deathful wound.
To France, sweet Suffolk! Let me hear from thee;

390. breathe] *Q1, 3;* breath *Q2, F.* 392. his] *Q;* its *F.* 393. thy] *Q1, 2, F;* my *Q3.* 402. Though] *ASC;* Away: Though *F.*

380. *an hour's poor loss*] The Cardinal, at his age, has lost only a very short period of his life, and this is no great cause for grief.

381. *Omitting*] ignoring.

387 ff. *If I depart . . .*] This speech is influenced by Ovid, *Tristia*, 3. 3. 43–4, 61–2, in which he writes to his wife of his death in exile, without her to close his eyes (394), of his soul flying aloft into the air (390, 396), and ends with "Farewell" (355). See also n. at 361 above. Ovid writes: "nec mandata dabo, nec cum clamore supremo / labentes *oculos condet* amica manus; . . . / nam si morte carens vacua *volat* altus *in aura / spiritus*, . . ."

393. *Where, from*] whereas, out of.

398. *Elysium*] "In the poets Elysium is part of the lower world, and the residence of the shades of the Blessed" (Smith).

402. *corrosive*] a caustic remedy (usually in medicine); something that eats into the mind; cf. *1 H 6*, III. iii. 3, as adj. used "of acids that consume by chemical action" (Lyly, 2. 568). Cf. Jonson, *EMO.*, I. I. 7; *Underwoods*, 26. 2, "I send nor Balmes, nor Cor'sives to your wound."

403. *applied*] adapted, suitable.
deathful] deadly, mortal.

For wheresoe'er thou art in this world's globe,
I'll have an Iris that shall find thee out.
Away!
Suf. I go.
Queen. And take my heart with thee. [*She kisses him.*
Suf. A jewel, lock'd into the woefull'st cask
That ever did contain a thing of worth.
Even as a splitted bark so sunder we:
This way fall I to death.
Queen. This way for me.
[*Exeunt severally.*

SCENE III.—*A bedchamber.*

Enter the KING, SALISBURY, WARWICK, *to the Cardinal in bed.*

King. How fares my lord? Speak, Beaufort, to thy sovereign.
Car. If thou be'st death, I'll give thee England's treasure,
Enough to purchase such another island,
So thou wilt let me live, and feel no pain.
King. Ah, what a sign it is of evil life
Where death's approach is seen so terrible!

407. Away!] *ASC; om. F. See n.* 407. S.D. *She . . . him.*] *Q (subst.); om. F.*

Scene III

Locality.] *edd.* Entry.] *F;* Enter King and *Salsbury*, and then the Curtaines be drawne, and the Cardinall is discouered in his bed, rauing and staring as if he were madde. *Q.*

406. *Iris*] Juno's messenger, and the goddess of the rainbow; cf. Ovid, *Metam.*, I. 270–1: "Nuntia Iunonis varios induta colores / Concipit Iris aquas alimentaque nubibus adfert."

407. *Away!*] see collation at 402. Misplaced by the printer, probably through use of amended Q copy. The rest of the speech, as amended, had to be transferred from the previous page in Q, while "Away!" would be written in the margin. By some error, the two were transposed, and "Away!" put at the beginning instead of at the end of the speech.

408. *into*] in.

cask] casket.

Scene III

For the Cardinal's death, see Hall, 210–11 (Appendix I). His speeches should be compared with those of Macbeth to the ghost of Banquo.

Note the irony: the Cardinal dies in the same house, and bed, as his victim Gloucester.

2. *England's treasure*] Hall, 211; cf. also Hall, 139, "by a bull legatyne, whiche he purchased at Rome, he gathered so much treasure, that no man in maner had money but he." Cf. IV. i. 74.

War. Beaufort, it is thy sovereign speaks to thee.
Car. Bring me unto my trial when you will.
Died he not in his bed? Where should he die?
Can I make men live whe'r they will or no?
O, torture me no more! I will confess.
Alive again? Then show me where he is:
I'll give a thousand pound to look upon him.
He hath no eyes, the dust hath blinded them.
Comb down his hair; look! look! it stands upright,
Like lime-twigs set to catch my winged soul.
Give me some drink; and bid the apothecary
Bring the strong poison that I bought of him.
King. O thou eternal Mover of the heavens!
Look with a gentle eye upon this wretch;
O! beat away the busy meddling fiend
That lays strong siege unto this wretch's soul,
And from his bosom purge this black despair.
War. See how the pangs of death do make him grin!
Sal. Disturb him not; let him pass peaceably.
King. Peace to his soul! if God's good pleasure be.
Lord Cardinal, if thou think'st on heaven's bliss,
Hold up thy hand, make signal of thy hope.
He dies, and makes no sign. O God, forgive him!

10. whe'r] *edd.;* where *F.*

14. *dust*] Vaughan suggests that the dust came from the beds, between which Hall says he may have been smothered. "In some parts of the country up to this time there is a bed in common use made of some selected parts of straw, cut up into comparatively fine sections . . . called a 'dust-bed'. As the bed must have been held with utmost force over the victim's face, whatever its materials, it might well be supposed . . . to blind his eyes, and leave in them what might be called 'dust'."

16. *lime-twigs*] twigs smeared with bird-lime. The metaphor has been much used earlier in the play, e.g. I. iii. 88; II. iv. 54.

19. *eternal Mover*] applied by Aristotle to God as the Primus Motor or First Cause, moving the universe, himself unmoved. Cf. Marlowe, *Jew*, 397; *1 Tamb.*, 1452.

21. *meddling*] intruding on the concerns of others, especially the souls it hopes to gain.

22. *lays strong siege*] cf. *F.Q.*, 2. 11. 5, 9, where the enemies of Temperance "lay strong siege" to her castle; but cf. Hall, 171, "environed the toune about with a *strong siege*", and Fabyan, 605.

24. *pangs of death*] *2 Sam.*, 22. 5; *Ps.*, 18 (Bishops'), 3.

25. *pass*] die.

28. *signal*] token, sign; cf. *1 H 6*, II. iv. 121: "In signal of my love to thee . . . / Will I . . . wear this rose."

War. So bad a death argues a monstrous life.
King. Forbear to judge, for we are sinners all.
Close up his eyes, and draw the curtain close;
And let us all to meditation. [*Exeunt.*

30. *argues*] evinces, betokens; cf. *3 H 6*, II. ii. 25.

31. *Forbear to judge*] "Peccantes culpare cave, nam labimur omnes, / Aut sumus, aut fuimus, vel possumus esse, quod hic est." (Singer). Cf. *Matt.*, 7. 1 "Judge not"; *Romans*, 3. 23 "all have sinned". An archaism = "abstain from judging".

32. *Close up his eyes*] a mark of affection and respect.

33. *meditation*] religious contemplation; prayer. An early and Biblical usage. The conclusion is characteristically religious and ineffectual.

ACT IV

SCENE I.—*The coast of Kent.*

Alarum. Fight at sea. Ordnance goes off. Enter a Lieutenant, a Master, a Master's Mate, WALTER WHITMORE, *and soldiers; with* SUFFOLK, *disguised, and two gentlemen, prisoners.*

Lieu. The gaudy, blabbing, and remorseful day
Is crept into the bosom of the sea,
And now loud-howling wolves arouse the jades
That drag the tragic melancholy night;
Who with their drowsy, slow, and flagging wings
Clip dead men's graves, and from their misty jaws
Breathe foul contagious darkness in the air.

ACT IV

Scene I

Locality.] *Pope.* Entry.] *edd.* (*subst.*)*; Alarum . . . Enter Lieutenant, Suffolke, and others. F;* Alarmes within, and the chambers be discharged, like as it were a fight at sea. And then enter the Captaine of the ship and the Maister, and the Maisters Mate, & the Duke of Suffolke disguised, and others with him, and Water Whickmore. *Q.* Walter] Water *Q* (*throughout*). 1–11.] *F; for Q, see App. 4.* 1. *Lieu.*] *F* (*throughout*)*; Cap. Q* (*throughout*). 6. Clip] Cleape *F;* Clap *Pope.*

Source: Hall, 219 (Appendix 1).

1–7.] Criticized by Hart as an excrescence "inartistically joined to the scene by the word 'therefore' "; and described by Singer as "exquisitely beautiful". Johnson says, "Guilt, if afraid of light, considers darkness as a natural shelter, and makes night the confidant of those actions which cannot be trusted to the *tell-tale day.*" Which goes to show how artistic appreciation may depend on textual theory and preconceptions.

1. *blabbing*] giving away secrets. Cf. "Revealing day", *Lucr.*, 1086.

remorseful] full of sorrow and pity. Cf. *Gent.*, IV. iii. 13.

3. *jades*] horses, in a contemptuous sense. Here = dragons: cf. *Troil.*, V. viii. 17 "dragon wing of night"; *Cym.*, II. ii. 48, "Swift, swift, you dragons of the night . . ."; *MND.*, III. ii. 379, "night's swift dragons". Hecate was often identified with Night, and presented with the dragons of Ceres; cf. D. Bush, *Ph. Q.* (1927), 6. 296–7.

5. *flagging wings*] cf. *F.Q.*, I. 11. 10, "flaggy wings", applied to a dragon.

6. *Clip*] strike; no doubt from the stroke or cut of shears.

7. *contagious darkness*] cf. *Caes.*, II. i. 265, "the vile contagion of the night", and *John*, V. iv. 34; *2 Tamb.*, 3892, "Contagious smels, and vapors to infect thee".

For the whole introduction to the

Therefore bring forth the soldiers of our prize,
For whilst our pinnace anchors in the Downs
Here shall they make their ransom on the sand,
Or with their blood stain this discolour'd shore.
Master, this prisoner freely give I thee;
And thou that art his mate make boot of this;
The other, Walter Whitmore, is thy share.
1 Gent. What is my ransom, master? let me know.
Mast. A thousand crowns, or else lay down your head.
Mate. And so much shall you give, or off goes yours.
Lieu. What! think you much to pay two thousand crowns,
And bear the name and port of gentlemen?
Cut both the villains' throats—for die you shall:
The lives of those which we have lost in fight
Be counterpois'd with such a petty sum!
1 Gent. I'll give it, sir; and therefore spare my life.
2 Gent. And so will I, and write home for it straight.
Whit. I lost mine eye in laying the prize aboard,
And therefore to revenge it shalt thou die; [*To Suffolk.*
And so should these, if I might have my will.
Lieu. Be not so rash: take ransom; let him live.
Suf. Look on my George; I am a gentleman.

8. Therefore . . . prize] *F;* Bring forward these prisoners that scorn'd to yeeld, / Vnlade their goods with speed and sincke their ship. *Q.* 22. sum!] *Grant White;* summe. *F.* 26. *To Suffolk.*] *Rowe; om. Q, F.* 29. George] *F;* ring *Q. See n.*

scene, cf. Marlowe, *Jew of Malta*, 640 ff: "Thus like the sad presaging Raven that tolls / The sicke mans passeport in her hollow beake, / And in the shadow of the silent night / Doth shake contagion from her sable wings".

9. *Downs*] a roadstead off the coast of Kent, protected by the Goodwin Sands, between the N. and S. Forelands.

11. *discolour'd*] used proleptically = this shore which will thus be discoloured.

13. *make boot of*] profit by. Cf. *Ant.*, IV. i. 9.

18. *think . . . much*] regard as onerous.

19. *port*] style of living, social station. Cf. Harrison, 2. 5, "whosoever can live without manuall labour, and thereto is able and will beare the port, charge and countenance of a gentleman, he will for monie have a cote and arms bestowed by the heralds."

25. *laying . . . aboard*] boarding' attacking at close quarters by laying one ship alongside the other.

28. *rash*] overhasty.

29. *George*] An equestrian badge of St George and the dragon, worn pendant from a blue riband, or jewelled collar, was one of the insignia of the Order of the Garter. Suffolk had been made a Knight of the Garter by Henry V. The ring (in Q) was probably substituted on the stage for the

Rate me at what thou wilt, thou shalt be paid.
Whit. And so am I; my name is Walter Whitmore.
How now! why starts thou? What doth thee affright?
Suf. Thy name affrights me, in whose sound is death.
A cunning man did calculate my birth,
And told me that by water I should die:
Yet let not this make thee be bloody-minded;
Thy name is Gualtier, being rightly sounded.
Whit. Gualtier or Walter, which it is, I care not.
Never yet did base dishonour blur our name
But with our sword we wip'd away the blot;
Therefore, when merchant-like I sell revenge,
Broke be my sword, my arms torn and defac'd,
And I proclaim'd a coward through the world!
Suf. Stay, Whitmore, for thy prisoner is a prince,
The Duke of Suffolk, William de la Pole.
Whit. The Duke of Suffolk, muffled up in rags!
Suf. Ay, but these rags are no part of the Duke:
Jove sometime went disguis'd, and why not I?

32. starts] *F;* start'st *edd.* thee] *ASC, Vaughan conj.;* death *F.* 48. Jove ... I?] *Pope, from Q; om. F.*

George, as more in keeping with Suffolk's disguise: see French, 158 ff; cf. Scott-Giles, 169.

30. *Rate*] value, estimate.

31. *Walter*] pronounced *Water*, the "l" being silent.

32. *starts*] Abbott, 340; Franz, 152; cf. III. ii. 328; v. i. 130.

thee] see collation. Vaughan conjectures an almost identical anticipation, "death/thou", from the line following, in *R 2*, v. v. 105: "How now? what meanes Death in this rude assalt? / Villaine, thine owne hand yeelds thy deaths instrument, . . ." Here the influence of *doth* and of *death* just below accounts for the error. "It is clear that Suffolk 'started' at the name 'Walter Whitmore' and that he did not appear to start at the name or thought of 'death' for two reasons. When he started Whitmore had made no allusion to 'death'; and, when Whitmore had some time before told him that he must die, Suffolk had not started. Whitmore could not therefore reasonably suppose that Suffolk, starting as he did at his answer, started from fear of death."

Both passages were set by compositor B.

34. *cunning man*] wizard, fortune-teller.

calculate] viz. by casting his horoscope.

35. *by water*] referring to the prophecy at I. iv. 32. The pun depends on the Elizabethan pronunciation of "Walter"; cf. 31.

39. *our name*] see n. to 50 below.

42. *arms*] coat of arms; armorial ensigns.

torn and defac'd] one of the commonest "abatements" or marks of disgrace in heraldry—obliterated.

48. *Jove . . .*] Hart compares *1 Tamb.*, 394, "Jove sometime maskèd in a shepherd's weed".

Lieu. But Jove was never slain, as thou shalt be.
Suf. Obscure and lowly swain, King Henry's blood,
The honourable blood of Lancaster,
Must not be shed by such a jaded groom.
Hast thou not kiss'd thy hand and held my stirrup?
And bare-head plodded by my foot-cloth mule,
And thought thee happy when I shook my head?
How often hast thou waited at my cup,
Fed from my trencher, kneel'd down at the board,
When I have feasted with Queen Margaret?
Remember it and let it make thee crest-fall'n,
Ay, and allay this thy abortive pride,
How in our voiding lobby hast thou stood
And duly waited for my coming forth.
This hand of mine hath writ in thy behalf,
And therefore shall it charm thy riotous tongue.

50. *Suf.*] *Pope, from Q; line continued to Lieu. F.* lowly] *Pope + edd., from Q;* lowsie *F, Wilson.* 51. The] *Pope; Suf.* The *F.* 53. kiss'd] *Q, F* (kist). 54. And bare-head] *Capell, from Q;* Bare-headed *F. See n.* 64. it] *F;* I *Vaughan conj., from Q.*

50. *lowly*] see collation. F "lowsie" has been defended by Wilson, who quotes Cade's "lowsy lynage" in e.g. Hall, 221. F, however, was here probably set up from corrected Q, and "lowsie" is an error easily made from *printed* copy.

King Henry's blood] a false claim. "His mother was a remote cousin of Henry VI" (A. W. Ward). But Hall says Suffolk assumed a good ancestry.

52. *jaded*] base-bred, ignoble, regarded with contempt like the lowest kind of horse.

54. *And bare-head*] see collation; the F *bare-headed* is probably due to a typical duplication, of compositor B, with *plodded*; cf. *1 H 4*, II. iv. 137 "fatch paunch". The omission of *And* may have been due either to negligence, or to subsequent regularization of the metre. See Introduction, p. xlviii, and Alice Walker, *SB.*, 6 (1954), 45–59.

foot-cloth] long ornamental housings or hangings for horses, used, in peace-time, by nobles, judges and others, especially in state-processions. Cf. IV. vii. 47; *R 3*, III. iv. 86.

55. *thee*] reflexive = thyself.

shook my head] not clear, unless it means, as Dover Wilson suggests, that "the wretched groom is grateful for any sign of recognition, even disapproval." Q reads "when I smilde on thee".

59. *crest-fall'n*] humbled; probably punning on (*a*) the plume of feathers on a helmet, (*b*) the tuft on the head of e.g. a hawk, a horse. Cf. "a meagre crestfaln hawk" in Howell's *Vocabulary*, Sect. iv (1659) (Hart).

60. *abortive*] untimely and monstrous.

61. *voiding lobby*] corridor for entrance or exit; waiting-room.

63. *writ . . . behalf*] *scil.* letters of recommendation.

64. *charm*] keep silent, as by an invocation.

riotous] unrestrained.

Whit. Speak, Captain, shall I stab the forlorn swain?
Lieu. First let my words stab him, as he hath me.
Suf. Base slave, thy words are blunt, and so art thou.
Lieu. Convey him hence, and on our long-boat's side
Strike off his head.
Suf. Thou dar'st not for thine own.
Lieu. Poole!
Suf. Poole?
Lieu. Ay, kennel, puddle, sink, whose filth
Troubles the silver spring where England drinks;
Now will I dam up this thy yawning mouth
For swallowing the treasure of the realm.
Thy lips, that kiss'd the Queen, shall sweep the ground;
And thou that smil'dst at good Duke Humphrey's death,
Against the senseless winds shalt grin in vain,
Who in contempt shall hiss at thee again:
And wedded be thou to the hags of hell,

69. thine] *Q; thy F. See n.* 70. *Lieu.* Poole . . . Ay] *Alexander; Cap.* Yes Poull. / *Suffolke.* Poull. / *Cap.* I *Q; Lieu. Poole,* Sir *Poole*? Lord, / I *F; Cap.* Yes, Poole. *Suf.* Poole! *Cap.* Ay, *P. Z. Round.* whose filth] *ASC, conj. Brooks;* and durt *Q;* whose filth and dirt *F.* 76–102.] *F;* Shalt liue no longer to infect the earth. Q.

65. *forlorn*] wretched, unhappy.

swain] (*a*) fellow, (*b*) lover (of the Queen).

66–7. *stab . . . blunt*] note the pun.

69. *thine*] see collation. F probably used "thy" to justify the line.

70. *Poole*] see collation, and Alexander in *Shakespeare Survey,* v (1952), 7–8. Alexander argues that the Q and F readings, which editors usually conflate, are equivalent and alternative, thus:

Q *Cap.* Yes Poull. *Suffolke.* Poull. *Cap.*
F *Lieu.* Poole. *Sir* *Poole*? Lord,

F "Sir" is thus a misprint for *Suf.*, and "Lord" for "*Lieu.*". The compositor was confused by his copy, and should have read as in the text. Punning on (*a*) poll, (*b*) pool, (*c*) Pole, Poole.

kennel] street gutter or open drain. Also "channel". Cf. *2 H 4,* II. i. 52; *Cor.*, III. i. 97; *Ed. 2,* 188.

puddle, sink] from the Homilies, e.g. "he that nameth rebellion . . . nameth the whole *puddle* and *sink* of all sins against God and man" (*Against Disobedience and Wilful Rebellion*); "that most filthy lake, foul puddle, and stinking sink" (*Against Adultery*).

The QF phrase "and dirt" (see collation) is hypermetrical in F; and is not in the Homilies. It is best explained as a phrase for which "whose filth" was meant to be substituted by the corrector, but which was erroneously reproduced in F.

73. *For swallowing . . .*] for fear of its swallowing. See Appendix I (Hall, 217); "wasting of the treasure of . . . the realm" (*Homily against . . . Rebellion*).

the treasure of the realm] Hall, 9, in the charges against Richard II. Cf. III. iii. 2 above.

76. *Against*] exposed to. Cf. *Sonn.*, 73, 3, "those boughs which shake *against* the cold."

senseless] insensible.

grin] grimace.

78. *hags of hell*] the Furies.

For daring to affy a mighty lord
Unto the daughter of a worthless king,
Having neither subject, wealth, nor diadem.
By devilish policy art thou grown great,
And, like ambitious Sylla, overgorg'd
With gobbets of thy mother's bleeding heart.
By thee Anjou and Maine were sold to France,
The false revolting Normans thorough thee
Disdain to call us lord, and Picardy
Hath slain their governors, surpris'd our forts,
And sent the ragged soldiers wounded home.
The princely Warwick, and the Nevils all,
Whose dreadful swords were never drawn in vain,
As hating thee, are rising up in arms:
And now the house of York, thrust from the crown
By shameful murder of a guiltless king,
And lofty proud encroaching tyranny,
Burns with revenging fire; whose hopeful colours
Advance our half-fac'd sun, striving to shine,
Under the which is writ "Invitis nubibus".
The commons here in Kent are up in arms;
And to conclude, reproach and beggary
Is crept into the palace of our King,
And all by thee. Away! convey him hence.

Suf. O! that I were a god, to shoot forth thunder

84. mother's] *Rowe;* Mother- *F.* 92. are] *Rowe;* and *F.*

79. *to affy . . .*] to affiance, betroth. Cf. *Shr.*, IV. iv. 49.

For this and the other accusations against Suffolk, cf. above, e.g. I. i. 108–9.

82. *policy*] in the Machiavellian sense; cf. above, n. to I. i. 83.

83. *Sylla*] Lucius Cornelius Sulla (138–78 B.C.) conducted a civil war against Marius, became dictator, and carried out the first great proscription in Roman history. Rome is thus metaphorically his "mother" and its citizens the "gobbets".

84. *gobbets*] pieces of raw flesh. Cf. *F.Q.*, I. I. 20; Golding's *Ovid*, 6. 815.

thy mother's] England's.

86. *thorough*] through.

87. *Picardy*] source unidentified.

94. *murder . . . guiltless king*] the misfortunes of the House of York are consistently attributed, in Hall and Shakespeare, to the usurpation of Henry IV and the murder of Richard II; cf. e.g. *R 2*, V. i. 55 ff, *2 H 4*, III. i. 70 ff.

97. *Advance*] raise on high.

97, 98. *half-fac'd sun . . . nubibus*] the sunburst, or "rays of the sun dispersing themselves out of a cloud" (Camden) which Edward III had used as a personal badge. Latin unidentified.

101. *palace . . . King*] Cf. *Ps.*, 45. 16 (Sternhold and Hopkins), "brought / . . . Into the palace of the king."

Upon these paltry, servile, abject drudges.
Small things make base men proud: this villain here,
Being captain of a pinnace, threatens more
Than Bargulus, the strong Illyrian pirate.
Drones suck not eagles' blood but rob bee-hives.
It is impossible that I should die
By such a lowly vassal as thyself.
Thy words move rage and not remorse in me.

Lieu. Ay, but my deeds shall stay thy fury soon.

107. Bargulus . . . pirate] *F;* mightie Abradas, / The great Masadonian Pyrate, *Q.* 112. *Lieu.* Ay . . . soon.] *ASC; Cap.* I . . . soone. *Q; om. F. See n.*

104. *drudges*] men in mean service—a term of reproach. Cf. IV. ii. 149.

106. *pinnace*] a ship of small burthen, built for speed.

107. *Bargulus*] from Cicero's *Offices*, 2. 11, a work much studied in Elizabethan schools. Farmer characteristically notes that Shakespeare might have derived the expression from either of two translations—Robert Whytinton, 1533, "Bargulus, a pirate upon the see of Illyry"; or N. Grimoald (*c.* 1553) "Bargulus, the Illyrian robber". Hart notes that the Q equivalent "Abradas" was taken from Greene, who twice uses identical words about him: "Abradas the great Macedonian Pirat thought every one had a letter of mart that bare sayles in ye Ocean" (*Penelope's Web*, Grosart, 5. 197; and *Menaphon*, 6. 77–8); and suggests that this may have been one of the feathers that Shakespeare was accused of plucking; see Introduction, p. xliv, and Greg, *The Shakespeare First Folio*, 184.

108. *Drones . . . eagles' blood*] an ancient piece of mythical natural history. Cf. *Ed. 3*, I. i. 94–5: "like the lazy drone / Crept up by stealth unto the eagle's nest;". Armstrong, *Shakespeare's Imagination*, quotes, "The Beetle is bred of putrid things. . . Though the eagle, its proud and cruel enemy, do make havoc and devour this creature of so mean a rank, yet as soon as it gets an opportunity it returneth like for like. For it flieth up nimbly into her nest . . . and in the absence of the old she-eagle bringeth out of the nest the eagle's eggs one after another, which, falling and being broken, the young ones are deprived of life" (Mouffet, *Theater of Insects*, 1658); and compares Lyly, *Endymion*, 5. 1. 130, "There might I behold Drones, or Beetles, . . . creeping under the winges of a princely Eagle, who being carried into her neast, sought there to sucke that veine, that woulde have killed the Eagle."

Note the antithesis between the "princely" eagle, and the drone or beetle, one of the lowest forms of life; and the image *crept* at 101.

rob bee-hives] another piece of folklore. Cf. *Per.*, II. i. 46–7, "these drones, that rob the bee of her honey"; and George Gascoigne (Arber, 20), 1577, "As the Drone the hony hive doth rob". Probably derived from Pliny, *Nat. Hist.*, 11. 57, "video . . . aliquos existimare, sicut furibus, grandissimis inter illos . . . ita appellatis quia furtim devorant mella."

112. Lieu. . . *soon.*] see collation. This line was probably dropped out (cf. 48 above), and the prefix wrongly attached to 115 (cf. 132), where F "Water: W." is really the speech prefix. Q misplaces 111–12, and, in the transfer to their correct position, the second has been overlooked—a common error in setting up from amended

Suf. I go of message from the Queen to France.
I charge thee waft me safely 'cross the Channel.
Whit. Come, Suffolk, I must waft thee to thy death.
Suf. *Pene gelidus timor occupat artus:*
'Tis thee I fear.
Whit. Thou shalt have cause to fear before I leave thee.
What! are ye daunted now? Now will ye stoop?
1 Gent. My gracious lord, entreat him, speak him fair.
Suf. Suffolk's imperial tongue is stern and rough,
Us'd to command, untaught to plead for favour.
Far be it we should honour such as these
With humble suit: no, rather let my head
Stoop to the block than these knees bow to any
Save to the God of heaven, and to my king;
And sooner dance upon a bloody pole
Than stand uncover'd to the vulgar groom.
True nobility is exempt from fear:
More can I bear than you dare execute.
Lieu. Hale him away, and let him talk no more.
Suf. Come, soldiers, show what cruelty ye can,
That this my death may never be forgot.
Great men oft die by vile bezonians.
A Roman sworder and banditto slave
Murder'd sweet Tully; Brutus' bastard hand

113. *Suf.*] *ASC; om. F.* 115. *Whit.* Come] *ASC; Lieu.* Water: W. Come *F.* 116. *Pene*] *Malone;* Pine *F;* Poenae *Theobald;* Perii! *Wilson, Thomson conj.* 118, 142. *Whit.*] *Wal. F.* 132. *Suf.*] *Hanmer; before line 133 F.*

Q copy: cf. e.g. *H 5*, IV. iii. 48.

113. *of*] expressing the motive of the message; cf. *Wiv.*, I. iv. 69, "He came of an errand".

114. *waft*] used of a sea-passage = convey by water.

115. Whit. *Come*] see 112 n., above.

116.] Possibly a confused and inaccurate recollection of *Æneid*, 7. 446 (cf. 11. 424): "subitus tremor occupat artus" and Lucan, *Pharsalia*, 1. 246: "gelidos pavor occupat artus." Cf. J. A. K. Thomson, *Shakespeare and the Classics*, 89–90.

127. *pole*] cf. the pun at 70 above.

128. *vulgar groom*] base fellow.

131. *Hale*] haul.

132. *show . . . cruelty*] cf. Hardyng, 401, "Hym (Suffolk) slewe and heded with great cruelte . . ."

134. *bezonians*] base fellows, beggars. It. *bisogno*, need. Cf. *2 H 4*, V. iii. 115. See Gascoigne, *Works*, 2. 597, or Pollard, *Tudor Tracts*, 446.

135. *sworder . . . slave*] "i.e. Herennius a centurion, and Popilius Laena, tribune of the soldiers" (Steevens). See Plutarch's *Lives*, Cicero.

136. *Brutus' bastard hand*] "Brutus was popularly credited, in error, with being Julius Caesar's bastard son, owing to the fact that his mother,

Stabb'd Julius Cæsar; savage islanders
Pompey the Great; and Suffolk dies by pirates.
[*Exeunt Whitmore and others with Suffolk.*

Lieu. And as for these whose ransom we have set,
It is our pleasure one of them depart:
Therefore come you with us, and let him go.
[*Exeunt all but the First Gentleman.*

Re-enter WHITMORE, *with* SUFFOLK'S *body.*

Whit. There let his head and lifeless body lie,
Until the Queen his mistress bury it. [*Exit.*

1 Gent. O barbarous and bloody spectacle!
His body will I bear unto the King:
If he revenge it not, yet will his friends;
So will the Queen, that living held him dear.
[*Exit with the body.*

138. S.D. *and others*] *Capell; om. F.* 139–41. And as . . . go] *F; Cap.* Off with his head, and send it to the Queene, / And ransomlesse this prisoner shall go free, / To see it safe deliuered vnto her. / Come lets goe. *Exet omnes. Q.* 141. S.D. *Exeunt . . . body.*] *Capell; Exit Lieutenant, and the rest. Manet the first Gent. Enter Walter with the body. F.* 142–7.] *F; om. Q.* 143. S.D. *Exit.*] *Exit Walter. F.* 147. S.D. *Exit . . .*] *Capell; om. F.*

Servilia, after her lawful husband's death, and his birth, became Caesar's mistress" (Ward). The implication is clear in Plutarch's *Lives*, Brutus.

137–8. *islanders / Pompey*] Pompey was actually killed on reaching the Egyptian coast, by hirelings of King Ptolemy—former centurions of his own—with whom he was seeking asylum. His head was thrown into the sea. In Chapman's *Caesar and Pompey* (pr. 1631), Pompey is murdered on the island of Lesbos (Wilson). But the error may well be due to Plutarch (Brutus), who attributes the incitement of the Egyptians to the murder to "Theodotus, that was born in the *Isle* of Chios"; whence the "islanders".

138. *dies by pirates*] cf. Marlowe, *Massacre*, 1021: "*Guise.* To dye by Pesantes, what a greefe is this?"

139–41.] for the alternative Q passage, see collation. The alteration was possibly due to censorship or vamping; see Introduction, p. xxvii.

142–7.] omitted in Q, as unnecessary and laborious stage-business. There is no need to look for signs of revision in these QF variations, as do e.g. C. A. Greer, *PMLA* (1933), 681 ff and Prouty, *Contention*, 16 ff.

145. *body*] with the head, of course, which he takes to the Queen; cf. IV. iv. 5–6.

SCENE II.—*Blackheath.*

Enter GEORGE BEVIS *and* JOHN HOLLAND.

Bevis. Come, and get thee a sword, though made of a lath: they have been up these two days.

Holland. They have the more need to sleep now then.

Bevis. I tell thee, Jack Cade the clothier means to dress the commonwealth, and turn it, and set a new nap upon it.

Hol. So he had need, for 'tis threadbare. Well, I say it was never merry world in England since gentlemen came up.

Bevis. O miserable age! Virtue is not regarded in handicraftsmen.

Hol. The nobility think scorn to go in leather aprons.

Bevis. Nay, more; the King's Council are no good workmen.

Hol. True; and yet it is said, "Labour in thy vocation": which is as much to say as, "Let the magistrates be labouring men"; and therefore should we be magistrates.

Bevis. Thou hast hit it; for there's no better sign of a brave mind than a hard hand.

Hol. I see them! I see them! There's Best's son, the tanner of Wingham,—

Scene II

Locality.] *Capell.* Entry.] *F* (*om.* George); Enter two of the Rebels with long staues. *Q.* 1, etc. *Bevis.*] *F; George. Q.* 3, etc. *Holland*] *F; Nicke Q.* 21–30.] *F; for Q, see App. 4.*

Bevis, John Holland] Holland was an actor, who appears in the cast of *2 Seven Deadly Sins* (Greg, *Dramatic Documents*) about 1590. Bevis was probably also a minor actor, which is corroborated by the gag preserved in Q at II. iii. 88. It seems probable that Shakespeare used their names here for convenience, or through a slip.

1. *lath*] the weapon carried by the Vice in the old Morality plays.

2. *up*] *scil.* in arms.

8. *merry world*] cf. *Tw. N.*, III. i. 109.

gentlemen] John Ball's theme in the Peasants' Revolt (Hol., 2. 749): "When Adam delu'd, and Eue span / Who was then a gentleman?"

8–9. *came up*] came into fashion.

12. *leather aprons*] worn by mechanics and workmen. Cf. *Caes.*, I. i. 7.

15. *Labour in thy vocation*] from the *Homily against Idleness*, "Apply yourselves, every man in his vocation, to honest labour and business."

22. *Wingham*] a village near Canterbury.

Bevis. He shall have the skins of our enemies to make dog's-leather of.

Hol. And Dick the butcher,—

Bevis. Then is Sin struck down like an ox, and Iniquity's throat cut like a calf.

Hol. And Smith the weaver,—

Bevis. *Argo*, their thread of life is spun.

Hol. Come, come; let's fall in with them.

Drum. Enter CADE, DICK *Butcher*, SMITH *the Weaver, and a Sawyer, with infinite numbers.*

Cade. We John Cade, so term'd of our suppos'd father,—

But. [*Aside*.] Or rather, of stealing a cade of herrings.

Cade. For our enemies shall fall before us, inspir'd with the spirit of putting down kings and princes,—Command silence.

But. Silence!

Cade. My father was a Mortimer,—

But. [*Aside*.] He was an honest man, and a good bricklayer.

Cade. My mother a Plantagenet,—

But. [*Aside*.] I knew her well; she was a midwife.

Cade. My wife descended of the Lacies,—

But. [*Aside*.] She was, indeed, a pedlar's daughter, and sold many laces.

Weaver. [*Aside*.] But not of late, not able to travel with her furr'd pack, she washes bucks here at home.

Cade. Therefore am I of an honourable house.

But. [*Aside*.] Ay, by my faith, the field is honourable, and

30. S.D.] *F;* Enter *Iacke Cade, Dicke Butcher, Robin, Will, Tom, Harry* and the rest, with long staues. *Q*. 32, etc. *Aside*] *Capell*. 33. fall] *F4;* faile *F1–3*.

24. *dog's-leather*] for gloves. Shakespeare's father was a glover.

29. Argo] a corruption of L. *ergo* = therefore.

30. S.D. with infinite numbers] a literary direction, and therefore probably Shakespeare's.

32. *cade*] barrel of 500 herring.

33. *fall*] a pun on Cade—L. *cado*, I fall (Johnson). Note succeeding puns on laces, 44; field, 48; cage, 50, etc.

37. *Mortimer*] cf. III. i. 359.

46. *furr'd pack*] "wallet or knapsack of skin with the hair turned outward" (Johnson).

bucks] quantity of clothes put through the "buck" or lye; hence, quantity washed (Onions).

48. *field*] probably a pun on the heraldic sense (Steevens); "vert plein" was used of the background of an escutcheon; and an allusion to *Heb*.,

there was he born, under a hedge; for his father had never a house but the cage.

Cade. Valiant I am.

Weaver. [*Aside*.] A must needs, for beggary is valiant.

Cade. I am able to endure much.

But. [*Aside*.] No question of that, for I have seen him whipp'd three market-days together.

Cade. I fear neither sword nor fire.

Weaver. [*Aside*.] He need not fear the sword, for his coat is of proof.

But. [*Aside*.] But methinks he should stand in fear of fire, being burnt i' th' hand for stealing of sheep.

Cade. Be brave then; for your captain is brave, and vows reformation. There shall be in England seven halfpenny loaves sold for a penny; the three-hoop'd pot shall have ten hoops; and I will make it felony to drink small beer. All the realm shall be in common, and in Cheapside shall my palfrey go to grass. And when I am king, as king I will be,—

All. God save your Majesty!

Cade. I thank you, good people—there shall be no money; all shall eat and drink on my score, and I will apparel them all in one livery, that they may agree like brothers, and worship me their lord.

But. The first thing we do, let's kill all the lawyers.

55. whipp'd] *Q*, *F* (whipt).

13. 4, "Marriage and the bed undefiled are honourable."

50. *cage*] "Little places of prison, set commonly in the market place, for harlots and vagabonds, we call cages" (Baret). Cf. *AYL.*, III. ii. 389.

52. *valiant*] alluding to the current term "valiant beggar". See Tanner, *Tudor Constitutional Documents*, 479–81.

55. *whipp'd*] as a rogue, vagabond, or offender; cf. II. i. 135 ff above.

58. *of proof*] a quibble on (*a*) reliable, tested, as a coat of mail, (*b*) well-worn.

60. *burnt i' th' hand*] with T for "thief". Cf. Strype, *Annals*, 4. 404, "those that be burnt in the hand, 35" (Calendar of the Assizes, Somerset, 1596).

63. *three-hoop'd pot*] bands were placed at equal intervals on wooden drinking-vessels. "Cade means that for a quart he will get over three quarts, just as for a penny he will get more than three loaves" (Hart).

66. *Cheapside*] as its name implies (*O.E. ceap*—buying and selling), the chief market centre of London, a street leading from St Paul's Churchyard on the west, to the Poultry on the east.

73. *lawyers*] "destroie first the great lords of the realme, and after the iudges and lawiers" (Hol., 2. 740).

Cade. Nay, that I mean to do. Is not this a lamentable thing, that of the skin of an innocent lamb should be made parchment? that parchment, being scribbled o'er, should undo a man? Some say the bee stings; but I say, 'tis the bee's wax, for I did but seal once to a thing, and I was never mine own man since. How now! Who's there?

Enter some, bringing forward the Clerk of Chartham.

Wea. The clerk of Chartham: he can write and read and cast accompt.

Cade. O monstrous!

Wea. We took him setting of boys' copies.

Cade. Here's a villain!

Wea. H'as a book in his pocket with red letters in 't.

Cade. Nay, then he is a conjurer.

But. Nay, he can make obligations, and write courthand.

Cade. I am sorry for 't. The man is a proper man, of mine honour; unless I find him guilty, he shall not die. Come hither, sirrah, I must examine thee. What is thy name?

Clerk. Emmanuel.

But. They use to write it on the top of letters. 'Twill go hard with you.

Cade. Let me alone. Dost thou use to write thy name? Or

76. that] *F;* that that *J. C. Maxwell conj.* 80. S.D. *Enter . . .*] *Capell; Enter a Clearke. F;* Enter Will with the Clarke of Chattam. *Q.* *Chartham*] Chartam *F* (*81*); Chattam *Q.* 86. H'as] *Rowe;* Ha's *F;* hee has *Q;* Has *Dyce;* He'as *Pope.*

79. *mine own man*] my own master. Hart quotes Nares, "He is his owne man; he liveth as he list; he is under no man's controlment."

81. *Chartham*] near Canterbury, on the road to Ashford.

84. *boys' copies*] "One of the standard words to practise letters on was till a recent date Emmanuel" (Hart).

86. *a book . . . with red letters*] probably a copy of the *Primer*, used in schools, and having capitals in red.

88. *make obligations*] draw up bonds. *courthand*] "Used in the law-courts till George II, when it was abolished by statute." (Craig). This is the hand in which scriveners would engross bonds. Dapper, the lawyer's clerk in Jonson's *Alchemist*, I. I, says, "By this hand of flesh, / Would it might never write good court-hand more . . ."

93. *Emmanuel*] "formerly prefixed to letters, deeds, etc., to convey the impression of piety" = "God with us" (Hart). Cf. 84 n. above.

hast thou a mark to thyself, like an honest plain-dealing man?

Clerk. Sir, I thank God I have been so well brought up that I can write my name.

All. He hath confess'd: away with him! he's a villain and a traitor.

Cade. Away with him, I say: hang him with his pen and ink-horn about his neck. [*Exit one with the Clerk.*

Enter MICHAEL.

Mich. Where's our general?

Cade. Here I am, thou particular fellow.

Mich. Fly, fly, fly! Sir Humphrey Stafford and his brother are hard by, with the King's forces.

Cade. Stand, villain, stand, or I'll fell thee down. He shall be encount'red with a man as good as himself. He is but a knight, is a?

Mich. No.

Cade. To equal him, I will make myself a knight presently. [*Kneels.*] Rise up Sir John Mortimer. [*Rises.*] Now have at him!

Enter Sir HUMPHREY STAFFORD, *and his brother, with drum and soldiers.*

Staf. Rebellious hinds, the filth and scum of Kent,
Mark'd for the gallows, lay your weapons down;
Home to your cottages, forsake this groom:

97. an] *F2–4;* a *F1.* 104. S.D. Michael] *F;* Tom *Q.* 113–15.] *F* (*subst.*); *for Q, see App. 4.* 114. S.D. *Kneels.*] *Collier + edd.* *Rises.*] *Dyce + edd.* 115. S.D.] *Q, F* (*subst.*).

103–4. *pen and ink-horn*] among the rebels in 1381 "it was dangerous . . . to be knowne for one that was lerned, and more dangerous, if any man were found with a penner and inkhorne at his side: for such seldome escaped from them with life" (Hol., 2. 746).

106. *particular*] private, punning on "general".

112. *No*] answering the negative implied in "but"; cf. *OED.*, "but", 6a = northern dialect "nobbut".

113. *presently*] usual Elizabethan sense = immediately.

115. S.D. Stafford] for source, see Appendix 1.

117. *Mark'd for the gallows*] cf. *Tp.*, I. i. 31, "He hath no drowning mark upon him: his complexion is perfect gallows."

The King is merciful, if you revolt.
Bro. But angry, wrathful, and inclin'd to blood,
If you go forward: therefore yield, or die.
Cade. As for these silken-coated slaves, I pass not:
It is to you, good people, that I speak,
Over whom, in time to come, I hope to reign;
For I am rightful heir unto the crown.
Staf. Villain! thy father was a plasterer;
And thou thyself a shearman, art thou not?
Cade. And Adam was a gardener.
Bro. What of that?
Cade. Marry, this: Edmund Mortimer, Earl of March,
Married the Duke of Clarence' daughter, did he not?
Staf. Ay, sir.
Cade. By her he had two children at one birth.
Bro. That's false.
Cade. Ay, there's the question; but I say, 'tis true.
The elder of them, being put to nurse,
Was by a beggar-woman stol'n away;
And, ignorant of his birth and parentage,
Became a bricklayer when he came to age:
His son am I; deny it if you can.
But. Nay, 'tis too true; therefore he shall be king.
Wea. Sir, he made a chimney in my father's house, and the bricks are alive at this day to testify; therefore deny it not.

128. What] *ASC;* And what *F.* 129. Marry, this:] Marry, this *F.* 142. testify] *Q1, 2;* testify it *Q3, F.*

119. *revolt*] in the literal sense of "return", "turn again". Cf. Cotgrave, s.v. "revolter"—to return, make a new turn; and Golding's *Ovid*, 10, 68, "And then revolted to the place in which he had her found" (Hart).

122. *silken-coated*] "in allusion to their emblazoned surcoats" (French, 166).

I pass not] I care not. Cf. *Ed. 2*, 438, "I pass not for their anger." *Lyly*, 3. 589, suggests an explanation from the sense of "budge", "stir", "be altered or affected by".

127. *shearman*] one who shears the nap from cloth in its final stages of manufacture; cf. 5–6 above. "The Shermen were one of the gilds who acted in the *Chester Plays*" (Hart).

128. *Adam . . . gardener*] cf. IV. ii. 8, and *Ham.*, V. i. 308.

140. *he shall be king*] "we would have created kings, as Wat Tiler in Kent, and other in other countries" (Hol., 2. 751).

142. *bricks . . . alive . . . testify*] cf. *Gesta Romanorum* (tr. Swan, 1877), 306, "the lady, borne along by a diabolical spirit, flew away, carrying along with her a portion of the chapel

Staf. And will you credit this base drudge's words,
That speaks he knows not what?
All. Ay, marry, will we; therefore get ye gone.
Bro. Jack Cade, the Duke of York hath taught you this.
Cade. [*Aside.*] He lies, for I invented it myself.—
Go to, sirrah, tell the King from me, that for his father's sake, Henry the Fifth, in whose time boys went to span-counter for French crowns, I am content he shall reign; but I'll be Protector over him.

But. And furthermore, we'll have the Lord Say's head for selling the dukedom of Maine.

Cade. And good reason; for thereby is England main'd and fain to go with a staff, but that my puissance holds it up. Fellow kings, I tell you that that Lord Say hath gelded the commonwealth and made it an eunuch; and more than that, he can speak French; and therefore he is a traitor.

Staf. O gross and miserable ignorance!

Cade. Nay, answer if you can: the Frenchmen are our enemies; go to then, I ask but this: can he that speaks with the tongue of an enemy be a good counsellor, or no?

All. No, no; and therefore we'll have his head.

155. main'd] *F;* maimde *Q.* 157. kings] *F;* knight *Vaughan conj.* 166–8. *All.* No . . . King.] *F; for Q, see App. 4.*

. . . and part of the very tower is yet standing, in testimony . . ." Hart compares Ovid, *Metam.* (tr. Golding), 8. 902–5.

testify] see collation; *it* was probably adopted by F from Q3 copy. In Q3, *it* is missing from 140 (twas Q1, 2; was Q3; 'tis F) whence it has probably been imported in Q3, 142.

144. *drudge*] mean fellow: a term of contempt.

151. *span-counter*] played with marbles or counters thrown to come within a span of the opponents'.

French crowns] a favourite Elizabethan pun on the crown of the head, and the baldness produced by "the French disease", and, of course, the coin.

153–4. *Say . . . Maine*] see Hall, 217 and 219 (Appendix 1).

155. *main'd*] another pun. "An accepted early spelling of 'maimed'. Malone quotes Daniel's *Civil Wars*, 1595, 'Aniou and Maine, the maim that foul appears' " (Hart).

157. *Fellow kings*] from *2 Tamb.*, 2720, "Loving friends and fellow-kings". Cf. 140 n. above.

158. *gelded the commonwealth*] from Cicero, *De Oratore*, 3. 41, quoted in Talaeus's *Rhetorica* (then used in schools), "Nolo dici morte Africani castratam esse rem publicam" (Anders, 38). Generally condemned as an offence against the Renascence ideal of "decorum", but probably meant to fit Cade. But cf. *R 2*, II. i. 237.

Bro. Well, seeing gentle words will not prevail,
Assail them with the army of the King.
Staf. Herald, away; and throughout every town
Proclaim them traitors that are up with Cade;
That those which fly before the battle ends
May, even in their wives' and children's sight,
Be hang'd up for example at their doors.
And you that be the King's friends, follow me.
[*Exeunt the two Staffords and Forces.*
Cade. And you that love the commons, follow me.
Now show yourselves men; 'tis for liberty.
We will not leave one lord, one gentleman:
Spare none but such as go in clouted shoon,
For they are thrifty honest men, and such
As would, but that they dare not, take our parts.
But. They are all in order, and march toward us.
Cade. But then are we in order when we are most out of order. Come: march forward! [*Exeunt.*

SCENE III.—*Another Part of Blackheath.*

Alarums to the fight, wherein both the STAFFORDS *are slain. Enter* CADE *and the rest.*

Cade. Where's Dick, the butcher of Ashford?
But. Here, sir.
Cade. They fell before thee like sheep and oxen, and thou behaved'st thyself as if thou hadst been in thine own

174. S.D. *Exeunt . . .*] *edd.; Exit. F; Exet Stafford* and his men. *Q.* 183. S.D. *Exeunt.*] *om. F.*

Scene III

Locality.] *edd.* Entry.] *F;* Alarums to the battaile, and (where *Q3*) sir *Humphrey Stafford* and his brother is slaine (brother are both slaine. *Q3*). Then enter (enters *Q3; om. Q2*) Iacke Cade againe and the rest. *Q.*

177. *gentleman*] cf. n. to 128 above, and IV. ii. 8.

178. *clouted*] hobnailed. "Clouted shoon" came to be a name for boors and country bumpkins; cf. Greene, *Quippe* (Grosart, 10, 237), "An up-start, *quasi* start up from clouted shoon" (Hart).

182–3. *in order . . . out of order*] a favourite Shakespearean paradox; cf. *Rom.*, I. i. 125, "most sought where most might not be found."

slaughter-house. Therefore thus will I reward thee—the Lent shall be as long again as it is; thou shalt have licence to kill for a hundred lacking one.

But. I desire no more.

Cade. And, to speak truth, thou deserv'st no less. [*He puts on Sir Humphrey's armour.*] This monument of the victory will I bear; and the bodies shall be dragg'd at my horse heels till I do come to London, where we will have the mayor's sword borne before us.

But. If we mean to thrive and do good, break open the gaols and let out the prisoners.

Cade. Fear not that, I warrant thee. Come; let's march towards London. [*Exeunt.*

6. thou] *Q1, 2;* and thou *Q3, F.* 7. licence] *Q;* a License *F.* one] *F;* one a week *Q, Malone. See n.* 9–10. S.D. *He . . . armour.*] *edd.* (*subst.*), *from the Chronicles; om. Q, F.* 16–17.] *F; for Q, see App. 4.*

6. *thou*] see collation; "and" was probably adopted by F from Q3.

7. *licence to kill*] Butchers were forbidden to kill meat during Lent (in Elizabeth's reign), excepting by special licence for a certain number each week for those who could not do without animal food (Malone). Cf. Strype, *Whitgift*, 2. 456.

The restriction had the aims and advantages of economizing in meat, encouraging the fisheries, and maintaining the numbers of ships, seamen, and port facilities, as a reservoir for the navy.

lacking one] as in the usual term of a lease, e.g. 99 years. Omission of Q "a week" must be due to the corrector.

10. *This monument*] Hart suggests, with probability, that this refers specially to Sir Humphrey Stafford's helmet, or salade, and points to the pun in "sallet" at IV. x. 10. He quotes Fabyan, 623, "And as soon as Iak Cade had thus over comyn the Staffordes, he anone apparaylled hȳ with the Knyghtes apparyll, and dyd on hym his briganders set with gylt nayle, and his salet and gylt sporys."

11–12. *at my horse heels*] a suggestion of Achilles and Hector?

14. *do good*] succeed, prosper; cf. *Wint.*, II. ii. 54.

15. *gaols . . . prisoners*] see Appendix 1 (Hall, 222); and Hol., 2. 737 ff for details taken from the Peasants' Revolt of 1381.

16. *Fear not that*] don't be alarmed; that will be done. Cf. *Caes.*, II. i. 202, "Never fear that."

I warrant thee] I'll guarantee it.

SCENE IV.—*London. The palace.*

Enter the KING *with a supplication, and the* QUEEN *with* SUFFOLK'S *head, the Duke of* BUCKINGHAM, *and the Lord* SAY.

Queen. [*Aside.*] Oft have I heard that grief softens the mind,
And makes it fearful and degenerate;
Think therefore on revenge, and cease to weep.
But who can cease to weep and look on this?
Here may his head lie on my throbbing breast;
But where's the body that I should embrace?
Buck. What answer makes your Grace to the rebels' supplication?
King. I'll send some holy bishop to entreat;
For God forbid so many simple souls
Should perish by the sword! And I myself,
Rather than bloody war shall cut them short,
Will parley with Jack Cade their general.
But stay, I'll read it over once again.
Queen. [*Aside.*] Ah! barbarous villains! hath this lovely face
Rul'd like a wandering planet over me,

Scene IV

Locality.] *Capell + Camb.* Entry.] *F;* Enter the King reading of a Letter, and the Queene, with the Duke of *Suffolkes* head, and the Lord *Say,* with others. *Q.* 1, 15, 55. *Aside.*] *Collier; om. Q, F.*

This action follows, but without the necessary adjustment, from the end of IV. i, the alteration of which (see Introduction, p. xxvii, and IV. i. 142–3) has left an "inconsistency" regarding the fate of Suffolk's head and body. But since IV. i. 142–3 were probably cut in performance (they are not in Q), no inconsistency would appear, or at least adjustment would not seem necessary.

2. *fearful*] full of fear.

3. *revenge*] the first statement of the revenge motif which is later to dominate the part of Margaret.

5. *throbbing*] *scil.* with grief; "with passionate desire" (Partridge, *Shakespeare's Bawdy*).

7–8.] This speech is probably misprinted for two lines of blank verse, the second reading "Unto . . . supplication".

supplication] Hall, 220.

9. *some holy bishop*] another "inconsistency". The bishop is in the Chronicles (Hall, 226). If a bishop was one of the original envoys to the rebels, he has probably been replaced by Buckingham, whose name fits badly into some of the later blank verse. The reference had probably been cut (cf. head-note) and there would thus be no inconsistency on the stage.

11. *perish by the sword*] *Job*, 33. 18; 36, 12; *Matt.*, 26, 52. Cf. *1 Tamb.*, 1566, "perish by our swords".

12. *cut them short*] pun, as at III. i. 81 above; cf. *2 Kings*, 10. 32.

16. *Rul'd like a wandering planet*] a

And could it not enforce them to relent,
That were unworthy to behold the same?
King. Lord Say, Jack Cade hath sworn to have thy head.
Say. Ay, but I hope your Highness shall have his.
King. How, madam! Still lamenting Suffolk's death?
I fear me, love, if that I had been dead,
Thou wouldest not have mourn'd so much for me.
Queen. My love; I should not mourn, but die for thee.

Enter a Messenger.

King. How now! What news? Why com'st thou in such haste?
Mess. The rebels are in Southwark; fly, my lord!
Jack Cade proclaims himself Lord Mortimer,
Descended from the Duke of Clarence' house,
And calls your Grace usurper, openly
And vows to crown himself in Westminster.
His army is a ragged multitude
Of hinds and peasants, rude and merciless:
Sir Humphrey Stafford and his brother's death
Hath given them heart and courage to proceed.
All scholars, lawyers, courtiers, gentlemen,
They call false caterpillars, and intend their death.
King. O graceless men! they know not what they do.
Buck. My gracious lord, retire to Killingworth,
Until a power be rais'd to put them down.

21–4.] *as verse F; as prose Q.* 21–2.] *ASC; King*. How now, Madam? / Still lamenting and mourning for Suffolkes death? / I feare me (Loue) if that I had beene dead, *Q* (*subst., as prose, reading* my loue), *F. See n.* 23. wouldest] *Theobald;* would'st *F, Q* (*subst.*); woldst *Q3.* 24. My loue] *ASC;* No my loue *Q, F.* 24. S.D.] *Q, F.*

relic of astrology, according to which the star in the ascendant ruled the fortunes of those born under it. Cf. *1 Tamb.*, 874.

21–4.] The text has been contaminated by use of Q "copy". See collation. The QF words now omitted are common memorial intrusions, or suggested by the passage itself.

31–2. *multitude . . . rude*] Hall, 230, "a multitude of euil rude . . . persones".

36. *caterpillars*] "oppressors . . . flatterers, suckers of his purse and robbers of his subiects" (Hall, 220). A pun on "pillars" and "pillers" (robbers). Cf. *R 2*, II. iii. 166, "caterpillars of the commonwealth".

37. *graceless . . . do*] characteristic of Henry's religious cast of mind and expression. Cf. *Luke* 23. 34.

38. *Killingworth*] Kenilworth.

39. *power*] army.

Queen. Ah, were the Duke of Suffolk now alive,
These Kentish rebels would be soon appeas'd!
King. Lord Say, the traitors hateth thee,
Therefore away with us to Killingworth.
Say. So might your Grace's person be in danger.
The sight of me is odious in their eyes;
And therefore in this city will I stay,
And live alone as secret as I may.

Enter another Messenger.

2 Mess. Jack Cade hath almost gotten London Bridge;
The citizens fly and forsake their houses;
The rascal people, thirsting after prey,
Join with the traitor; and they jointly swear
To spoil the city and your royal court.
Buck. Then linger not, my lord; away! take horse.
King. Come, Margaret: God, our hope, will succour us.
Queen. [*Aside.*] My hope is gone, now Suffolk is deceas'd.
King. Farewell, my lord: trust not the Kentish rebels.
Buck. Trust nobody, for fear you be betray'd.
Say. The trust I have is in mine innocence,
And therefore am I bold and resolute. [*Exeunt.*

SCENE V.—*London. The Tower.*

Enter Lord SCALES *upon the Tower, walking. Then enter two or three Citizens below.*

Scales. How now! Is Jack Cade slain?

48. almost] *Q; om. F.* 57. be betray'd] *F2;* betraid *F1.*

Scene v

Locality.] *edd.* Entry.] *F;* Enter the Lord *Skayles* (*Lord Scayles Q2; Sord Skayles Q3*) vpon the Tower walles walking. *Q;* Enter three or foure Citizens below. *Q1, 2; om. Q3.*

42. *hateth*] for his part in the surrender of Anjou and Maine, cf. IV. ii. 154 above.

50. *rascal people*] Hall, 29.

58–9.] Cf. Gloucester at II. iv. 59–63.

Scene v

The text was set up from Q, slightly amended. Hence prose printed as verse, similarly divided in Q and F. See Introduction, pp. xxx–xxxi.

1 Cit. No, my lord, nor likely to be slain; for they have won the bridge, killing all those that withstand them. The Lord Mayor craves aid of your Honour from the Tower to defend the city from the rebels.

Scales. Such aid as I can spare you shall command;
But I am troubled here with them myself;
The rebels have assay'd to win the Tower.
But get you to Smithfield and gather head,
And thither I will send you Matthew Goffe;
Fight for your king, your country, and your lives;
And so farewell, for I must hence again. [*Exeunt.*

SCENE VI.—*London. Cannon Street.*

Enter JACK CADE *and the rest, and strikes his staff on London Stone.*

Cade. Now is Mortimer lord of this city. And here, sitting upon London Stone, I charge and command that, of the city's cost, the pissing-conduit run nothing but

2–5.] *Q, F, as verse, divided* . . . slaine, / . . . bridge, / . . . them. / . . . Tower, / . . . Rebels. 8. assay'd] *F;* attempted *Q.* 9. But get . . . and] *Q,F;* Get . . . and there *ASC conj.* 10. I will] *Q1, 2, F;* will I *Q3.*

Scene VI

Locality.] *Theobald* + *edd.* Entry.] *F* (*Enter . . . staffe* on . . . London stone.); Enter . . . sword vpon . . . London stone. *Q.* 1–6.] *Q, F as verse, similarly divided. See Introduction, pp. xxx–xxxi.*

Source: Hall, 221 (Appendix 1).

S.D. Lord *Scales* . . . Tower] Hall, 221. Scales was left behind to "kepe the Towre", when the King went to Kenilworth; he was not Constable or Governor of the Tower, as usually described. See French, 163.

Tower] i.e. the upper stage.

9. *gather head*] collect their forces.

Scene VI

Set up from amended Q, like IV. v.

S.D. staff] only a sword is mentioned in the Chronicles; cf. IV. x. 1, 55. This is probably not an error, as Wilson thinks, since both staff and sword are present in Q, though transposed. Note the "long staves" of the rebels in the Q S.DD. at IV. ii. 1 and 30.

London Stone] Hall, 221 (Appendix 1). A rounded block of stone in Cannon Street. "Portions of it, having been built into the street wall of St Swithin's Church, still survive" (Ward). See also French, 174; Sugden, 317.

2. *charge and command*] Hall, 232.

3. *pissing-conduit*] Hart quotes Stow, "The little Conduite called the *pissing Conduite*, by the Stokes Market"; and refers to Steevens's note, illustrating are expression from French historical

claret wine this first year of our reign. And now henceforward it shall be treason for any that calls me other than Lord Mortimer.

Enter a Soldier, running.

Sold. Jack Cade! Jack Cade!

Cade. Knock him down there. [*They kill him.*

But. If this fellow be wise, he'll never call ye Jack Cade more: I think he hath a very fair warning. My lord, there's an army gathered together in Smithfield.

Cade. Come then, let's go fight with them. But first, go and set London bridge afire, and, if you can, burn down the Tower too. Come, let's away. [*Exeunt.*

SCENE VII.—*London. Smithfield.*

Alarums. MATTHEW GOFFE *is slain, and all the rest. Then enter* JACK CADE, *with his company.*

Cade. So, sirs. Now go some and pull down the Savoy;

6. S.D. *running.*] *F; om. Q.* 8. S.D. *They kill him.*] *Q, F.* 9–11.] *F* (*But.* If ... warning. *Dicke.* My Lord, ... Smithfield.)*; Dicke.* My Lord, ... Smythfield. *Q.* 12–14.] *Q, F as verse, divided* ... them: / ... fire, / ... too. / ... away. 12. go] *F;* go on *Q.* 13. afire] *Q1, 3;* on fire *Q2, F.* 14. S.D. *Exeunt.*] *edd.; Exeunt omnes. Q2, F; Exet omnes. Q1; Exit omnes. Q3.*

Scene VII

Locality.] *Theobald + edd.* Entry.] *F;* Alarmes, and then *Mathew* ... rest with him. Then ... *Cade* again, and his ... *Q.* 1–2.] *Q, F as verse, divided* ... Sauoy: / ... all.

records, date 1453. A place from which the lower classes fetched water. See Sugden, 127–8.

9–11.] see collation: F insertion of a duplicate speech-prefix is another sign of setting up from amended Q copy. See Introduction, p. xxxv.

11. *Smithfield*] "a place called Smithfield, whereas every Friday there is a market of horses" (Froissart, 258).

13. *set London bridge afire*] the bridge and the houses built along each side of it were then built of wood.

afire] see collation: Q2, followed by F, reads "*on* fire"; the Q2 variation being probably due to the previous "on" in line 12 (see collation).

Scene VII

Set up from amended Q as far as line 4.

1, 2. *Savoy* ... *Inns of Court*] probably from Fabyan's account (530) of

others to the Inns of Court: down with them all.

But. I have a suit unto your lordship.

Cade. Be it a lordship, thou shalt have it for that word.

But. Only that the laws of England may come out of your mouth.

Hol. [*Aside.*] Mass, 'twill be sore law then; for he was thrust in the mouth with a spear, and 'tis not whole yet.

Wea. [*Aside.*] Nay, John, it will be stinking law; for his breath stinks with eating toasted cheese.

Cade. I have thought upon it; it shall be so. Away! burn all the records of the realm; my mouth shall be the parliament of England.

Hol. [*Aside.*] Then we are like to have biting statutes, unless his teeth be pull'd out.

Cade. And henceforward all things shall be in common.

Enter a Messenger.

Mess. My lord, a prize, a prize! here's the Lord Say, which sold the towns in France; he that made us pay

7, 15. *Hol.*] *Camb.; Iohn F.* 7, 10, 15. *Aside.*] *Capell; om. Q, F.* 10. *Wea.*] *ASC; Smith. F.* 15–16.] *F, as verse, divided* . . . Statutes / . . . out.

the 1381 rising (Holinshed does not mention the Inns of Court): "They . . . came vnto ye Duke of Lancasters place standyng without ye Temple Barre, callyd *Savoy*, & spoylyd yt was therin, & after set it vpon fyre & brent it; . . . Than they entryd the cytie & serchid the Temple and other innes of court, & spoylyd theyr placys & brent theyr bokys of lawe, & slewe as many men of lawe & questmongers as they myght fynde; & that done they went to Seynt Martyns ye Graunde, & toke with them all seyntwary men, & the prysons of Newgate, Ludgate, & of bothe Counters, & distroyed theyr registers & bokis, & in lyke maner they dyd with the prysoners of the Marshalse & Kynges Benche in Southwerke." The leaders are named as 'Iacke Strawe, Wyl Wawe, Watte Tyler, Iacke Shepeherde, Tomme Myller, and Hobbe Carter." The *Contention* gives a Will and a Tom (Hart).

The reference to the Savoy is here anachronistic, since it was destroyed by Wat Tyler, and not rebuilt till 1505.

1–2.] see collation; prose identically divided as verse in Q and F, evidence of F use of Q copy.

5–6. *laws . . . mouth*] "putting his (Tyler's) hands to his lips, that within foure daies all the lawes of England should come foorth of his mouth" (Hol., 2. 740).

13. *records*] see n. to 1 above (Fabyan, 530; Hol., 2. 737, 738, 746). Wilson (unaccountably) says Holinshed does not mention records.

15. *biting*] severe.

18. *Say*] Hall, 219, 221 (Appendix 1).

one-and-twenty fifteens, and one shilling to the pound, the last subsidy.

Enter GEORGE, *with the Lord* SAY.

Cade. Well, he shall be beheaded for it ten times. Ah, thou say, thou serge, nay, thou buckram lord! now art thou within point-blank of our jurisdiction regal. What canst thou answer to my Majesty for giving up of Normandy unto Mounsieur Basimecu, the Dauphin of France? Be it known unto thee by these presence, even the presence of Lord Mortimer, that I am the besom that must sweep the court clean of such filth as thou art. Thou hast most traitorously corrupted the youth of the realm in erecting a grammar-school; and whereas, before, our forefathers had no other books but the score and the tally, thou hast caus'd printing to be us'd; and contrary to the King

23. serge] *Rowe;* Surge *F;* George *Q.*

20. *one-and-twenty fifteens*] a humorous exaggeration. Cf. Hall, 220.

21. *subsidy*] special assessment for the Queen's supply.

George] generally taken to refer to Bevis; cf. IV. ii. 1.

23. *say*] a kind of silk cloth resembling serge. Another pun.

buckram] the end of the anticlimax. Coarse linen cloth stiffened with glue (Schmidt). Used for making bags, curtains, giants for the stage (Hart).

24. *point-blank*] *scil.* range, reach (from gunnery).

26. *Basimecu*] *bus mine cue* (Q). "In reference to the Dauphin's fawning manners, *Basimecu* constitutes a pun on *baise mon cul*, 'kiss my backside!'" (Partridge).

27–8. *Be it known . . . presence*] the usual phrase for opening a declaration or bond; cf. "Noverint omnes per presentes", *AYL.*, I. ii. 132.

29. *besom*] brush, broom. "and I will sweep it with the besom of destruction" (*Isaiah*, 14. 23).

30–1. *corrupted the youth*] the accusation made against Socrates and his teaching.

31–2. *grammar-school*] Hol., 2. 746, says that in 1381 the rebels obliged "teachers of children in *grammer schooles* to sweare neuer to instruct any in their art".

33. *score . . . tally*] a stick with transverse notches or scores to mark accounts of moneys lent, etc. When split lengthwise, one half was kept by the debtor, the other by the creditor. The halves should thus correspond, or tally.

34. *printing*] an anachronism.

34–5. *King . . . crown . . . dignity*] a standard legal phrase; cf. the submission of John Udal (Strype, *Annals*, 4. 36), "a certain book . . . wherein false, slanderous and seditious matters are contained against her majesty's prerogative royal, her crown and dignity." Cf. Marlowe, *Massacre*, 561–2; *Err.*, I. ii. 144; Hall, 12.

his crown, and dignity, thou hast built a paper-mill. It will be prov'd to thy face that thou hast men about thee that usually talk of a noun, and a verb, and such abominable words as no Christian ear can endure to hear. Thou hast appointed justices of peace, to call poor men before them about matters they were not able to answer. Moreover, thou hast put them in prison; and because they could not read, thou hast hang'd them; when, indeed, only for that cause they have been most worthy to live. Thou dost ride in a foot-cloth, dost thou not?

Say. What of that?

Cade. Marry, thou ought'st not to let thy horse wear a cloak, when honester men than thou go in their hose and doublets.

But. And work in their shirt too; as myself, for example, that am a butcher.

Say. You men of Kent—

But. What say you of Kent?

Say. Nothing but this: 'tis "bona terra, mala gens."

Cade. Away with him! away with him! he speaks Latin.

Say. Hear me but speak, and bear me where you will.
Kent, in the Commentaries Cæsar writ,

39. of] *Q1, 2, F;* of the *Q3.* 50, 53, 87, 120. *But.*] *Dicke F* (*Dicke, Dic.*). 54–5. terra . . . Latin.] *Cade.* Bonum terrum, sounds whats that? / *Dicke.* He speaks French. / *Will.* No tis Dutch. / *Nicke.* No tis outtalian, I know it well inough. *Q.*

35. *paper-mill*] another anachronism. "In 1588 Thomas Churchyard published *A Sparke of Friendship and Warme Good-will* . . . with a description and commendation of a Paper-Mill, now and of late set up (neere the Town of Darthford) by an High Germayn, called M. Spilman, Jeweller to the Qu. most excellent Majestie" (Hart).

42. *could not read*] that is, were not entitled to "benefit of clergy". Prisoners who could say their "neck-verse" (in Latin) could claim exemption from hanging and other penalties, as did e.g. Ben Jonson.

45. *foot-cloth*] cf. n. at IV. i. 54. Often made of velvet, and embroidered with gold lace, and thus specially obnoxious to Cade and his followers.

52–4. *Kent . . . gens.*] Cf. Andrew Borde, *The First Booke of the Introduction of Knowledge* (*c.* 1548), I. ii, "The Italyen and the Lombarde say *Anglia terra bona terra, mala gent* [sic]."

57–8. *Kent . . . place*] "Ex his omnibus sunt humanissimi qui Cantium incolunt" (*Commentaries*, bk. 5). Translated by Golding (1565), and quoted by Lyly, *Euphues* (1580), 2. 32. 17, 18, in the form: "Of all the inhabitants of this isle the civilest are the Kentish-

Is term'd the civil'st place of all this isle:
Sweet is the country, because full of riches;
The people liberal, valiant, active, wealthy;
Which makes me hope you are not void of pity.
I sold not Maine, I lost not Normandy;
Yet, to recover them, would lose my life.
Justice with favour have I always done;
Prayers and tears have mov'd me, gifts could never.
When have I aught exacted at your hands,
But to maintain the King, the realm, and you?
Large gifts have I bestow'd on learned clerks,
Because my book preferr'd me to the King,
And seeing ignorance is the curse of God,
Knowledge the wing wherewith we fly to heaven,
Unless you be possess'd with devilish spirits,
You cannot but forbear to murder me:
This tongue hath parley'd unto foreign kings
For your behoof,—

Cade. Tut, when struck'st thou one blow in the field?

Say. Great men have reaching hands: oft have I struck

59. because] *F; om. Q;* beauteous, *Hanmer;* bounteous, *Vaughan conj.;* pleasant, *Kinnear conj.;* plenteous, *ASC conj. See n.* 60. wealthy] *F;* worthy *Hanmer.* 66–7. hands, / But] *Rann* (*Johnson conj.*); hands? / Kent *F.* 76. Tut] *F;* Tut, tut *Hanmer.* struck'st] *F;* struckest *Dyce.*

folke" (Lyly—"Kentishmen"). Cf. *3 H 6*, I. ii. 41–3.

59. *because*] see collation. An adjective seems required to complete the series and balance that of l. 60. Allowing for the carelessness of compositor B, and the writing of "en" as "ẽ", I suggest "plenteous"="possessing or having abundance; abundantly provided or supplied; rich". Prynne, *Sov. Power Parl.*, 2. 55, "It had beene long evill ruled by evill Officers, so that the Land could not be *plenteous* neither with Merchandize, chaffer, nor riches" (*OED.*). Cf. Fabyan, 10, "Brute . . . serched the lande [Albyon] ouer all, & founde it full fertyle & *plenteous* of wode & of grasse, & granysshed with many fayre Ryuers & stremes." Cf. *Lr.*, I. i. 64.

61. *void*] devoid; cf. *Mer. V.*, IV. i. 5.

66–7. *exacted . . . you?*] Say was Lord Treasurer in 1449.

68. *clerks*] scholars, learned men (L. *clericus*).

69. *book*] learning.

preferr'd] recommended for promotion, brought to notice. Cf. *Ed. 2*, 734.

72. *possess'd with devilish spirits*] cf. *Mark*, I. 32, "them that were possessed with devils".

77. *Great men . . . reaching hands*] a paraphrase of the classical proverb "Kings have long hands". See e.g. Ovid, *Her.*, 17. 166, "An nescis longas regibus esse manus?"; and Lyly, *Euphues*, I. 221. Cf. *Ham.*, II. i. 64, "we . . . of reach".

Those that I never saw, and struck them dead.
Geo. O monstrous coward! What, to come behind folks!
Say. These cheeks are pale with watching for your good.
Cade. Give him a box o' th' ear, and that will make 'em red again.
Say. Long sitting, to determine poor men's causes,
Hath made me full of sickness and diseases.
Cade. Ye shall have a hempen caudle then, and pap with a hatchet.
But. Why dost thou quiver, man?
Say. The palsy, and not fear, provokes me.
Cade. Nay, he nods at us; as who should say, "I'll be even with you": I'll see if his head will stand steadier on a pole or no. Take him away and behead him.
Say. Tell me: wherein have I offended most?
Have I affected wealth or honour? speak.
Are my chests fill'd up with extorted gold?
Is my apparel sumptuous to behold?
Whom have I injur'd, that ye seek my death?
These hands are free from guiltless blood-shedding,
This breast from harbouring foul deceitful thoughts.
O! let me live.
Cade. [*Aside.*] I feel remorse in myself with his words; but I'll bridle it: he shall die, and it be but for pleading so well for his life. Away with him! he has a familiar

80. with] *F2–4;* for *F1.* 85. caudle] *F4;* Candle *F1–3.* 85–6. pap with a hatchet] *ASC; Farmer conj.;* the help of hatchet *F. See n.* 100. *Aside.*] *Capell; om. F.*

81. *box o' th' ear*] "From the title of Lyly's "Pappe with an Hatchet. Alias, A figge for my God sonne. Or, Cracke me this nut. Or, A Countrie cuffe, that is, a sound *boxe of the eare*," etc. (Hart). See also next notes.

85. *caudle*] a warm gruel, mixed with wine, and sweetened, for the sick. A "caudle of hempseed", or "hempen caudle", was a euphemism for hanging, as "pap with a hatchet" was for beheading. The two are exactly matched.

85–6. *pap with a hatchet*] proverbial for rough treatment (of children); cf. Lyly, *Mother Bombie*, 3. 539, "They give us pap with a spoone, and when we speake for what we love, *pap with a hatchet*." Lord Say is to be hanged first, and beheaded, for the pole, afterwards, according to an Elizabethan custom. Cf. n. to 85 above.

pap with a] see collation; a graphical error due to MS. similarity of *Pappe* to *Helpe*, and subsequent editorial rationalization.

97. *guiltless blood-shedding*] shedding of guiltless blood.

102. *familiar*] a demon supposed to attend at call; cf. *1 Sam.*, 28. 7.

under his tongue; he speaks not a God's name. Go, take him away, I say, and strike off his head presently; and then break into his son-in-law's house, Sir James Cromer, and strike off his head, and bring them both upon two poles hither.

All. It shall be done.

Say. Ah! countrymen, if when you make your prayers,
God should be so obdurate as yourselves,
How would it fare with your departed souls?
And therefore yet relent and save my life.

Cade. Away with him! and do as I command ye.

[*Exeunt one or two with the Lord Say.*

The proudest peer in the realm shall not wear a head on his shoulders, unless he pay me tribute; there shall not a maid be married, but she shall pay to me her maidenhead, ere they have it. Men shall hold of me in capite; and we charge and command that their wives be as free as heart can wish or tongue can tell.

But. My lord, when shall we go to Cheapside and take up commodities upon our bills?

Cade. Marry, presently.

All. O! brave.

104. say,] *F;* say, to the Standard in Cheapside, *Q*. 105. then] *F;* then to the Mile-end green and *Q*. 113. S.D. *Exeunt* . . .] *Q* (*reading* Exit . . .)*; om. F.* 119.] *Q continues,* Enter *Robin* . . . Sargiant. *See App. 4.*

103. *a*] obsolete form of *in*.

104.] *Standard in Cheapside* Q. "A water-conduit in Cheapside . . . in the form of a pillar with a dome shaped top . . . often used as a place of execution" (Sugden, 485).

105.] *Mile-end Green* Q. Froissart, 256, calls it "a fair place . . . whereas the people of the city did sport them in the summer season". Criminals were also hung in chains there (Sugden, 346).

Both references were omitted, apparently with intention, from F.

110. *obdurate*] accented on the second syllable.

116–17. *married . . . maidenhead*] the ancient custom of signorial *Ius primae noctis*.

118. *in capite*] in chief; a pun on tenant "in capite"—one who held his land direct from the king, at the *head* of the feudal pyramid.

119. *as free . . . tell*] Halliwell found this phrase in several ancient grants in verse (*Cont., Shakespeare Lib.*). Cf. Hall, 181, "the prouision was more then toung could speake, or harte could thinke." *Mirror, Add.*, 98, has "as harte can thinke, or tonge can tell".

The Q variant has been affected by the recollection of a similar passage in Kyd, *Sp. Tr.*, I. I. 57–8, "I saw more sights then thousand tongues can tell, / Or pennes can write, or mortall harts can think."

120–1. *take up . . . bills?*] note the pun.

Enter one with the heads.

Cade. But is not this braver? Let them kiss one another; for they loved well when they were alive. Now part them again, lest they consult about the giving up of some more towns in France. Soldiers, defer the spoil of the city until night; for with these borne before us, instead of maces, will we ride through the streets; and at every corner have them kiss. Away! [*Exeunt.*

SCENE VIII.—*Southwark.*

Alarum and retreat. Enter again CADE *and all his rabblement.*

Cade. Up Fish Street! down Saint Magnus' Corner! kill and knock down! throw them into Thames! [*Sound a parley.*] What noise is this I hear? Dare any be so bold to sound retreat or parley, when I command them kill?

Enter BUCKINGHAM *and* OLD CLIFFORD.

Buck. Ay, here they be that dare and will disturb thee:
Know, Cade, we come ambassadors from the King
Unto the commons, whom thou hast misled;
And here pronounce free pardon to them all
That will forsake thee and go home in peace.

Clif. What say ye, countrymen? Will ye relent
And yield to mercy, whilst 'tis offer'd you,

123. S.D. *Enter* . . .] *F;* Enter two with the Lord *Sayes* head, and sir Iames Cromers, vpon two poles. *Q.* 124–30.] *F, as verse, divided* . . . brauer: / . . . well / . . . againe, / . . . vp / . . . Soldiers, / . . . night / . . . Maces, / . . . Corner / . . . Away. 130. S.D. *Exeunt.*] *Rowe; Exit. F; the scene is continued in Q.*

Scene VIII

Locality.] *Theobald.* Entry.] *F.* 2. S.D. *Sound* . . .] *F; om. Q.* 3–5.] *F, as verse, divided* . . . heare? / . . . Parley / . . . kill? 6–54.] *F; for Q, see App. 4.*

1. *Fish Street* . . . *Saint Magnus' Corner*] on the north side of the Thames, opposite Southwark (25). St Magnus' Church (Hall, 222; not in Holinshed) stood at the bottom of Fish Street, London Bridge.

Or let a rebel lead you to your deaths?
Who loves the King, and will embrace his pardon,
Fling up his cap, and say "God save his Majesty!"
Who hateth him, and honours not his father,
Henry the Fifth, that made all France to quake,
Shake he his weapon at us, and pass by.

All. God save the King! God save the King!

Cade. What! Buckingham and Clifford, are ye so brave?
And you, base peasants, do ye believe him? Will you needs be hang'd with your pardons about your necks? Hath my sword therefore broke through London gates, that you should leave me at the White Hart in Southwark? I thought ye would never have given out these arms till you had recover'd your ancient freedom; but you are all recreants and dastards, and delight to live in slavery to the nobility. Let them break your backs with burdens, take your houses over your heads, ravish your wives and daughters before your faces. For me, I will make shift for one, and so God's curse light upon you all!

All. We'll follow Cade, we'll follow Cade!

Clif. Is Cade the son of Henry the Fifth,
That thus you do exclaim you'll go with him?
Will he conduct you through the heart of France,
And make the meanest of you earls and dukes?
Alas! he hath no home, no place to fly to;
Nor knows he how to live but by the spoil,
Unless by robbing of your friends and us.
Were't not a shame, that whilst you live at jar,

13. rebel] *Singer + edd.;* rabble *F, Hart.* 26. out] *F;* over *Walker conj.* 33.] Wee'l . . . *Cade,* / . . . *Cade. F.* 40. Unless] *F;* And lives *Vaughan conj.*

13. *rebel*] see collation; "rabble" is probably a misprint from a spelling "rebell" or "rebbell", possibly influenced by "rabblement" at the head of the scene.

18. *Shake he his weapon*] for this gesture as a signal of choice, cf. *1 Tamb.*, 2408.

20. *brave*] audacious, overbearing; cf. *Cor.*, IV. v. 19.

23. *therefore*] therefor, to that end.

26–7. *ancient freedom*] Hall, 123 (Oracion of . . . Alaunson), from which this passage seems to have been adapted, "Bedford . . . entendyng . . . to bryng to extreme bondage all vs our *wiues and children* . . . and you also *slaues* & bondmen . . . Where is . . . the *auncient fredome?*" Cf. also Hall, 208 (Appendix 1).

41. *live at jar*] quarrelling; cf. I. i. 254.

The fearful French, whom you late vanquished,
Should make a start o'er seas and vanquish you?
Methinks already in this civil broil
I see them lording it in London streets,
Crying "Villiago!" unto all they meet.
Better ten thousand base-born Cades miscarry
Than you should stoop unto a Frenchman's mercy.
To France, to France! and get what you have lost;
Spare England, for it is your native coast.
Henry hath money, you are strong and manly;
God on our side, doubt not of victory.

All. A Clifford! a Clifford! we'll follow the King and Clifford.

Cade. [*Aside.*] Was ever feather so lightly blown to and fro as this multitude? The name of Henry the Fifth hales them to an hundred mischiefs, and makes them leave me desolate. I see them lay their heads together to surprise me. My sword make way for me, for here is no staying.—In despite of the devils and hell, have through the very midst of you! and heavens and honour be witness, that no want of resolution in me, but only my followers' base and ignominious treasons, make me betake me to my heels. [*Exit.*

Buck. What, is he fled? Go some, and follow him;
And he that brings his head unto the King
Shall have a thousand crowns for his reward.
[*Exeunt some of them.*

53.] A . . . , a Clifford, / . . . Clifford. *F.* 55. *Aside.*] *Dyce, Staunton; om. F.* 64. S.D. *Exit.*] *F;* He runs through them with his staffe, and flies away. *Q.*

42. *fearful*] full of fear.

43. *start*] sudden outburst.

46. *Villiago*] villain. Florio (1598) has "Vigliacco, a raskal, a villain, a base, vile, abiect skurvie, a scoundrell". Cf. Jonson, *EMO*, 5. 3. 68. Possibly a survival from "Fuora villiacco!" the watchword of the Spaniards at the sack of Antwerp, 1574 (A. F. Pollard, *Tudor Tracts*, 432).

47. *miscarry*] die prematurely; be killed.

53. *A Clifford!*] The authorities have treated the "A" as the indefinite article (Franz, 278; *OED.*). But see Gösta Langenfelt, in *Studier i Modern Språkvetenskap*, 18 (1953), 55–64, and the case for treating "a" as French "à".

55. *Was ever feather . . .*] This thought is developed in *3 H 6*, III. i. 84–9 (Hart).

59. *surprise*] capture, take prisoner.

67. *crowns*] *marks* in the Chronicles. Possibly from Q "copy"; but perhaps a slip of Shakespeare's; cf. *Elianor* (*Nell*) for *Margaret* (*Meg*) in III. ii.

Follow me, soldiers: we'll devise a mean
To reconcile you all unto the King. [*Exeunt.*

SCENE IX.—*Kenilworth Castle.*

Sound trumpets. Enter KING, QUEEN, *and* SOMERSET, *on the terrace.*

King. Was ever king that joy'd an earthly throne,
And could command no more content than I?
No sooner was I crept out of my cradle
But I was made a king at nine months old;
Was never subject long'd to be a king
As I do long and wish to be a subject.

Enter BUCKINGHAM *and* CLIFFORD.

Buck. Health and glad tidings to your Majesty!
King. Why, Buckingham, is the traitor Cade surpris'd?
Or is he but retir'd to make him strong?

Enter multitudes, with halters about their necks.

Clif. He is fled, my lord, and all his powers do yield,
And humbly thus, with halters on their necks,
Expect your Highness' doom, of life, or death.
King. Then, heaven, set ope thy everlasting gates,

Scene IX

Locality.] *Theobald + edd.* Entry.] *F* (*reading Tarras*); Enter King *Henry*, *and* the Queene, and *Somerset*. *Q*. 1–21.] *F; for Q, see App. 4.* 6, 9. S.DD.] *F;* Enter the Duke of *Buckingham* and *Clifford*, with the Rebels, with halters about their necks. *Q*.

S.D. on the terrace] i.e. above; on the upper stage.

1–5. *Was ever . . . Was never*] a favourite device of Spenser; cf. *1 H 6*, Introduction, xxxii (Old Arden, ed. Hart).

1. *joy'd*] enjoyed.

4. *made a king*] Hall, 114–15, "proclaimed kyng of Englande and of Fraunce".

at nine months old] cf. *3 H 6*, III. i. 76; but also *1 H 6*, III. iv. 17, where Henry remembers his father's advice, at that age.

8. *surpris'd*] captured, taken prisoner.

9. S.D., with halters . . . necks] cf. Hall, 120, "with a halter about his necke."

12. *doom*] judgment.

13. *set ope . . . gates*] *Ps.*, 24 (Sternhold and Hopkins), 7, 9: "Ye princes ope your gates, and stand ope / the everlasting gate".

To entertain my vows of thanks and praise!
Soldiers, this day have you redeem'd your lives,
And show'd how well you love your Prince and country:
Continue still in this so good a mind,
And Henry, though he be infortunate,
Assure yourselves, will never be unkind:
And so, with thanks and pardon to you all,
I do dismiss you to your several countries.

All. God save the King! God save the King!

Enter a Messenger.

Mess. Please it your Grace to be advertised
The Duke of York is newly come from Ireland,
And with a puissant and a mighty power
Of gallowglasses and stout kerns
Is marching hitherward in proud array;
And still proclaimeth, as he comes along,
His arms are only to remove from thee
The Duke of Somerset, whom he terms a traitor.

King. Thus stands my state, 'twixt Cade and York distress'd;
Like to a ship that, having scap'd a tempest,
Is straightway calm'd, and boarded with a pirate.
But now is Cade driven back, his men dispers'd,

26. stout] *F;* stout Irish *Collier* (*Mitford conj.*). 33. calm'd] *F4;* calme *F1–3.*

14. *entertain*] receive favourably.

21. *countries*] localities; cf. Holinshed, quoted at IV. ii. 140.

23. *advertised*] informed, accented on the second syllable.

26.] Metrically defective, probably owing to a compositor's omission. See collation.

gallowglasses . . . kernes] cf. III. i. 310. "The *Galloglasses* useth a kind of pollax for his weapon. These men are grim of countenance, big of limme, lusty of body, wel and strong timbered. The *kerne* is an ordinary foot-soldier, using for weapon his sword and target, and sometimes his piece, being commonly good markmen" (Singer, from Stanihurst's *Description of Ireland*, c. viii, f. 21). Shakespeare could have found the words in Holinshed (on Macbeth) or *The Mirror for Magistrates*.

28–30. *still proclaimeth . . . remove . . . Somerset*] Hall, 225–6 and 231 (Appendix 1). Somerset was twice released, and twice met by York and his army.

29. *arms*] armed bands; cf. III. i. 378; V. i. 18, 39.

31. *my state*] my condition; the state of me, who am distressed.

33. *calm'd*] becalmed. See collation; an *e : d* error in F.

34. *But now*] just now; not used adversatively. Cf. *R 2*, III. ii. 77: "But now the blood of twenty thousand men / Did triumph in my face."

And now is York in arms to second him.
I pray thee, Buckingham, go and meet him,
And ask him what's the reason of these arms.
Tell him I'll send Duke Edmund to the Tower,
And, Somerset, we will commit thee thither,
Until his army be dismiss'd from him.

Som. I'll yield, my lord, to prison willingly,
Or unto death, to do my country good.

King. In any case, be not too rough in terms,
For he is fierce and cannot brook hard language.

Buck. I will, my lord; and doubt not so to deal
As all things shall redound unto your good.

King. Come, wife, let's in, and learn to govern better;
For yet may England curse my wretched reign.
[*Flourish. Exeunt.*

SCENE X.—*Kent. Iden's Garden.*

Enter CADE.

Cade. Fie on ambitions! fie on myself, that have a sword, and yet am ready to famish! These five days have I hid me in these woods and durst not peep out, for all the country is laid for me; but now am I so hungry,

36. meet] *F;* meet with *Rowe.* 41. I'll yield . . . prison] *ASC;* My Lord, / Ile yeelde my selfe to prison *F. See n.* 47–8.] *F; for Q, see App. 4.* 48. S.D. *Flourish. Exeunt.*] *F; Exet* (*exeunt Q2; Exit Q3*) *omnes. Q.*

Scene x

Locality.] *Capell.* Entry.] *F;* Enter *Iacke Cade* at one doore, and at the other maister *Alexander Eyden* and his men, and *Iacke Cade* lies downe picking of hearbes and eating them. *Q.* 1–23.] *F; for Q, see App. 4.*

35. *York* . . .] Shakespeare reverses the order of Somerset's imprisonment and York's arrival from Ireland; cf. Hall, 221–2 (Appendix 1).

36.] metrically defective. Cf. 26.

41. *my lord*] see collation. Probably written in above "myself" as a correction in the MS., and so printed above it as a separate line in F.

43. *rough . . . terms*] violent . . . language.

44. *brook*] endure.

48. *yet*] so far; till now.

Scene x

The garden is in Hall but not Holinshed.

S.D.] see collation. Iden's five men, in Q, and in F at 39, were presumably cut in performance.

4. *is laid*] warrants and watches are issued and sent out. Cf. Kyd, *S.P.*, 2.

that if I might have a lease of my life for a thousand years, I could stay no longer. Wherefore, on a brick wall have I climb'd into this garden, to see if I can eat grass, or pick a sallet another while, which is not amiss to cool a man's stomach this hot weather. And I think this word "sallet" was born to do me good: for many a time, but for a sallet, my brain-pan had been cleft with a brown bill; and many a time, when I have been dry and bravely marching, it hath serv'd me instead of a quart-pot to drink in; and now the word "sallet" must serve me to feed on.

Enter IDEN.

Iden. Lord! who would live turmoiled in the court,
And may enjoy such quiet walks as these?
This small inheritance my father left me
Contenteth me, and worth a monarchy.
I seek not to wax great by others' waning,
Or gather wealth I care not with what envy:
Sufficeth, that I have maintains my state,
And sends the poor well pleased from my gate.

Cade. [*Aside.*] Here's the lord of the soil come to seize me

20. waning] *Rowe;* warning *F.* 24. *Aside.*] *Dyce, Staunton; om. F.*

I. 333: "that he may not scape / Weele lay the ports and havens round about", and Hardyng, 530, "in everie coaste and corner of the realme laied wondrefull wayte and watche to take ... the said duke" (Hart).

8, 11. *sallet*] (*a*) salad, (*b*) a light round head-piece (Fr. *salade*). Hart refers to Fabyan, 623; see n. at IV. iii. 10. For the same pun, see *Thersites* (Dodsley, I. 396–7). Brutus has a drink from a sallet (Steevens, referring to North's *Plutarch*).

12. *brown bill*] pike or halberd carried by watchmen and constables. Cf. Lyly, *Pappe with an Hatchet*, 2. 406, "all weapons, from the taylors bodkin to the watchman's browne bil"; Middleton, *Father Hubbard's Tale* (Works, 8. 99) "the tweering constable of Finsbury with his Bench of Browne bill men." The colour was due to bronzing for prevention of rust.

16. *turmoiled*] worried. Cf. Golding, *Ovid*, 7. 152–3, "their boyling brests / Turmoyling with the firie flames enclosed in their chests".

19. *Contenteth . . . monarchy*] on the relation between kingship and content, cf. *3 H 6*, III. i. 64; II. v. 20–54; *2 H 4*, III. i. 30, 31, etc.

22. *Sufficeth, that I have*] it is sufficient that what I have . . .

24–5. *lord of the soil . . . stray . . . fee-simple*] typical of Shakespeare's background of familiarity with the law; cf. e.g. Fripp, *Shakespeare, Man and Artist*, 138 ff. A fee-simple is an estate which belongs absolutely to the "lord of the soil" and his heirs for ever. The

for a stray, for entering his fee-simple without leave. —Ah, villain, thou wilt betray me, and get a thousand crowns of the King by carrying my head to him; but I'll make thee eat iron like an ostrich, and swallow my sword like a great pin, ere thou and I part.

Iden. Why, rude companion, whatsoe'er thou be,
I know thee not; why then should I betray thee?
Is't not enough to break into my garden,
And like a thief to come to rob my grounds,
Climbing my walls in spite of me the owner,
But thou wilt brave me with these saucy terms?

Cade. Brave thee! ay, by the best blood that ever was broach'd, and beard thee too. Look on me well: I have eat no meat these five days; yet, come thou and thy five men, and if I do not leave you all as dead as a door-nail, I pray God I may never eat grass more.

26. Ah] *F* (A); *edd.* 38. these] *F;* this *Q.* 39. five] *Q*, *F;* fine *Collier.*

"lord" had the right to impound "strays", animals wandering out of their own bounds on his estate. Perhaps from Fabyan, 593.

27. *crowns*] a "discrepancy" due to a slip by Shakespeare or the F editor. See n. at IV. viii. 67 above.

28. *eat iron like an ostrich*] Hart compares Lyly, *Pappe*, 3. 399, "his conscience hath a cold stomacke. Cold? Thou art deceived, twil digest a Cathedral Church as easilie, as an Estritch a two penie naile."; *Euphues*, 1. 260, "the estridge digesteth harde yron to preserve his healthe". Bond quotes *Barth. Angl.*, 12, 33, "and [the ostryche] is so hote, that he swoloweth and defyeth [i.e. digests] and wastyth yren." Cf. Dekker, *The Wonderful Year*, 1603, "so hungry is the ostrich disease (the plague) that it will devour even iron."

The heralds and Bestiaries commonly depict the ostrich as carrying "a horseshoe, a fetterlock, or a Passion nail: . . . An ostrich with Passion nail in its beak was the badge of Ann of Bohemia" (Rothery).

30. *companion*] common fellow, in a bad sense. Cf. Kyd, *Sp. Tr.*, 3. 2. 115, "better its that base companions dye."

35. *saucy*] overbearing, insolent.

37. *beard thee*] defy thee to thy face.

39. *five men*] see head-note. Wilson suggests that this may be "not to refer to persons present, since Iden certainly enters soliloquizing at 15, but as an insulting suggestion that this petty squire had but five men on his estate." The Q entry, however, is definite enough, as is the Q command of Iden, "Sirrha, fetch me weopons, and stand you all aside." It is probable that the five men were "cut" at some time before the printing of F, and the reference here to the five men overlooked. The insult was probably implied just the same.

"Cade here says that 'though he has eaten no meat these *five* days, he is nevertheless more than a match for Iden and his *five* men.' . . . in his next speech, after being stabbed, he says, '. . . let *ten* thousand devils come against me, and give me but the *ten* meals I have lost, and I'd defy them all." (Dyce, *Strictures*, 136–7).

Iden. Nay, it shall ne'er be said, while England stands,
That Alexander Iden, esquire of Kent,
Took odds to combat a poor famish'd man.
Oppose thy steadfast-gazing eyes to mine,
See if thou canst outface me with thy looks:
Set limb to limb, and thou art far the lesser;
Thy hand is but a finger to my fist;
Thy leg a stick compared with this truncheon;
My foot shall fight with all the strength thou hast;
And if mine arm be heaved in the air
Thy grave is digg'd already in the earth.
As for words, whose greatness answers words,
Let this my sword report what speech forbears.

Cade. By my valour, the most complete champion that ever I heard! Steel, if thou turn the edge, or cut not out the burly-bon'd clown in chines of beef ere thou sleep in thy sheath, I beseech God on my knees thou may'st be turned to hobnails. [*Here they fight. Cade falls.* O, I am slain! Famine and no other hath slain me: let ten thousand devils come against me, and give me but the ten meals I have lost, and I'd defy them all. Wither, garden; and be henceforth a burying-place to all that do dwell in this house, because the unconquer'd soul of Cade is fled.

Iden. Is 't Cade that I have slain, that monstrous traitor?

41. shall ne'er] *F* (. . . nere); shall neuer *Q3;* never shall *Q1, 2.* 42. Iden] *ASC;* Iden an *Q, F.* 52. As for] *F;* But as for *Dyce;* And as for *Keightley;* As for more *Rowe, Hanmer;* As for mere *Mason conj.;* As for thy *Perring conj.* 57. God] *Q, Malone;* Ioue *F.* 58. may'st be] *F;* maist (mightst *Q3*) fal into some smiths hand, and be *Q, ASC conj.* 58. S.D. *Cade falls.*] *Capell; om. F;* and *Cade* fals downe. *Q.*

42. *esquire*] see collation; Hall, 222, is alone of the chroniclers in reading "esquire of Kent". The F insertion of the article was probably due to the use of Q "copy" at this point. See Introduction, pp. xxxix ff.

43. *Took odds*] Note Iden's chivalry; cf. Cade's comment, 54, and Iden's attitude on discovering Cade's identity, 65 ff.

52–3.] "Words" and "sword" continue the contrast of the previous lines between Iden and Cade. For the sentiment, Perring compares *Mac.*, v. viii. 7: "I have no words: / My voice is in my sword.", and *Cym.*, IV. ii. 78: "Have not I / An arm as big as thine? a heart as big? / Thy words, I grant, are bigger, for I wear not / My dagger in my mouth."

57. *God*] cf. F *Iove*, and a similar modification at v. iii. 29 below.

65. *monstrous*] like a monster; unnatural.

Sword, I will hallow thee for this thy deed,
And hang thee o'er my tomb when I am dead:
Ne'er shall this blood be wiped from thy point,
But thou shalt wear it as a herald's coat,
To emblaze the honour that thy master got.

Cade. Iden, farewell; and be proud of thy victory. Tell Kent from me, she hath lost her best man, and exhort all the world to be cowards; for I, that never fear'd any, am vanquish'd by famine, not by valour. [*Dies*.

Iden. How much thou wrong'st me, heaven be my judge.
Die, damned wretch, the curse of her that bare thee!
And as I thrust thy body in with my sword,
So wish I I might thrust thy soul to hell.
Hence will I drag thee headlong by the heels
Unto a dunghill, which shall be thy grave,
And there cut off thy most ungracious head;
Which I will bear in triumph to the King,
Leaving thy trunk for crows to feed upon. [*Exit*.

74. S.D. *Dies*.] *F;* He dies. *Q*. 79. headlong] *F;* endlong *Vaughan conj*.

66–70. *Sword* . . .] the hanging of arms and armorial insignia on tombs was a feature of the age. Cf. *Ham.*, IV. v. 210; *Ant.*, V. ii. 134.

67. *hang thee*] i.e. have thee hung.

70. *emblaze*] set forth, as his master's device on a herald's coat.

79. *headlong*] head downwards (horizontally), i.e. presumably by the heels.

ACT V

SCENE I.—*Fields between Dartford and Blackheath.*

Enter YORK *and his army of Irish, with drum and colours.*

York. From Ireland thus comes York to claim his right,
And pluck the crown from feeble Henry's head:
Ring, bells, aloud; burn, bonfires, clear and bright,
To entertain great England's lawful king.
Ah! sancta majestas, who'd not buy thee dear?
Let them obey that knows not how to rule;
This hand was made to handle nought but gold:
I cannot give due action to my words,
Except a sword or sceptre balance it.
A sceptre shall it have, have I a sword,
On which I'll toss the fleur-de-luce of France.

ACT V

Scene I

Locality.] *Malone, from the Chronicles.* Entry.] *F;* Enter the Duke of *Yorke* with Drum and souldiers. *Q.* 2.] *F; om. Q.* 5. who'd] *ASC;* who wold *Q, F.* 6. knows] *F;* know *Rowe + edd.* 10. sword] *ASC (Johnson conj.); soule F.* 11. fleur] *F* (Fleure); flower *edd.*

Source: Hall, 225–6 (Appendix I).

3. *bells . . . bonfires*] cf. *1 Tamb.*, 1335–6; *1 H 6*, I. vi. 11.

4. *entertain*] receive, welcome. Cf. *2 Tamb.*, 2985, "To entertain divine Zenocrate."

5. *sancta majestas*] Ovid, *Ars Am.*, 3. 407–8 (J. A. K. Thomson): "Sanctaque maiestas et erat venerabile nomen / Vatibus et largae saepe dabantur opes."

6. *that knows*] the relative with a singular verb, even where the antecedent is plural; Abbott, 247.

7. *gold*] the royal ceremonial sword, with hilt of gold.

10. *sword*] see collation; continues the balance of "sword" and "sceptre" in 9. York will win the sceptre with the sword. "Soul" is inept here.

11. *toss*] bear aloft on the point of a pike; cf. *1 H 4*, IV. ii. 71; *3 H 6*, I. i. 244. "Toss" was the technical term for the management of the pike, to which the sceptre is here compared.

fleur-de-luce] the heraldic lily, borne upon the royal arms of France (Onions). "One of the royal sceptres shown on Henry V's seal is topped with a fleur-de-lys, perhaps in allusion to his claim to the French crown." (Scott-Giles, 136).

Enter BUCKINGHAM.

Whom have we here? Buckingham, to disturb me?
The King hath sent him, sure: I must dissemble.
Buck. York, if thou meanest well, I greet thee well.
York. Humphrey of Buckingham, I accept thy greeting.
Art thou a messenger, or come of pleasure?
Buck. A messenger from Henry, our dread liege,
To know the reason of these arms in peace;
Or why thou, being a subject, as I am,
Against thy oath and true allegiance sworn,
Should raise so great a power without his leave,
Or dare to bring thy force so near the court.
York. [*Aside.*] Scarce can I speak, my choler is so great:
O, I could hew up rocks and fight with flint,
I am so angry at these abject terms;
And now, like Ajax Telamonius,
On sheep or oxen could I spend my fury.
I am far better born than is the King,
More like a king, more kingly in my thoughts;
But I must make fair weather yet awhile,
Till Henry be more weak, and I more strong.—
Buckingham, I prithee, pardon me,
That I have given no answer all this while;

23. *Aside.*] *Rowe.*

18. *arms*] armed bands; cf. III. i. 378; IV. ix. 29.

26. *Ajax Telamonius*] "Ajax, son of Telamon, destroyed a flock of sheep, in a fit of blind fury, believing them to be his enemies, after Ulysses was awarded Achilles' arms in preference to himself. He then committed suicide. The event is not touched upon in Ovid's account in the *Metamorphoses*, where Ajax is credited with immediate self-destruction." (Hart).

"We have here a plain allusion to the *Ajax* of Sophocles, of which no translation was extant in the time of Shakespeare. In that piece, Agamemnon consents at last to allow Ajax the rites of sepulture, and Ulysses (Laertes' son) is the pleader, whose arguments prevail in favour of his remains." (Malone).

Cf. "brazen caves", above, III. ii. 88; "Rhesus' fatal steeds", *3 H 6*, IV. ii. 19–21; Anders, 285, suggests a similar use of the *Hecuba* of Euripides in *Tit.*, I. i. 136–9. Root refers to Horace, *Sat.*, 2. 3. 202.

D. Bush, *Ph. Q.* (1927), 6. 296, gives references to Adlington, *Golden Asse*, *Fennes Frutes*, Marlowe's *Elegies of Ovid*, and J. Tortelli's *Orthographia*, to illustrate 16th century acquaintance with this version of the story.

30. *make fair weather*] go with the times. Cf. *Ado*, I. iii. 25; North's *Plutarch* (Tudor Trans., I. 318), "So make fayre weather again with the governour."

My mind was troubled with deep melancholy.
The cause why I have brought this army hither
Is to remove proud Somerset from the king,
Seditious to his Grace and to the state.

Buck. That is too much presumption on thy part:
But if thy arms be to no other end,
The king hath yielded unto thy demand:
The Duke of Somerset is in the Tower.

York. Upon thine honour, is he prisoner?

Buck. Upon mine honour, he is prisoner.

York. Then, Buckingham, I do dismiss my powers.
Soldiers, I thank you all; disperse yourselves:
Meet me to-morrow in Saint George's Field,
You shall have pay, and every thing you wish.
[*Exeunt soldiers.*
And let my sovereign, virtuous Henry,
Command my eldest son, nay, all my sons,
As pledges of my fealty and love;
I'll send them all as willing as I live:
Lands, goods, horse, armour, any thing I have,
Is his to use, so Somerset may die.

Buck. York, I commend this kind submission:
We twain will go into his Highness' tent.

Enter KING *and Attendants.*

King. Buckingham, doth York intend no harm to us,
That thus he marcheth with thee arm in arm?

York. In all submission and humility
York doth present himself unto your Highness.

King. Then what intends these forces thou dost bring?

York. To heave the traitor Somerset from hence,
And fight against that monstrous rebel, Cade,

47. S.D. *Exeunt soldiers.*] *Q2; Exet* souldiers. *Q1, 3* (*subst.*); *om. F.*

46. *Saint George's Field*] *2 H 4*, III. ii. 207. "An open space of great extent, on the Surrey side of the Thames, lying between Southwark and Lambeth, and so called from the adjoining church of St. George the Martyr in Southwark. . . It was one of the chief drill-grounds for the trained bands" (Hart).

51. *as willing as I live*] "with all the pleasure in life" (Ward).

53. *so*] provided that.

60. *intends*] see Abbott, 333.

62. *fight . . . Cade*] note the irony of

Who since I heard to be discomfited.

Enter IDEN, *with* CADE'S *head.*

Iden. If one so rude and of so mean condition
May pass into the presence of a king,
Lo! I present your Grace a traitor's head,
The head of Cade, whom I in combat slew.
King. The head of Cade! Great God, how just art Thou!
O, let me view his visage, being dead,
That living wrought me such exceeding trouble.
Tell me, my friend, art thou the man that slew him?
Iden. I was, an 't like your Majesty.
King. How art thou call'd? And what is thy degree?
Iden. Alexander Iden, that's my name;
A poor esquire of Kent, that loves his king.
Buck. So please it you, my lord, 'twere not amiss
He were created knight for his good service.
King. Iden, kneel down. [*He kneels.*] Rise up a knight.
We give thee for reward a thousand marks;
And will that thou henceforth attend on us.
Iden. May Iden live to merit such a bounty,
And never live but true unto his liege.

Enter QUEEN *and* SOMERSET.

King. See, Buckingham, Somerset comes with th' Queen:
Go, bid her hide him quickly from the Duke.
Queen. For thousand Yorks he shall not hide his head,

63. heard] *F;* hear *Capell.* 72. I was] *F;* I was the man *Vaughan conj.* 78. S.D. *He kneels.*] *Johnson; om. Q, F.* Rise] *F;* and rise thou *Hanmer;* Iden, rise *Dyce;* and now rise *Vaughan conj.*

this addition to the Chronicles, when compared with York's instigation of Cade's rebellion.

64. *rude*] L. *rudis*: uncultured, unrefined.

69–70. *his visage . . . / That*] L. construction = the visage of him that . . .

78. *kneel down. Rise up*] cf. the knighting of Walworth and others in the Peasants' Revolt in Hol., 2. 747; and its treatment in *Jack Straw*, Dodsley, 5. 413: "Kneel down, William Walworth, and receive, / By mine own hand the Order of Knighthood: / Stand up, Sir William, first knight of thy degree".

79. *a thousand marks*] as in the Chronicles; but "crowns" at IV. viii. 67, and IV. x. 26 above. Cf. *Ed. 3*, V. i. 94–6: "Kneel therefore down; now rise, King Edward's knight: / And, to maintain thy state, I freely give / Five hundred marks a year to thee and thine."

But boldly stand and front him to his face.
York. How now! is Somerset at liberty?
Then, York, unloose thy long-imprison'd thoughts
And let thy tongue be equal with thy heart.
Shall I endure the sight of Somerset?
False king! why hast thou broken faith with me,
Knowing how hardly I can brook abuse?
King did I call thee? No, thou art not king;
Not fit to govern and rule multitudes,
Which dar'st not, no, nor canst not rule a traitor.
That head of thine doth not become a crown;
Thy hand is made to grasp a palmer's staff,
And not to grace an awful princely sceptre.
That gold must round engirt these brows of mine,
Whose smile and frown, like to Achilles' spear,
Is able with the change to kill and cure.
Here is a hand to hold a sceptre up,
And with the same to act controlling laws.
Give place: by heaven, thou shalt rule no more
O'er him whom heaven created for thy ruler.
Som. O monstrous traitor! I arrest thee, York,
Of capital treason 'gainst the king and crown.
Obey, audacious traitor; kneel for grace.
York. Would'st have me kneel? First let me ask of these
If they can brook I bow a knee to man.

88 ff.] *F; for Q, see App. 4.* 109. these] *Theobald;* thee *F.*

86. *front*] confront.

97. *palmer's staff*] a sign of extreme piety.

98. *awful*] inducing awe.

100. *Achilles' spear*] a post-Homeric commonplace of classical literature, according to which Telephus, wounded with the spear of Achilles, was cured by the application of its rust. See e.g. Ovid, *Amores*, 2. 9; *Rem. Am.*, 47; *Metam.*, 12. 112; 13. 171–2; Propertius, 2. 1. 63–4; Pliny, *Nat. Hist.*, 25. 19 and 34. 45 (cited by Bond, *Lyly*) where the cure was "by some explained of the verdigris which he scraped off the spear with his sword, as represented in some pictures". Elizabethan sources and references are also numerous, e.g. Newton's Seneca, *Troas*, 2. 3; *Ed. 3*, II. i. 392–3; *Lucr.*, 1424; Greene, *Tullie's Love* (Grosart, 7. 109.)

101. *the change*] *scil.* from frown to smile and vice versa.

103. *act*] enact, put into action.

109. *these*] see collation; probably his sons, though it might be taken to refer to his troops. His sons may be assumed to be just off-stage, but within sight; cf. 147, where Warwick and Salisbury are similarly called, and enter immediately.

Sirrah, call in my sons to be my bail: [*Exit Attendant.*
I know ere they will have me go to ward,
They'll pawn their swords for my enfranchisement.

Queen. Call hither Clifford; bid him come amain,
To say if that the bastard boys of York
Shall be the surety for their traitor father. [*Exit Attendant.*

York. O blood-bespotted Neapolitan,
Outcast of Naples, England's bloody scourge!
The sons of York, thy betters in their birth,
Shall be their father's bail; and bane to those
That for my surety will refuse the boys!

Enter EDWARD *and* RICHARD.

See where they come: I'll warrant they'll make it good.

Enter CLIFFORD *and his Son.*

Queen. And here comes Clifford, to deny their bail.

Clif. Health and all happiness to my lord the King! [*Kneels.*

York. I thank thee, Clifford: say, what news with thee?
Nay, do not fright us with an angry look:
We are thy sovereign, Clifford, kneel again;
For thy mistaking so, we pardon thee.

Clif. This is my King, York; I do not mistake;
But thou mistakes me much to think I do.

111. sons] Q (sonnes); sonne *F.* 111. S.D.] *Capell; om. Q, F.* 113. for] *F2;* of *F1.* 116. S.D.] *Dyce; om. Q, F; Exit Buckingham. Capell + edd.* 120. bane] *F;* bale *Theobald.* 121. S.D.] *F; Enter . . . Richard. om. Q.* 122. S.D.] *Enter* Clifford. *F;* Enter the Duke of *Yorkes* sonnes, *Edward* the Earle of *March,* and crook-backe *Richard,* at the one doore, with Drumme and soldiers, and at the other doore, enter *Clifford* and his sonne, with Drumme and souldiers, and *Clifford* kneeles to *Henry,* and speakes. *Q.* 124. S.D. *Kneels.*] *Johnson, from Q; om. F.*

111. *call . . . bail*] cf. 49–50, where York offers his sons as "pledges" of his fealty.

sons] actually children at this time.

117. *Neapolitan*] cf. I. i. 46–7, "daughter unto Reignier, king of Naples". Reignier claimed the throne of Naples, which his father had held, but never succeeded in attaining it.

118. *England's bloody scourge*] cf. *1 H 6,* IV. ii. 16, where Talbot is the "bloody scourge" of France; and I. ii. 129, where Joan of Arc is "the English scourge". In this respect Margaret is her true successor. Cf. *2 Tamb.* "the scourge of God" (3048); and Virgil, *Æneid,* 8. 703, "sanguineo . . . flagello", (of Bellona).

120. *bane*] destruction.

121, 122. S.DD.] see collation; the soldiers have been cut in F, here and at 147.

130. *mistakes*] Franz, 152; cf. III. ii. 328; IV. i. 32.

To Bedlam with him! Is the man grown mad!
King. Ay, Clifford; a bedlam and ambitious humour
Makes him oppose himself against his king.
Clif. He is a traitor; let him to the Tower,
And chop away that factious pate of his.
Queen. He is arrested, but will not obey:
His sons, he says, shall give their words for him.
York. Will you not, sons?
Edw. Ay, noble father, if our words will serve.
Rich. And if words will not, then our weapons shall.
Clif. Why, what a brood of traitors have we here!
York. Look in a glass, and call thy image so;
I am thy king, and thou a false-heart traitor.
Call hither to the stake my two brave bears,
That with the very shaking of their chains
They may astonish these fell-lurking curs:
Bid Salisbury and Warwick come to me.

Enter the Earls of WARWICK *and* SALISBURY.

Clif. Are these thy bears? We'll bait thy bears to death,
And manacle the bear'ard in their chains,
If thou dar'st bring them to the baiting-place.
Rich. Oft have I seen a hot o'erweening cur

146. fell-lurking] *F;* fell-barking *Roderick conj.* 147 S.D. *Enter* . . .] *F;* Enter at one doore, the Earles of *Salsbury* and *Warwicke*, with Drumme and souldiers. And at the other, the Duke of *Buckingham*, with Drumme and souldiers. *Q.* 149. bear'ard] *Wilson, F* (Berard). *Cf. 211.*

131. *Bedlam*] "an hospital for distracted people" (Stow). Cf. III. i. 51 above.

132. *humour*] temperament, state of mind.

139. *if our words will serve*] cf. *2 Tamb.*, 3089, "If words might serve". Briggs compares *Ed. 2*, 289, "I, if words will serve; if not, I must".

142. *glass*] mirror.
image] reflection.

143. *false-heart*] false-hearted. Cf. *Troil.* v. i. 95.

144. *two brave bears*] another allusion to the muzzled bear rampant and ragged staff, the badge of the house of Warwick; cf. 202; *3 H 6*, v. vii. 10 11. The Spaniards speak similarly of "a brave bull".

146. *astonish*] terrify, dismay; cf. *Lucr.*, 1730.

144, 148, 149. *stake . . . bait . . . bears . . . chains*] a favourite analogy in Shakespeare. For an account of bear-baiting, Hart refers to Laneham's *Letter* (1575) describing the Queen's entertainment at Kenilworth.

151. *Oft* . . .] Hart notes the beginning of Richard's use of tropes and figures, afterwards (*3 H 6, R 3*) abundant, and gaining him the name of "currish Æsop".

Run back and bite, because he was withheld;
Who, being suffer'd, with the bear's fell paw
Hath clapp'd his tail between his legs and cried:
And such a piece of service will you do,
If you oppose yourselves to match Lord Warwick.

Clif. Hence, heap of wrath, foul indigested lump,
As crooked in thy manners as thy shape!

York. Nay, we shall heat you thoroughly anon.

Clif. Take heed, lest by your heat you burn yourselves.

King. Why, Warwick, hath thy knee forgot to bow?
Old Salisbury, shame to thy silver hair,
Thou mad misleader of thy brain-sick son!
What! wilt thou on thy death-bed play the ruffian,
And seek for sorrow with thy spectacles?
O! where is faith? O! where is loyalty?
If it be banish'd from the frosty head,
Where shall it find a harbour in the earth?
Wilt thou go dig a grave to find out war,
And shame thine honourable age with blood?
Why art thou old and want'st experience?
Or wherefore dost abuse it, if thou hast it?
For shame! in duty bend thy knee to me,
That bows unto the grave with mickle age.

153. suffer'd,] *ASC, Vaughan conj.*; suffer'd *F.* 167. banish'd] *F* (banisht).

153. *suffer'd*] allowed, in antithesis to "withheld". Cf. III. i. 32, III. ii. 261; *3 H 6*, IV. viii. 7–8, "A little fire . . . / Which, being suffered, rivers cannot quench."

157. *foul indigested lump*] Ovid's "rudis indigestaque moles", *Metam.*, I. 7. Cf. *Sonn.*, 114, "monsters and things indigest".

158. *crooked*] for Richard's appearance, see Hall, 421, in Boswell-Stone, 423.

160. *heat . . . burn*] "In probable allusion to Nebuchadnezzar's furnace which was so hot that it slew his servants" (Noble).

162–74. *silver hair . . son . . . death-bed . . . sorrow . . . frosty head . . . honourable age . . . old . . . unto the grave . . . age*] a series of images and recollections or associations from the story of Jacob and Benjamin, *Genesis*, 42. 38; 44. 29, 31: "And he said, My son shall not go down with you; for his brother is dead, and he is left alone: if mischief befall him . . . then shall ye bring down my gray head with sorrow to the grave", and perhaps *Lev.* 19. 32, "Thou shalt rise up before the hoary head, and honour the face of the old man." Cf. also II. iii. 18–20 and *1 Tamb.*, 1862–3: "Pitie olde age within whose *silver haires*, / Honor and reverence evermore have raign'd".

165. *spectacles*] organs of sight; cf. III. ii. 111.

172. *abuse*] use ill, disgrace, dishonour.

174. *mickle*] a northern form = much. Common in Eliz. writers.

Sal. My lord, I have consider'd with myself
The title of this most renowned duke;
And in my conscience do repute his Grace
The rightful heir to England's royal seat.
King. Hast thou not sworn allegiance unto me?
Sal. I have.
King. Canst thou dispense with heaven for such an oath?
Sal. It is great sin to swear unto a sin,
But greater sin to keep a sinful oath.
Who can be bound by any solemn vow
To do a murd'rous deed, to rob a man,
To force a spotless virgin's chastity,
To reave the orphan of his patrimony,
To wring the widow from her custom'd right,
And have no other reason for this wrong
But that he was bound by a solemn oath?
Queen. A subtle traitor needs no sophister.
King. Call Buckingham, and bid him arm himself.
York. Call Buckingham, and all the friends thou hast,
Both thou and they shall curse this fatal hour;
I am resolv'd for death or dignity.
Clif. The first I warrant thee, if dreams prove true.
War. Thou were best to go to bed and dream again,
To keep thee from the tempest of the field.
Clif. I am resolv'd to bear a greater storm
Than any thou canst conjure up to-day;
And that I'll write upon thy burgonet,

194.] *Q; om. F. See n.* 195.] *F; om. Q.* or] *Rowe*; and *F.* 197. Thou were] *ASC;* You were *F;* You had *Q. See n.*

181. *dispense with*] make an arrangement with, come to terms with, for an offence.

187. *reave*] bereave.

188. *custom'd right*] the widow's right, by custom, to the life-rent of part of her husband's estate. Cf. *Mirror*, 437.

191. *sophister*] "a cunning, cavilling disputer" (Cotgrave).

194.] see collation. The F omission of this line is either one of compositor B's frequent lapses; or may be due to the marginal insertion in the Q copy of 195, and the compositor's mistaking the insertion for a substitution.

197. *Thou were*] see collation. F "you" is due, either to imperfect amendment of Q, or an alteration to suit the apparent syntax required by "were". See Franz, 152.

201. *burgonet*] "a small Burgundian steel cap, as distinct from the more ponderous helmet, but both alike crowned with its crest or badge" (Rothery).

Might I but know thee by thy housed badge.
War. Now, by my father's badge, old Nevil's crest,
The rampant bear chain'd to the ragged staff,
This day I'll wear aloft my burgonet,—
As on a mountain top the cedar shows
That keeps his leaves in spite of any storm,—
Even to affright thee with the view thereof.
Clif. And from thy burgonet I'll rend thy bear,
And tread it under foot with all contempt,
Despite the bear'ard that protects the bear.
Y. Clif. And so to arms, victorious father,
To quell the rebels and their complices.
Rich. Fie! charity for shame! speak not in spite,
For you shall sup with Jesu Christ to-night.
Y. Clif. Foul stigmatic, that's more than thou canst tell.
Rich. If not in heaven, you'll surely sup in hell.
[*Exeunt severally.*

202. housed] *F;* Household *Q;* household *Malone.* 211. bear'ard] *Wilson, F* (Bearard). 212. father] *F;* Soueraigne *Q, ASC conj.* 217. S.D. *severally.*] *Theobald; om. F.*

202, 203. *housed badge . . . father's badge*] the emblem of the family; cf. n. to 144 above.

204. *rampant bear . . .*] Hart refers to Whitney's *Emblems*, 105–7, for the device and a dedicatory poem in praise of Warwick and Leicester. He might also have referred to the Frontispiece, which carried this design. The staff was used to thrust into the mouth of the bear when required, presumably to rescue the dogs.

206. *cedar*] a symbol of royalty.

208. *Even to affright*] continuous with 205, after the "cedar" parenthesis.

215. *sup . . . to-night*] from the *Grace before Supper* in the *Primer* or *Book of Private Prayer* of 1553: "He that is King of glory, and Lord over all, / Bring us to the supper of the life eternall." (Baldwin). Cf. *Ham.*, IV. iii. 17–18; "It is an instance of the consistency with which Shakespeare has drawn Richard's character throughout the plays, that thus early after his first introduction he should utter 'old odd ends stol'n out of Holy Writ' " (Noble). Cf. n. to 151 above.

216. *stigmatic*] branded deformity. Applied to a criminal branded or "stigmatized" with a hot iron.

SCENE II.—*Saint Albans.*

Alarums to the battle. Enter WARWICK.

War. Clifford of Cumberland, 'tis Warwick calls:
And if thou dost not hide thee from the bear,
Now, when the angry trumpet sounds alarum,
And dead men's cries do fill the empty air,
Clifford, I say, come forth and fight with me!
Proud northern lord, Clifford of Cumberland,
Warwick is hoarse with calling thee to arms.

Enter YORK.

How now, my noble lord! what! all afoot?
York. The deadly-handed Clifford slew my steed;
But match to match I have encounter'd him,
And made a prey for carrion kites and crows
Even of the bonny beast he loved so well.

Enter CLIFFORD.

War. Of one or both of us the time is come.
York. Hold, Warwick! seek thee out some other chase,

Scene II

Locality.] *Capell.* Entry. *Alarums . . . battle.*] *Q; om. F.* 8. S.D.] *F;* Clifford speakes within. / Warwicke stand still, and view the way that Clifford hewes with / his murthering Curtelaxe, through the fainting troopes to finde / thee out. / Warwicke stand still, and stir not till I come. / Enter *Yorke. Q.* 8. How] *edd.; War.* How *Q, F.* 12.] *Q continues:* The boniest gray that ere was bred in North. 14–30.] *F; for Q, see App. 4.*

Source: Hall, 251. This main account of Clifford's death is developed here, and in *3 H 6,* I. i. 54–5 and I. iii. 5, from the hint supplied by Hall, "thy father slew myne". The casual and contradictory account in *3 H 6,* I. i. 9, where he is "by the hands of common soldiers slain", was derived from Hall, 233, and would pass unnoticed by the audience, as it probably did by Shakespeare.

3. *sounds alarum*] sounds the call to arms; cf. *1 H 6,* I. ii. 18, and above, II. iii. 90. More common as a stage-direction.

4. *dead men's cries*] prolepsis.

cries . . . fill . . . air] cf. *Jack Straw,* Dodsley, 5. 395: "troops of men / That filled the air with cries and fearful noise:" and *2 Tamb.,* 3865: "Fill all the aire with troublous bellowing"; and *F.Q.*, I. 8. 17, "scourging the emptie ayre with his long trayne".

8. *afoot*] in motion and action.

11. *kites*] another instance of a standard Shakespearean image-cluster: kite . . . crow . . . deadly . . . soul (18) . . . empty (4). Cf. above, III. i. 249; III. ii. 190.

13 ff.] For censorship here, see version in App. 4; and Intro., p. xxviii.

14. *chase*] game; cf. *Wint.*, III. iii. 57.

For I myself must hunt this deer to death.
War. Then, nobly, York; 'tis for a crown thou fight'st.
As I intend, Clifford, to thrive to-day,
It grieves my soul to leave thee unassail'd. [*Exit.*
Clif. What seest thou in me, York? Why dost thou
pause?
York. With thy brave bearing should I be in love,
But that thou art so fast mine enemy.
Clif. Nor should thy prowess want praise and esteem,
But that 'tis shown ignobly and in treason.
York. So let it help me now against thy sword
As I in justice and true right express it.
Clif. My soul and body on the action both!
York. A dreadful lay! Address thee instantly.
Clif. *La fin couronne les œuvres.*
[*They fight, and Clifford falls and dies.*
York. Thus war hath given thee peace, for thou art still.
Peace with his soul, heaven, if it be thy will! [*Exit.*

Enter Young CLIFFORD.

Y. Clif. Shame and confusion! all is on the rout:
Fear frames disorder, and disorder wounds
Where it should guard. O war, thou son of hell,
Whom angry heavens do make their minister,
Throw in the frozen bosoms of our part

18. S.D. *Exit.*] *Exet Warwicke. Q; Exit War. F.* 19.] What . . . Yorke? / Why . . . pause? *F.* 28. *couronne les œuvres.*] *edd.; Corrone les eumenes. F.* 28. S.D. *They fight . . . dies.*] *edd.;* Alarmes, and they fight, and *Yorke* kils *Clifford. Q; om. F1;* Dies. *F2.* 29. thou] y^{u} *F.* 30. *Exit.*] *Exit Yorke. Q; om. F.* S.D.] *Q, F* (*subst.*). 31–65.] *F; for Q, see App. 4.*

15. *I myself . . . death*] Singer compares *Iliad*, 22. 205, where Achilles expresses a similar determination about Hector. Cf. *3 H 6*, II. iv. 12–13.

20. *bearing*] behaviour; cf. *LLL.*, I. i. 272.

27. *lay*] wager, stake. A pun? Cf. *Oth.*, II. iii. 330.

Address thee] prepare thyself.

28. La fin . . .] "The end crowns all", *Troil.*, IV. v. 224; "the fine's the crown." *All's W.*, IV. iv. 35; "The end is crowne of every worke well done;" Kyd, *Sp. Tr.*, 2. 6. 8, etc.

29. *war . . . peace*] a typical Shakespearean paradox.

31. *confusion*] destruction, ruin, chaos.

32. *frames*] forms, makes. "Frame" had a much more extended use than it now has; cf. Golding's *Ovid*, 6. 599, 600, "Love gave him power to frame his talke at will".

33–4. *O war . . . minister*] Noble compares *Ezek.*, 14. 21 and 5. 13.

35. *part*] side, party.

Hot coals of vengeance! Let no soldier fly.
He that is truly dedicate to war
Hath no self-love; nor he that loves himself
Hath not essentially, but by circumstance,
The name of valour. [*Seeing his dead father.*
O! let the vile world end,
And the premised flames of the last day
Knit earth and heaven together;
Now let the general trumpet blow his blast,
Particularities and petty sounds

40. S.D. *Seeing . . . father.*] *Theobald; om. Q,F.*

36. *Hot coals of vengeance*] *Ps.*, 140. 10, "hot burning coals": Bishops' Bible (Noble).

37. *dedicate*] a common Elizabethan form of pa.pple. of a verb ending in "t" or "d". See Franz, 159.

39. *essentially . . . by circumstance*] a relic of the mediaeval distinction between essence and accident.

40. *the vile world*] Bible and Prayer Book. Cf. *Sonn.*, 71. 3, 4: "fled / From this vile world, with vilest worms to dwell."

40–51. *O! let . . . stony.*] A regular Shakespearean group of images, compounded from various sources, and centring on the Last Judgement, as presented in mediaeval art and thought. The situation is always one of horror aroused by the death of a dear friend or relative, and the effect on the bereaved that of chaos come again; cf. *Mac.*, II. iii. 63 ff (on the murder of Duncan):

Macd. O *horror*! *horror*! *horror*!
Confusion . . . destroy your sight
With a new *Gorgon*. . . up, up, and see
The great doom's image!—Malcolm! Banquo!
As from your graves rise up, and walk like sprites
To countenance this *horror*!
Bell rings.
Lady M. What's the business
That such a hideous *trumpet* . . .

and *Lr.*, v. iii. 257 ff (after the three trumpets of the duel, and the death of Cordelia):

Lear. O you are men of *stone:*
Had I your tongue and eyes, I'ld use them so
That *heaven's* vault should *crack* . . .
She's dead as *earth.*
Kent. Is this the *promis'd end*?
(? premis'd)
Edg. Or image of that *horror*?
Alb. Fall and *cease.*

41. *premised*] predestined; foreordained; included in the premisses of Creation. "He asks to have them now; he doesn't say they have come (sent before their time), as the commentators have it, but that he wants them" (Hart); cf. "ordain'd", 45.

41–2. *flames of the last day . . . together*] Cf. Ovid, *Metam.*, I. 256–8: Jove "remembered also that 'twas *in the fates* that a time would come when sea and *land* the unkindled palace of the *sky* and the beleaguered structure of the universe should be destroyed *by fire.*" (Loeb). Cf. also Ovid, *Amores*, I. 15, "when the same day shall give the world to destruction", and *2 Peter* 3. 10, 12. A more direct source for 40 and 42 is *2 Tamb.*, 4642 (last speech), "Meet *heaven & earth*, & here let al things *end.*"

43. *general trumpet*] Cf. *1 Cor.*, 15. 52.

44. *Particularities*] trifles, details, individual affairs; cf. *H 5*, III. ii. 142. Hart quotes Gabriel Harvey, *Letters*, "A fewe such particularities and dis-

To cease! Wast thou ordain'd, dear father,
To lose thy youth in peace, and to achieve
The silver livery of advised age,
And, in thy reverence and thy chair-days, thus
To die in ruffian battle? Even at this sight
My heart is turn'd to stone: and while 'tis mine
It shall be stony. York not our old men spares;
No more will I their babes: tears virginal
Shall be to me even as the dew to fire;
And beauty, that the tyrant oft reclaims,
Shall to my flaming wrath be oil and flax.
Henceforth I will not have to do with pity:
Meet I an infant of the house of York,
Into as many gobbets will I cut it
As wild Medea young Absyrtus did:
In cruelty will I seek out my fame.
Come, thou new ruin of old Clifford's house:
As did Æneas old Anchises bear,
So bear I thee upon my manly shoulders;
But then Æneas bare a living load,
Nothing so heavy as these woes of mine.
[*Exit, bearing off his father.*

Enter RICHARD *and* SOMERSET *to fight.* SOMERSET *is killed.*

65. S.D. *Exit, . . . father*] *Pope;* He takes him vp on his backe . . . *Exet* yoong *Clifford* with his father. *Q.; om. F.* *Somerset is killed.*] *Rowe;* Alarmes to the battaile, and then enter the Duke of *Somerset* and *Richard* fighting, and *Richard* kils him vnder the signe of the Castle in saint *Albones. Q.* (*after* v. i.); *om. F.*

tinctions compendiously and familiarly coursed over".

45. *ordain'd*] foreordained, predestined.

47. *silver livery . . . age*] cf. v. i. 162 n. *advised*] deliberate and wise.

48. *reverence*] L. *reverenda canities.*

50. *My heart . . . stone*] *1 Sam.*, 25. 37, "his heart died within him, and he became as a stone." The story of Nabal has been introduced above, III. ii. 183.

51–2. *York . . . old men . . . their babes*] a pointer to Clifford's revenge in the murder of young Rutland in *3 H 6*, I. i. 54, 55; I. iii. 5. Cf. head-note, and Hall, 251 (Appendix I).

54. *the tyrant . . . reclaims*] inversion.

58. *gobbets*] mouthfuls, lumps.

59. *Medea*] When Medea fled with Jason from Colchos, she murdered her brother Absyrtus, and cut his body into several pieces, that her father might for some time be prevented from pursuing her. See Ovid, *Trist.*, 3. 9. 25–8 (Malone).

62. *Æneas . . . bear*] cf. *Caes.*, I. ii. 112.

Rich. So, lie thou there;
For underneath an alehouse' paltry sign,
The Castle in Saint Albans, Somerset
Hath made the wizard famous in his death.
Sword, hold thy temper; heart, be wrathful still:
Priests pray for enemies, but princes kill. [*Exit.*

Fight. Excursions. Enter KING, QUEEN, *and others.*

Queen. Away, my lord! you are slow: for shame, away!
King. Can we outrun the heavens? Good Margaret, stay.
Queen. What are you made of? You'll nor fight nor fly;
Now is it manhood, wisdom, and defence,
To give the enemy way, and to secure us
By what we can, which can no more but fly.
[*Alarum afar off.*
If you be ta'en, we then should see the bottom
Of all our fortunes; but if we haply scape,—

66. there;] *F* (there:); there, and breathe thy last. *Q1, 2;* there, and tumble in thy blood, *Q3. See n.* 67. For] *F;* Whats here, the signe of the Castle? / Then the prophesie is come to passe, / For Somerset was forewarned of Castles, / The which he alwaies did obserue. / And *Q. See n.* 71. S.D. *Exit.*] *Q; om. F. Fight . . . others.*] *F;* Alarmes againe, and then enter three or foure, bearing the Duke of *Buckingham* wounded to his Tent. Alarmes still, and then enter the King and Queene. *Q.* 77. S.D. *Alarum . . .*] *F; om. Q.*

66.] see Q collation "*and breathe thy last*". The replacement, by conjecture, in Q3, must mean that the phrase dropped out at some stage of printing. The gap in F probably means that it was also set, at this point, from an exemplar of Q3, but one in which the gap still existed. It is impossible to say whether the phrase, which is an Elizabethan commonplace, is memorial or not.

67. *For*] indicates an omission, of which Q (see collation) almost certainly gives the substance; cf. Hall, 233, "For there died vnder the signe of the Castle, Edmond duke of Somerset, who long before was warned to eschew all Castles, . . ." If, as seems likely, Q3 copy was used, the F omission might be explained on the theory that 70–1, omitted in Q, were written marginally opposite the four lines, all six lines being intended for inclusion. Instead, the two were treated as alternative to the four, which were thus omitted in F. On the other hand, the omission may be just another piece of compositor B's carelessness.

68. *Castle* . . .] The prophecy is accomplished, and helps to round off and unify the events of the Chronicle.

71. *Priests . . . enemies*] Cf. *Luke*, 6. 27, 28 (Noble).

73. *outrun the heavens*] escape from, as in the expression "outrun the constable". Cf. *Amos.*, 9. 2, 3; *Ps.*, 139. 6, 7.

76. *secure us*] make ourselves safe; cf. *Cym.*, IV. iv. 8.

78. *bottom*] nadir, lowest point; cf. *1 H 4*, IV. i. 50.

As well we may, if not through your neglect,—
We shall to London get, where you are lov'd,
And where this breach now in our fortunes made
May readily be stopp'd.

Re-enter Young CLIFFORD.

Y. Clif. But that my heart's on future mischief set,
I would speak blasphemy ere bid you fly;
But fly you must; uncurable discomfit
Reigns in the hearts of all our present parts.
Away, for your relief! and we will live
To see their day and them our fortune give.
Away, my lord, away! [*Exeunt.*

SCENE III.—*Fields near Saint Albans.*

Alarum. Retreat. Enter YORK, RICHARD, WARWICK, *and Soldiers, with drum and colours.*

York. Old Salisbury, who can report of him,
That winter lion, who in rage forgets
Aged contusions and all brush of time,
And, like a gallant in the brow of youth,
Repairs him with occasion? This happy day
Is not itself, nor have we won one foot,
If Salisbury be lost.

83. S.D.] *Dyce; Enter Clifford. F.* 84 ff.] *F; for Q, see App. 4.* 87. parts] *F;* part *Dyce;* party *Warburton.*

Scene III

Locality.] *Malone.* Entry.] *F;* Alarmes, and then a flourish, and enter the Duke of *Yorke* and *Richard. Q;* (*Alarmes . . . Yorke, Edward and Richard. Q3*). *See further App. 4.* 1. Old] *Collier, from Q;* Of *F.*

81. *London . . . where you are lov'd*] Contrast *3 H 6*, I. i. 67, where Henry says, "The city favours *them*."

82–3. *breach . . . stopp'd*] cf. III. i. 288.

84 ff.] For the alteration in F, see Introduction, p. xxii, and Appendix 4.

86. *uncurable discomfit*] irretrievable defeat.

87. *parts*] a jingle with "hearts"; probably a misprint; see collation.

Scene III

S.D.] see collation; Edward's two lines in Q have probably been cut.

1. *who can report*] cf. *Mac.*, I. ii. 1.

2. *winter*] aged.

3. *Aged*] of age.

brush] hostile encounter (Onions).

4. *brow*] height, top, as in the *brow* of a hill (Steevens); cf. *John*, v. i. 49.

5. *Repairs him with occasion*] revives, is restored, with opportunity.

Rich. My noble father,
Three times to-day I holp him to his horse,
Three times bestrid him; thrice I led him off,
Persuaded him from any further act:
But still, where danger was, still there I met him;
And like rich hangings in a homely house,
So was his will in his old feeble body.
But, noble as he is, look where he comes.

Enter SALISBURY.

Sal. Now, by my sword, well hast thou fought to-day;
By the mass, so did we all. I thank you, Richard:
God knows how long it is I have to live;
And it hath pleas'd him that three times to-day
You have defended me from imminent death.
Well, lords, we have not got that which we have:
'Tis not enough our foes are this time fled,
Being opposites of such repairing nature.

York. I know our safety is to follow them;
For, as I hear, the King is fled to London,
To call a present court of Parliament:
Let us pursue him ere the writs go forth.
What says Lord Warwick? Shall we after them?

War. After them! Nay, before them, if we can.
Now, by my faith, lords, 'twas a glorious day:
Saint Albans battle, won by famous York,
Shall be eterniz'd in all age to come.
Sound drums and trumpets! and to London all:
And more such days as these to us befall! [*Exeunt.*

14. S.D.] *F;* Enter Salsbury and Warwicke. *Q.* 15. *Sal.*] *Q, F; before 16 Wilson conj.* 29. faith] *Q;* hand *F.* 32. drums] *Q, Hanmer;* Drumme *F.*

9. *bestrid*] straddled, in order to defend; cf. *1 H 4*, v. i. 121–2.

20. *we have not . . . we have*] "we have not secured that which we have acquired" (Singer); cf. *Lucr.*, 135, "Oft they have not that which they possess."

22. *opposites . . . repairing nature*] foes with such power of recovery (Hart). Cf. 5 above.

25. *court of Parliament*] the king and his councillors forming a Parliament.

26. *writs*] issued in the king's name, to call members of parliament.

29. *faith*] see collation; a sign of occasional removal of "oaths" from Q; cf. iv. x. 57 above.

31. *eterniz'd*] immortalized. Also "eternish", e.g. *Dido*, 108. Introduced about 1580.

Appendix I

SOURCE-MATERIAL

from

(*a*) Hall's *Chronicle* (1542, 1548, 1550; reprinted 1809)

Hall *2 H 6*

p. 2 [Introduction to Henry IV]. Edward the third...
had issue Edwarde his first begotten sonne prince of II. ii. 10 ff
Wales, Willyam of Hatfeld the second begotten sonne, Lionell duke of Clarence the iij. begotten sonne, Ihon of Gaunt duke of Lancaster the iiij. begotten sonne, Edmond of Langley duke of York the v. begotten sonne, Thomas of Wodstocke duke of Glocestre the vj. begotten sonne, and Willyam of Wynsor the vij. begotten sonne. The saied prince Edward died in y[e] life of his father kyng Edward the iij. & had issue Richard borne at Burdeaux, whiche after the death of kyng Edward the iij. as cosin and heire to hym ... succeded hym ... and died without issue, Lionell duke of Clarence ... had issue Philippe his only doughter whiche was maried to Edmond Mortymer erle of Marche and had issue Roger Mortymer erle of March: whiche Roger had issue Edmond Mortimer erle of Marche, Anne and Elienor, whiche Edmond and Elianor died without issue. And the saied Anne was maried to Richard erle of Cambridge sonne to Edmond of Langley duke of Yorke the fifth begotten sonne of the said kyng Edwarde the thirde whiche Richarde had issue thee famous prince Richard Plantagenet duke of Yorke...

22 [First year of Henry IV]. Owen Glendor.../... II. ii. 39
23 made ... warre on ... lorde Grey of Rithen and toke
him prisoner, promisyng hym libertee and dischargyng his raunsome, if he would espouse and marie his doughter ... The lorde Grey ... assented... But this false father in lawe ... kept hym with his wife

still in captivitee till he died. And not content with this heynous offence, made warre on lorde Edmond Mortimer erle of Marche, and . . . toke hym prisoner . . .

114 i. [Henry VI (1422–3)] . . . the politike Princes and I. i. 76 ff
sage Magestrates of . . . England . . . caused yong prince Henry, the sole orphane of his noble parent kyng Henry the fifth, beyng of the age of. ix.
115 monethes / openly to be proclaimed kyng of Englande and Fraunce . . . And the custody of this young prince was apoyncted to . . . Henry Beaufford bishopp of Wynchester; the duke of Bedford was deputed to be Regent of Fraunce, and the duke of Gloucester was assigned Protector of Englande. Whiche . . . called to hym wise and graue counsailers, . . . he drouided farther all thynges necessary . . . for . . . farther conquest of Fraunce. . . He gathered great somes of money to mainteine the men of warre. . . Bedford no lesse studied then toke payne, not onely to kepe the countrees and regions by king Henry late conquered . . . Bedford . . . made . . . oracion, admonishyng them . . . in no wise to be the occasioners or counsailers that young kyng Henry should be depriued from his fathers lawful inheritance . . . to call to their memory . . . And if they would . . . diligently persecute and set on his enemies . . . they should . . . receiue of hym condigne rewardes, ouer and beside immortall fame and renoune.

197 xx. [1442–3]. Now let us speake alitle of a smoke I. ii, iv
that rose in England, whiche after grewe to a greate fire, and a terrible flame, to the destruccion of many a noble man. You have heard before, how the Duke of Gloucester sore grudged at the proude doynges of the Cardinall of Wynchester, and howe the Cardinall likewise, sore envied and disdayned at the rule of the Duke of Gloucester, and how . . . eche was reconciled to other, in perfite love and amitie, to all mens out-
202 ward judgementes. . . But venyme will once breake oute, and inwarde grudge will sone appeare . . . for divers secret attemptes were advaunced forward this season, against the noble duke Humfrey of Glocester, a farre of, whiche in conclusion came so nere, that

they bereft hym both of lyfe and lande... For first this yere, dame Elyanour Cobham, wyfe to the sayd duke, was accused of treason, for that she, by sorcery and enchauntment, entended to destroy the kyng, to thentent to advaunce and to promote her husbande to the croune: upon this she was examined in sainct Stephens chappel, before the Bisshop of Canterbury, and there by examinacion convict & judged, to do open penaunce, in iij open places, within the citie of London, and after that adjudged to perpetuall prisone in the Isle of Man, under the kepyng of Sir Jhon Stanley, knyght. At the same season, wer arrested as ayders and counsailers to the sayde Duchesse, Thomas Southwel, prieste and chanon of sainct Stephens in Westmynster, Jhon Hum priest, Roger Bolyngbroke, a conyng nycromancier, and Margerie Jourdayne, surnamed the witche of Eye, to whose charge it was laied, y[t] thei, at the request of the duchesse, had devised an image of waxe, representyng the kynge, whiche by their sorcery, a litle and litle consumed, entendyng therby in conclusion to waist, and destroy the kynges person, and so to bryng hym death, for the which treison, they wer adjudged to dye, & so Margery Jordayne was brent in smithfelde, & Roger Bolyngbroke was drawen and quartered at tiborne, taking upon his death, that there was never no suche thyng by them ymagined, Jhon Hum had his pardon, & Southwel died in the toure before execution: the duke of Gloucester, toke all these thynges paciently, and saied litle.

203 xxii. [1444–5].... to appeace the mortall warre, so long contineuyng . . . there was a greate diete appoynted . . . and many thynges moved to come to a finall peace, and mutuall concord. But . . . a finall concord could not be agreed, but in hope to come to a peace, a certain truce aswell by sea as by land, was concluded by the commissioners, for xviii monethes. . . In the treatyng of this truce, the Erle of Suffolke, extendyng his commission to the uttermoste, without assent of his associates, imagened in his phantasie, that the nexte waie to come to a perfite peace, was to move some mariage, betwen the Frenche kyngs I. i

kynsewoman, and kyng Henry his sovereigne: & because the Frenche kyng had no doughter of ripe age
204 . . . he desired to have the Lady Margaret, / cosyn to the Frenche kyng, and doughter to Reyner duke of Aniow, callyng hymself kyng of Scicile, Naples, and Hierusalem, havyng onely the name and stile of the same, without any peny profite, or fote of possession. . . . The erle of Suffolke (I cannot saie) either corrupted with bribes, or to muche affectionate to this unprofitable mariage, condiscended and agreed to their mocion, that the Duchie of Aniow, and the countie of Mayne, should be released and delivered, to the kyng her father, demaundyng for her mariage, neither peny nor farthyng. . . Humfrey duke of Gloucester, Protector of the realme, repugned and resisted, as muche as in him laie, this new alliaunce and contriued matrimonie: alledgyng that it was neither consonaunt to the lawe of GOD nor man, nor honourable to a prince, to infringe and breake a promise or contracte, by hym made and concluded, . . . a mariage betwene his highnes, & the doughter of therle of Arminacke, upon condicions, both to hym and his realme, as muche profitable as honorable. . . The duke was not heard, but the Erles doynges, were condiscended unto, and allowed. Whiche facte engendered suche a flame, that it never went oute, till bothe the parties with many other were consumed and slain, to the great unquietnes of the kyng and his realme. . . The kyng, bothe for the honor of his realme, and to assure to hymself, more speciall frendes, he created Lorde Jhon Holand Erle of Huntyngdon, Duke of Excester, as his father was, and Humfrey Erle of Stafford, was made Duke of Buckyngham, and Henry Erle of Warwicke, was erected to the title of Duke of Warwicke, and the Erle of Suf-
205 folke, made Marques of / Suffolke, whiche Marques with his wife, & many honorable parsonages of men and women, richely adorned, bothe with apparell and Jeuels, havyng with them many costly chariottes, & gorgious horselitters, sailed into Fraunce, for the conveyaunce of the nominated Quene, into the realme of England. For kyng Reyner her father, for al his long stile, had to short a purse to sende

his doughter honorably, to the kyng her spouse.

xxiii. [1445–6]. This noble company, came to the citee of Toures in Tourayne, where they were honorably received, bothe of the French kyng, and of the kyng of Scicile. Wher the Marques of Suffolke, as procurator to Kyng Henry, espoused thesaid Ladie, in the churche of saincte Martyns. At whiche mariage were present . . . the dukes of Orleaunce, of Calaber, of Alaunson, and of Britayn vii. Erles, xii. Barons xx. Bishoppes, beside knightes and gentlemen. There wer triumphaunt Iusts, costly feastes, and delicate banquettes . . . these honorable ceremonies ended, the Marques had the Ladie Margaret to hym delivered, whiche in greate estate, he conveyed through Normandy to Deape, and so transported her into Englande, where she landed at Portsmouthe, in the monethe of Aprill. This woman excelled all other, aswell in beautie and favor, as in wit and pollicie, and was of stomack and corage, more like to a man, then a woman . . . she was conveyed to . . . Southwike in Hamshire, where she . . . was coupled in matrimony, to kyng Henry the vi. After whiche mariage, she was . . . conveyed to London, and so to Westminster, where upon the xxx. daie of May, she . . . was Crouned Quene. I. i. 5 ff I. i. 1

This marriage seemed to many, bothe infortunate, and vnprofitable to the realme of England, and that for many causes. First the kyng with her had not one peny, and for the fetchyng of her, the Marques of Suffolke, demaunded a whole fiftene, in open parliament: also for her marriage, the Duchie of Aniow, the citee of Mauns, and the whole countie of Mayne, were deliuered and released to King Reyner her father, whiche countreis were the very stayes, and backestandes to the Duchy of Normandy. Furthermore for this marriage, the Earle of Arminacke, toke suche displeasure, that he became vtter enemy to the realme of Englande and was the chief cause, that the Englishmen, wer expulsed out of the whole duchie of Aquitayne, and lost bothe the countreis of Gascoyn and Guyen. But moste of all it should seme, that God with this matrimony was not content. For after this

spousage the kynges frendes fell from hym, bothe in
Englande and in Fraunce, the Lordes of his realme,
fell in diuision emongst themselfes, the commons rebelled against their souereigne Lorde, and naturall
Prince, feldes wer foughten, many thousandes slain,
and finally, the kyng deposed, and his sonne slain,
and this Quene sent home again, with asmuche
misery and sorowe, as she was receiued with pompe
and triumphe, suche is worldly vnstablenes, and so
waueryng is false flattering fortune.

206 xxiiii. [1446–7] . . . it was concluded, that Nor- I. iii. 100–
mandy should be well furnished and strongly de- 206
fended, before the terme of the truce should be expired. . . For whiche consideracion, money was
graunted, men were appoynted, and a great army
gathered together and the duke of Somerset, was
appoynted Regent of Normandy, and the Duke of I. i. 63
Yorke thereof discharged.
207 This Marques thus gotten up, into fortunes trone, I. i. 62
not content with his degree, by the meanes of the
Quene, was shortely erected to the estate and degree
of a Duke, and ruled the Kyng at his pleasure. . .
This yere, an Armerars servaunt of London, appeled I. iii,
his master of treason, whiche offered to bee tried by II. iii. 47 ff
battaill. At the daie assigned, the frendes of the master, brought hym Malmesey and *Aqua vite*, to com-
forte hym with all, but it was the cause of his and
their discomforte: for he poured in so much that
when he came into the place in Smithfelde, where he
should fight, bothe his witte and strength failed hym:
208 and so he beyng a tall and / hardye personage, over-
laded with hote drynkes, was vanqueshed of his servaunt, beyng but a cowarde and a wretche, whose
body was drawen to Tiborne, & there hanged and
behedded.

xxv. [1447–8]. During the tyme of this truce . . . a I. iii. 41 ff
sodain mischief, and a long discorde, sprang out
sodainly, by the meanes of a woman: for kyng Henry
. . . was a man of a meke spirite, and of a simple witte,
preferryng peace before warre, rest before businesse,
honestie before profite, and quietnesse before

laboure... In hym reigned shamefastnesse, modestie, integritie, and pacience to bee marveiled at, takyng and sufferyng all losses, chaunces, displeasures, and suche worldely tormentes, in good parte, and with a pacient maner, as though they had chaunced by his awne fault or negligent oversight: yet he was governed of them whom he should have ruled, and brideled of suche, whom he sharpely should have spurred: He gaped not for honor, nor thirsted for riches, but studied onely for the health of his soule... But on the other parte, the Quene his wife, was a woman of a greate witte, and yet of no greater witte, then of haute stomacke, desirous of glory, and couetous of honor, and of reason, pollicye counsaill, and other giftes and talentes of nature, belongyng to a man, full and flowyng: of witte and wilinesse she lacked nothyng, nor of diligence, studie, and businesse, she was not unexperte: but yet she had one poynt of a very woman: for often tyme, when she was vehement and fully bente in a matter, she was sodainly like a wethercocke, mutable, and turnyng. This woman perceivyng that her husbande did not frankely rule as he would, but did all thyng by thadvise and counsaill of Humfrey duke of Gloucester, and that he passed not muche on the aucthoritie and governaunce of the realme, determined with her self, to take upon her the rule and regiment, bothe of the kyng and his kyngdome, & to deprive & evict out of al rule and auothoritie, thesaid duke, then called the lord protector of the realme: least men should saie & report, y[t] she had neither wit nor stomacke, whiche would permit & suffre her husband, beyng of perfect age & mans estate, like a yong scholer or innocent pupille to be governed by the disposicion of another man... This ... invencion ... was furthered and set forward by suche, as of long tyme had borne malice to the duke... Whiche venomous serpentes, and malicious Tygers, perswaded, incensed, and exhorted the quene, to loke well upon the expenses and revenues of the realme, and thereof to call an accompt: affirmyng plainly that she should evidently perceive, that the Duke of Gloucester, had not so muche advaunced & preferred the common/wealth and publique utili-

209 tie, as his awne private thinges & peculier estate. . .
And although she joyned her husbande with hir in
name, yet she did all, she saied all, and she bare the
whole swynge . . . and firste of all she excluded the
duke of Gloucester, from all rule and governaunce,
not prohibityng suche as she knewe to be his mortal
enemies, to invent and imagyne, causes and griefes,
against hym and his: so that by her permission, and
favor, diverse noblemen conspired against hym, of
the whiche . . . the Marques of Suffolke, and the duke
of Buckyngham to be the chiefe, not unprocured by
the Cardinall of Winchester, and the Archebishop of
Yorke. Diverse articles, bothe heynous and odious,
were laied to his charge in open counsaill, and in
especiall one, that he had caused men adjudged to
dye, to be put to other execucion, then the law of the
land had ordered or assigned. . . But his capitall
enemies and mortal foes, fearying that some tumulte
or commocion might arise, if a prince so well be-
loved of the people, should bee openly executed, and
put to death, determined to trappe & undoo hym. . .
So for the furtheraunce of their purpose, a parlia- II. iv. 70,
ment was somoned to be kept at Bery, whether re- III. i,
sorted all the peres of the realme, and emongst them, III. ii
the duke of Gloucester, whiche on the seconde daie of
the session, was by the lorde Beaumond, then high
Constable of Englande, accompanied by the duke of
Buckyngham, and other, arrested, apprehended, and
put in warde, and all his servauntes sequestered from
hym. . . The duke the night after his emprisonement,
was found dedde in his bed, and his body shewed to
the lordes and commons, as though he had died of a
palsey or empostome: but all indifferent persons
well knewe, that he died of no natural death but of
some violent force: some judged hym to be strangled:
. . . other write, that he was stiffeled or smoldered betwene twoo fetherbeddes. . . Thus was this noble
prince, sonne, brother, and uncle to kynges, whiche
had valeauntly and pollitiquely by the space of xxv.
yeres governed this Realme, and for his demerites,
called the good duke of Gloucester, . . . brought to his
. . . laste ende. . . It semeth to many men, that the
name and title of Gloucester, hath been unfortunate

and unluckie to diverse, whiche for their honor, have been erected by creacion of princes, to that stile and dignitie, as Hugh Spencer, Thomas of Woodstocke, sonne to kyng Edward the third, and this duke Humfrey, which thre persones, by miserable death finished their daies, and after them kyng Richard the iii. also, duke of Gloucester, in civill/warre was slain and
210 confounded: so y[t] this name of Gloucester, is taken for an unhappie and unfortunate stile. . . When the rumor of the dukes death, was blowen through the realme, many men wer sodainly appalled and amased for feare: many abhorred and detested y[e] faict, but all men reputed it an abhominable crueltie, and a shameful tiranny.

xxvi. [1448–9]. Rychard duke of Yorke, perceivyng the Kyng to be a ruler not Ruling, & the whole burden of the Realme, to depend in the ordinaunces of the Quene & the duke of Suffolke, began secretly to allure to his frendes of the nobilitie, and privatly declared to them, his title and right to the Crowne. . . II. ii

During these doynges, Henry Beaufford, bishop of Winchester . . . departed out of this world. . . This man was sonne to Jhon of Gaunte duke of Lancaster, discended of an honorable lignage, but borne in Baste, more noble of blodd, then notable in learning, haut in stomacke, and hygh in countenance, ryche above measure of all men, & to few liberal, disdaynfull to his kynne and dreadfull to his lovers, preferrynge money before frendshippe, many thinges beginning, and nothing perfourmyng. His covetous insaciable, and hope of long lyfe, made hym bothe to forget God, hys Prince and hym selfe, in his latter daies . . . he, lyeng on his death bed, said these wordes: 'Why should I dye, having so muche ryches, if the whole Realme would save my lyfe, I am able either by pollicie to get it, or by ryches to bye it? Fye! wyll not death be hyered, nor will money do/
211 nothyng? . . . I thought to encrease my treasure in hoope to have worne a tryple Croune.' III. iii

212 . . . which mischiefes (while the Kyng, as thinges of the worlde, and of no great moment, did neglect and omit, as he which preferred & extolled godly thinges,

213 above all worldly affaires . . .) / . . . dayly so much encreased . . . the Frenche nacion knew in what case the
state of the realme of Englande stode.

xxvii. [1449–50]. It was not enough, the realme of
England this season thus to be vexed and unquieted
with the busines of Normandy, but also a new rebel- III. i. 282
lion began in Irelande, to the great displeasure of the
Kynge and his counsaill: for repressinge whereof,
Richard duke of Yorke, with a convenient number
of men was sent thither, as lieuetenant to the Kyng,
which not onely appeased the fury of the wylde, and
savage people there, but also gat him suche love and
favour of the countrey and the inhabitauntes, that
their sincere love and frendly affeccion coulde never
be seperated from him and his lygnage.

215 xxviii. [1450–1]. The Duke of Somerset . . . made III. i. 82
an agrement with the Frenche kyng, that he would
rendre the toune so that he and all his might depart
216 in sauegard with all their / goodes and substaunce;
whiche offre, the Frenche Kyng gladly accepted . . .
Sir Davie Halle . . . departed to Chierburge and
from thence sailed into Irelande to the duke of Yorke
makyng relacion to hym . . . whiche thyng kyndeled
so greate a rancore in his harte & stomacke that he
never left persecutynge of the Duke of Somersette. . .
Nor rested English onely the toune of Chierburge. . .
Thus was the riche duchie of Normandy lost y[e]
whiche had continued in thenglishmennes possession
xxx. yeres, by the conquest of Kyng Henry the fifth.
. . . Other say, that the Duke of Somerset, for his
awne peculier profite, kept not halfe his nombre of
souldiors, and put their wages in his purse.
. . . the people of the Realme (aswell of the nobilitie, III. ii. 240
217 as of the meane sorte) . . . / . . . began to make exclamacion against the Duke of Suffolke, affirming him,
to be the onely cause of the delivery of Angeow &
Mayne, the chief procurer of the death of the good
duke of Gloucester, the verie occasion of the losse of
Normandy, the moste swallower up and consumer of
the kynges treasure, . . . the expeller from the kyng,
of all good and verteous counsailors . . . : So that the

duke was called in every mannes mouth, a traitor, a murderer, a robber of the kynges treasure, and worthy to bee put to moste cruell punishment. By reason of this exclamacion, the Quene somewhat fearyng the destruccion of the Duke, but more the confusion of her self, caused the Parliament . . . to be
219 adjourned . . . / whither came the Kyng and the Quene in great estate and with them the Duke of Suffolke, as chefe counsailor. . . When kyng Henry perceived, that the commons wer thus stomacked and bent, against the Quenes dearlynge William Duke of Suffolke, he playnly saw, that neither glosyng wolde serve, nor dissimulacion coulde appeace, the continual clamor of the importunate commons: . . . First he sequestred the lorde Say, beyng threasorer of Englande, and other the Dukes adherentes, from there offices, and authoritie, and after banished and put in exile the duke of Suffolke, as the abhorred tode, and common noysaunce of the Realme of Englande, for the terme of v. yeres: meanyng by this exile, to appease the furious rage of ye outragious people, and that pacified, to revocate him into his olde estate, as the Quenes chefe frend & counsailor. But fortune wold not, that this flagitious person, shoulde so escape: for when he shipped in Suffolke, entendynge to be transported into Fraunce, he was IV. i, iv
encontered with a shippe of warre apperteynyng to the duke of Excester, the Constable of the Towre of London, called the Nicholas of the Towre. The capitayne of the same barke with small fight entered into the dukes shyppe, and perceyvyng his person present, brought hym to Dovere Rode, & there on the one syde of a cocke bote caused his head to be stryken of, and left his body with the head upon the sandes of Dover, which corse was there founde by a chapelayne of his, and conveyed to Wyngfelde college in Suffolke, and there buried. This ende had William de la Pole, first duke of Suffolke, as men judge by Gods punyshment: for above all thinges he was noted to be the very organ, engine, and diviser of the destruccion of Humfrey the good duke of Gloucester, and so the bloudde of the Innocente man was with his dolorous death, recompensed and punished. But the death of

this froward person, and ungracious patron, brought
not the Realme quyete, nor delivered it from all
inward grudge. . . For although Rychard duke of II. ii
Yorke, was in pryson, (as the kynges deputie) in ye
Realm of Irelande, continually resyaunt there, yet
his breath puffed, and his wynde blew dayly, in
many partes of the Realme. For many of the nobilitie, and more of the meane estate, wisely ponderynge
the estate and condicion of the Realme, perceyvynge
more losse then encrease, more ruyne then avaunce-
ment, daily to ensue: Rememberyng also that
Fraunce was conquered, and Normandy was gayned,
by the Frenche people in shorte space, thought with
them selfes and imagened, that the falte of all these
miserable chaunces, happened, either because the
Kynge was not the true enheritor to the crowne, or
that he and his counsaill were not able of wit, pollicie,
and circumspeccion, to rule and gouerne so noble a
Realme, or so famous a region. Upon this conjecture
the frendes, kinsmen and alyes of the duke of Yorke,
which wer of no small number, began to practise the
governaunce of his title: Infusyng and puttyng into
mens heades secretely his right to ye crown, his pol-
litique governaunce, his gentle behavior, to all the
Iryshe nacion, affirmyng, that he whiche had
brought that rude and savage nacion, to civile
fashion, and Englishe urbanitie, wolde, (if he once
ruled in the Realme of England) depose evil coun-
saillors, correct evil judges, & reforme all matters
amisse, and unamended. And to set open the fludde
gates of these devises, it was thought necessary, to
cause some great commocion and rysyng of people to
be made against the King: so that if they prevayled,
then had the duke of Yorke and his complices, there
appetite and desire. And because the kentishmen be
impacient in wronges disdayning of to much oppression, and ever desirous of new chaung, and new
fangelnes. / The overture of this matter was put III. i. 331
fyrste furthe in Kent, and to thentent that it should
not be knowen, that the duke of Yorke or his frendes
were the cause of the sodayne rising: A certayn yong-
man of a goodely stature, and pregnaunt wit, was
entised to take upon him the name of Jhon Morty- IV. ii ff

mer, all though his name were Jhon Cade, and not for a small policie, thinking that by that surname, the lyne and lynage of the assistent house of the erle of Marche, which were no small number, should be to hym both adherent, and favorable. This capitayn not onely suborned by techers, but also enforced by privye scholemasters, assembled together a great company of talle personages: . . . promiysng them, that if . . . they might once take the kyng, the Quene, & other their counsaillers . . . neither fiftenes should hereafter be demaunded, nor once any imposicions, or tax should be spoken of. These perswasions, with many other fayre promises of libertie, (whiche the common people more affect & desire, rather then reasonable obedience, and due conformitie) so animated the Kentishe people, that they with their capitayne above named, in good order of battell (not in great number) came to the playne of Blackehethe . . . Wherupon the kyng assembled a great army, and marched toward them. . . The subtill capitayn Jack Cade, entendyng to bring the kyng farther, within the compasse of his net, brake up his Campe, and retyred backwarde to the towne of Sevenocke in Kent, and there exspectynge his pray, encamped him selfe, and made his abode. The Quene, which bare the rule, beyng of his retrayte well advertised, sent syr Humfrey Stafford knyght, and William his brother with many other gentlemen, to folow the chace of the Kentishmen, thinkynge that they had fledde, but verely, they were desceyved: for at the fyrst skyrmish, both the Staffordes were slayne, and all their companye shamfully discomfited. . . When the Kentish capitayn, or ye covetous Cade, had thus obteyned victory . . . he appareled hym selfe in their rych armure, and so with pompe and glory returned agayn to the playn of Blackeheath, and there strongly encamped him selfe: to whome were sent by the kynge, the Archebishop of Canterbury, and Humfrey duke of Buckyngham, to common with hym of
221 his greves and requestes. / . . . The kyng . . . havyng dayly reporte of the concurse and accesse of people, which continually resorted to him, doubtyng asmuch his familiar servauntes, as his unknowen sub-

jectes (which spared not to speake, that the capitaynes cause, was profitable for the common wealth)
departed in all haste to the castell of Kylyngworthe
in Warwyckeshyre, leavyng only behynd him ye lord IV. v
Scales, to kepe the Towre of London. The capitayn
beynge advertised of the kynges absence, came first
into Southwarke, and there lodged at the white hart,
prohibityng to all men, Murder, Rape, or Robbery:
by whiche colour he allured to hym the hartes of the
common people. But after that he entered into London, and cut the ropes of the drawbridge, strikyng
his sworde on London stone, saiyng: now is Mortymer lorde of this citie, and rode in every strete lyke a
lordly Capitayn. . . he caused syr James Fynes lord
Say . . . to be brought to the Gylde halle of London,
and there to be arrayned: whiche beyng before the IV. vii
kynges justices put to aunswere, desired to be tryed
by his peeres, for the lenger delay of his life. The
Capitayne perceivyng his dilatorie ple, by force toke
him from the officers, and brought him to the standard in Cheape, and there before his confession
ended, caused his head to be cut of, and pitched it on
a highe poole, which was openly borne before hym
through the stretes. And this cruell tyraunt not content with the murder of the lorde Say, wente to Myle
end, and there apprehended syr James Cromer, then
shreve of Kent, and sonne in law to the sayd lord
Say, & hym without confession or excuse heard,
caused there lykewise to be hedded, and his head to
be fixed on a poole, and with these two heddes, this
blody butcher entered into the citie agayn, and in
despyte caused them in every strete, kysse together,
to the great detestacion of all the beholders. . . He
also put to execution in Southwarke divers persons,
some for infryngyng his rules and preceptes, bycause
he wolde be sene indifferent, other he tormented of
his olde acquayntance, lest they shoulde blase &
declare his base byrthe, and lowsy lynage, dis-
paragyng him from his usurped surname of Mortymer. . . The wise Mayre, and sage magistrates of the
citie of London, perceyvyng themselfes, neither to be
sure of goodes nor of lyfe well warranted, determined
with feare to repel and expulse this mischievous

head, and hys ungracious company. And because the lord Scales was ordeyned keper of ye Towre of London, with Mathew Gough, the often named capitayne in Normandy . . . they purposed to make them pryvye both of their entent and enterprise. The lord Scales promised them hys ayde, with shotyng of ordinaunce, and Mathew Goughe was by hym appoynted, to assist the Mayre and the Londoners: bycause he was both of manhode, and experience renoumed and noysed. So ye Capitaynes of the citie appointed, toke upon them in the night to kepe the bridge of London, prohibiting the Kentishmen, either to passe or approche. The rebelles, which never soundly slepte, for feare of sodain chaunces, hearyng the brydge to be kept and manned, ran with greate haste to open their passage, where betwene bothe partes was a ferce and cruell encounter. Matthew Gough, . . . perceivyng the Kentishmen /
222 better to stande to their taclyng, then his imaginacion expected, advised his company no further to procede, toward Southwarke, till the day appered: to the extent, that the citezens hearing where the place of the jeopardye rested, might occurre their enemies, and releve their frendes and companions. But this counsaill came to small effect: for the multitude of ye rebelles drave the citezens from the stoulpes at the bridge foote, to the drawe bridge, and began to set fyre in divers houses . . . Yet the Capitayns nothing regarding these chaunces, fought on the draw bridge all the nighte valeauntly, but in conclusion, the rebelles gate the draw bridge, and drowned many, and slew . . . many other, beside Matthew Gough, a man of great wit, much experience in feates of chivalrie, the which in continual warres, had valeauntly served the kyng and his father, in the partes beyond the sea. . . This hard and sore conflict endured on the bridge, til ix. of the clocke in the morninge, in doutfull chaunce, and fortunes balaunce: for some tyme the Londoners were bet back to the stulpes at sainct Magnes corner, and sodaynly agayne the rebelles were repulsed and driven backe, to the stulpes in Southwarke, so that both partes, beyng faynte, wery and fatigate, agreed

to desist from fight, and to leve battail til the next day, upon condicion: that neither Londoners should passe into Southwarke, not the Kentishmen in to London.

After this abstinence of warre agreed, the lusty Kentishe Capitayne, hopyng on more frendes, brake up the gayles of the kinges benche and Marshalsea, and set at libertie, a swarme of galantes, both mete for his service and apte for his enterprise. The archebishop of Canterbury . . . called to him the bishop of Winchester. . . These two prelates seyng the fury of the Kentish people, by reason of their betyng backe, to be mitigate and minished, passed the ryver of Thamyse from the Towre, into Southwarke, bringing with them under the kynges great seale, a
general pardon unto all the offendors: which they IV. viii
caused to be openly proclaimed & published. Lorde how glad the poore people were of this Pardone . . . and how thei accepted the same, in so muche that the whole multitude, without biddyng farewel to their capitain, retired thesame night, every man to his awne home, as men amased, and striken with feare. But Jhon Cade desperate of succors, whiche by the frendes of the duke of Yorke wer to hym promised, and seyng his companie thus without his knowledge sodainly depart, mistrustyng the sequele of y[e] matter, departed secretly in habite disguysed, into Sussex; but all his metamorphosis or transfiguracion, little
prevailed. For after a Proclamacion made, that who- IV. x
soever could apprehende thesaied Jack Cade, should have for his pain, a M. markes, many sought for hym, but few espied hym, til one Alexander Iden, esquire of Kent found hym in a garden, and there in his defence, manfully slewe the caitife Cade, & brought his ded body to London, whose hed was set on London bridge. . .

After this commocion, the kyng himself came into Kent, & there sat in judgement upon the offendors, and if he had not mitigated his justice, with mercie and compassion, more than five C. by the rigor of his lawe, had been justely put to execucion: but he considered, bothe their fragilitie and innocencie, and how they with perverse people, were seduced and deceived: and so punished the stubburne heddes, and delivered the ignorant & miserable people, to the greate rejoysyng of all his subjectes.

225 xxx. [1452–3] . . . the duke of Yorke . . . mindyng IV. ix
no lenger to dreame in his waightie matter, nor to V.
kepe secrete his right and title, returned out of Irelande, and came to London in the Parliament tyme, where he deliberately consulted, with his especial frendes: as Jhon Duke of Norffolke, Richard Erle of Salisbury, and Lorde Richard his sonne, whiche after was Erle of Warwick . . . requiryng them bothe of advise and counsaill, how he might without spot of treason, or colour of usurpacion, set forth his title, and obtein his right.

After long consultacion, it was thought expedient, first to seke some occasion and picke some querell, to the duke of Somerset, whiche ruled the kyng, ordred the realme, and moste might do with the quene . . . declaring, that thei neither meant evil, nor thought harme, either to the kinges person, or to his dignitie: but that their intent was, for the revenging of great injuries doen to the publique wealth, and to persecute and reforme diverse rulers about the kyng. . .

When the duke of Yorke had thus framed thentery into his long intended jorney, he with helpe of his frendes, assembled a great army in the Marches of Wales. . . The kyng muche astonnied with this sodain
226 commocion, by / the advise of his counsail, raised a greate hoste, and marched forward toward the duke: but he being of his approche, credibly advertised, by his espials, diverted from the kynges waies, and toke his jorney toward London: and havyng knowledge, that he might not be suffered with his army, to passe through London, he crossed over the Thamese at Kyngston bridge, and so set forth toward Kent, where he knewe he had bothe frendes and good willers, and there, on brente Heath, a mile from Dertford, and x. miles from London, he embattailed himself, and encamped his army very strongly, bothe with trenches and artilery. The king thereof advertised, with greate diligence, brought his army to blacke Heath, & there pight his tentes. While both

tharmies lay thus embattailed, the kyng by thadvise of his counsaill, sent the bishoppes of Winchester and Elie to the duke, both to knowe, what was the cause of so greate a tumult and commocion, and also to make a concord, if the requestes of the duke and his company, semed to them consonant to reason, or profitable to the people. The duke hearyng ye message of the two bishops, either doubting the variable chaunce of mortal battaill, or lokyng for a better occasion, or a more lucky daie, aunswered the prelates, that his commyng was neither to dampnifie the kyng, neither in honor, nor in persone, nor yet any good man, but his intent was to remove from hym, certain evil disposed persons of his counsaill, which wer the bludsuckers of the nobilitie, the pollers of the cleargie, and oppressors of the poore people: emongst whom he chiefly named, Edmond duke of Somerset, whom if the kyng would commit to warde, to aunswere to suche articles, as against hym should in open parliament, be both proponed and proved, he promised not onely to dissolve his armie and dispatche his people, but also offered hymself, like an obedient subjecte, to come to the kynges presence, and to do him true and faithful service, accordyng to his truth & bounden duetie... The kyng... caused the duke of Somerset to be committed to ward, as some saie: or to kepe hymself privye in his awne house, as other write,... Whiche thyng doen, the duke of Yorke... dissolved his army, & brake up his campe, and came to the kynges tent, where beside his expectacion, and contrary to the promise made by the kyng, he found the duke of Somerset, set at large and at libertie, whom the duke of Yorke boldly accused, of treason, of bribery, oppression, and many other crimes. The duke of Somerset not onely made aunswere to the dukes objeccions, but also accused hym of treason... the kyng removed straight to London, and the duke of Yorke as a prisoner, rode before hym, & so was
227 kept awhile... / ... The kinges counsaill set the duke of Yorke at libertie, and permitted him to returne to his fayre Castel of Wigmore... ye duke of Somerset rose up in high favor w^{t} ye king & ye quene, & his worde only ruled, & his voyce was only hearde.

xxxii. [1454–5]. When the duke [of York] sawe
mennes appetites, and felt well their mindes, he
chiefly enterteined two Richardes, and bothe
231 Nevelles, the one of Salisbury, the other of Warwicke I. I. 188
beyng erle, the first the father, the second the sonne.
. . . This Richard . . . was a man of marvelous quali-
ties, but also from his youth . . . so set them forward,
with wittie and gentle demeanour . . . that emong all
sortes of people, he obteined greate love, muche
232 favor, and more credence: / whiche thynges daily
more encreased by his abundant liberalitie, and
plentifull house kepynge, then by his riches, aucthoritie, or high parentage: by reason of whiche doynges,
he was in suche favor and estimacion, emongst the
common people, that thei judged hym able to do all
thynges, and that, without hym, nothyng to be well
done.

xxiii. [1455–6]. When the duke of Yorke had fastened his chaine, betwene these twoo strong and
robustious pillers, he with his frendes, so seriously
wrought, and so pollitiquely handled his business,
that the Duke of Somerset, was arrested in the IV. ix. 14
Quenes greate chamber, and sent to the toure of
London . . .: against whom in open parliament, wer
laied diuerse and heinous articles of high treason, . . .
the kyng either of his awne mynde, or by the Quenes
procurement, caused the duke of Somerset, to be set
at libertie: by whiche doyng, grew great enuy and V. i. 87 ff
displeasure, betwene the king and diuerse of his
lordes, and in especiall between the duke of Yorke,
and the kynges linage. . . The duke of Yorke and his V. ii. iii
adherentes perceiuyng, that neither exhortacion
serued, nor accusement preuailed against the duke of
Somerset, determined to reuenge their querrell, and
obtein their purpose, by open warre and marciall
aduenture, and no lenger to slepe in so waightie a
businesse. So he beyng in the Marches of Wales, associate with his especiall frendes, the erles of Salisbury
and Warwicke, the lorde Cobham, and other,
assembled an army, and gathered a greate power,
and like warlike persones, marched toward London.
. . . The kyng beyng credebly informed, of the greate

army commyng toward hym, assembled an host,
intendyng to mete the duke in the Northe parte, because he had to many frendes about the citie of London, and for that cause, with greate spede and small
lucke, he beyng accompanied, with the Dukes of
Somerset, and Buckyngham, therles of Stafford,
Northumberlande, and Wiltshire, with the lorde
Clifford, and diuerse other barons, departed out of
Westminster, the xx. daie of May, toward the toune
of S. Albons: of whose doynges, the duke of Yorke
being aduertised, by his espials, with all his power
costed the countreys, and came to the same toune,
the third daie next ensuyng. The kyng hearyng of
their approchyng, sent to hym messengers, straightly
chargyng and commaundyng hym, as an obedient
subiect, to kepe the peace, and not as an enemy to his
naturall countrey, to murdre and slay his awne coun-
tremen and propre nacion. While kyng Henry more
desirous of peace then of warre, was sendyng furthe
his orators, at the one ende of the toune: the erle of
Warwicke with the Marchemen, entered at the other
gate of the toune, and fiersly set on the kynges fore-
ward, and theim shortly discomfited. Then came the
duke of Somerset, & all the other lordes with the
kynges power, whiche fought a sore and a cruell battaill, in the whiche, many a tall man lost his life: but
the duke of Yorke sent euer freshe-men, to succor the
wery, & put new men in the places of the hurt per-
233 sons, by whiche onely / pollicie, the kynges armie
was profligate and dispersed, & all the chieftaines of
the field almoste slain and brought to confusion. For
there died vnder the signe of the Castle, Edmond v. ii. 66
duke of Somerset, who long before was warned to
eschew all Castles, and beside hym, lay Henry the
second erle of Northumberland, Humfrey erle of
Stafford, sonne to the duke of Buckingham, Jhon
lorde Clifford, and viij. M. men and more. Humfrey duke of Buckyngham, beyng wounded, & James
Butler erle of Wiltshire & Ormond, seyng fortunes
loweryng chaunce, left the kyng poste a lone & with
a greate numbre fled away. This was thend of the
first bataill at S. Albons. . .

236 xxxv. [1457–8] . . . Quene Margarete, whose
breath ruled, and whose worde was obeyed above
the kyng and his counsail . . . entendyng the destruccion of the duke of Yorke and his frendes, which
devise she thought not mete to be practised nere to
the citie of London, . . . caused the kyng to make a
progresse into Warwyckeshire, for his health & re- I. ii. 56
creacion, and so with Hawkyng and Huntynge came II. i
to the citie of Coventrey, where were diuers ways
studied privelv, to bryng the quene to her hartes ease,
and long expectate desire: which was the death &
destruccion of the duke of Yorke, the erles of Salisbury and Warwycke . . . if these noblemen admonish-
ed by their frendes, had not sodaynly departed, their
lyfes threde had bene broken, . . . but . . . they
auoided this net and narrowly escaped the snare.

246 xxxviii. [1460–1] . . . Which kyng Richard, of that II. ii. 21 ff
name the second, was lawfully and justly possessed of
the croune, and diademe of this Realme and region,
till Henry of Derby, duke of Lancaster and Herd-
ford, sonne to Jhon duke of Lancaster . . . wrongfully
usurped and entruded upon the royall power and
high estate of this Realme and region, takyng on hym
ye name, stile, & aucthoritie of kyng and governor of
thesame. . . After whose piteous death . . . the right &
title of the croune . . . was lawfully . . . returned to
Rogier Mortimer, erle of Marche, sonne and heyre
to lady Philippe, the onely child of the above re-
hersed Lyonel, duke of Clarence, to which Rogiers
doughter called Anne, my . . . mother, I am the very
true and lineall heyre. . . Edmond erle of Marche, my
most welbeloved uncle, in the tyme of the first
usurpar, in dede, but not by right, called kyng
Henry the iiij. . . . he beyng then in captivitie, with
Owen Glendore, the rebell in Wales, made his title,
and righteous clayme, to the destruccion of both the
noble persons.

251 xxxix. [1461–2] . . . the yong erle of Rutland, ii.
sonne to the aboue named duke of Yorke, . . . the lord
Clifford marked him and sayde: by Gods blode, thy
father slew myne, and so wil I do the and all thy kyn,

and with that woord, stacke the erle to ye hart with his dagger, . . .

(*b*) John Fox, *Acts and Monuments* (ed. 1844), iii. 712–13

712 In the young days of this king Henry VI., being II. i. 61 ff
yet under the governance of this duke Humphrey,
his protector, there came to St. Alban's a certain
713 beggar with his wife, and was walking there / about
the town begging five or six days before the king's coming thither; saying, that he was born blind, and never saw in his life, and was warned in his dream, that he should come out of Berwick, where he said he had ever dwelled, to seek St. Alban; and that he had been at his shrine, and had not been holpen, and therefore he would go and seek him at some other place; for he had heard some say, since he came, that St. Alban's body should be at Cologne: and indeed such a contention hath there been; but of a truth, as I am surely informed, he lieth here, at St. Alban's, saving some relics of him, which they there show shrined. But, to tell you forth my tale, when the king was come, and the town full, suddenly this blind man, at St. Alban's shrine, had his sight again, and a miracle solemnly rung, and "Te Deum" sung; so that nothing was talked of in all the town, but this miracle. So happened it then, that duke Humphrey of Gloucester, a man no less wise than well learned, having great joy to see such a miracle, called the poor man unto him; and first showing himself joyous of God's glory so showed in the getting of his sight, and exhorting him to meekness, and to no [none?] ascribing of any part of the worship to himself, nor to be proud of the people's praise, who would call him a good and godly man thereby; at last, he looked well upon his eyes, and asked whether he could see nothing at all in his life before. And when his wife, as well as himself, affirmed falsely "no", then he looked advisedly upon his eyes again, and said, "I believe you very well, for me thinketh ye cannot see well yet." "Yea, sir," quoth he, "I thank God and his holy martyr, I can now see as well as any man." "You

can," quoth the duke, "What colour is my gown?" Then anon the beggar told him. "What colour," quoth he, "is *this* man's gown?" He told him also, and so forth: without any sticking he told him the names of all the colours that could be showed him. And when the duke saw that, he bade him "walk, traitor," and made him to be set openly in the stocks: for though he could have seen suddenly, by miracle, the difference between divers colours; yet could he not, by the sight, so suddenly tell the names of all these colours, except he had known them before, no more than the names of all the men, that he should suddenly see.

By this it may be seen, how duke Humphrey had not only a head, to discern and dissever truth from forged and feigned hypocrisy; but study also, and diligence, likewise, was in him, to reform that which was amiss.

And thus much, hitherto, for the noble prowess and virtues, joined with the like ornaments of knowledge and literature, shining in this princely duke: for which as he was both loved of the poor commons, and well spoken of, of all men, and no less deserving the same, being called the "good" duke of Gloucester; so neither wanted he his enemies and privy enviers. . .

Appendix 2

GENEALOGICAL TABLES

(*a*) The Seven Sons of Edward III

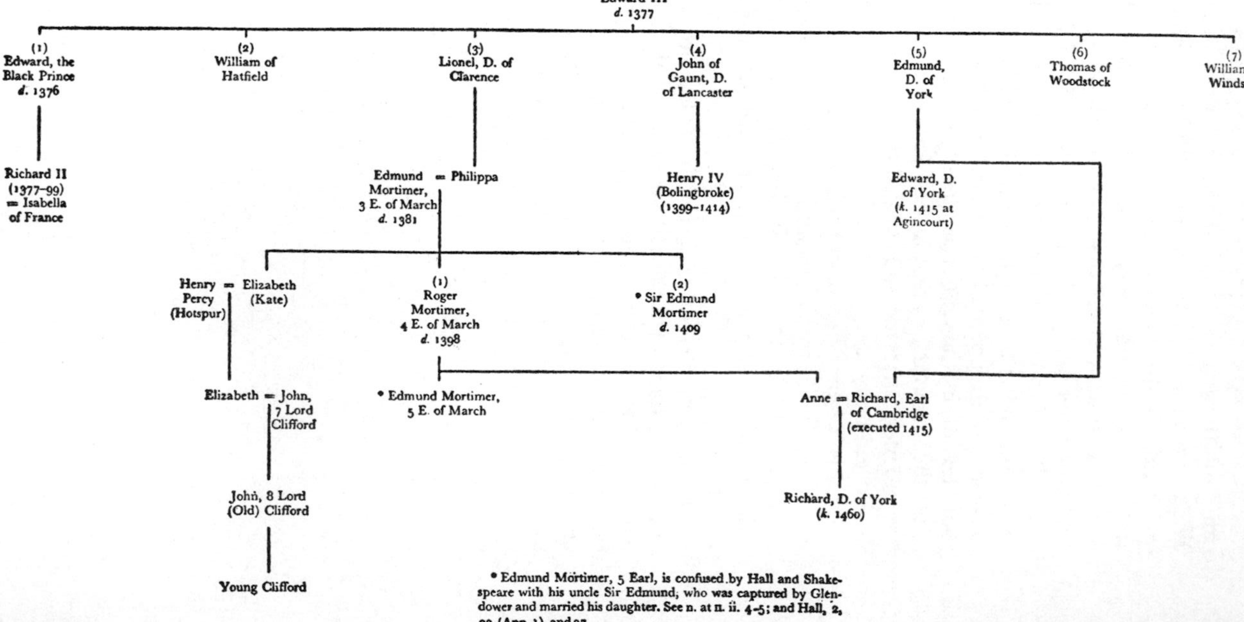

* Edmund Mortimer, 5 Earl, is confused by Hall and Shakespeare with his uncle Sir Edmund, who was captured by Glendower and married his daughter. See n. at II. ii. 4–5; and Hall, 2, 23 (App. 1), and 27.

(b) The Houses of York and Lancaster

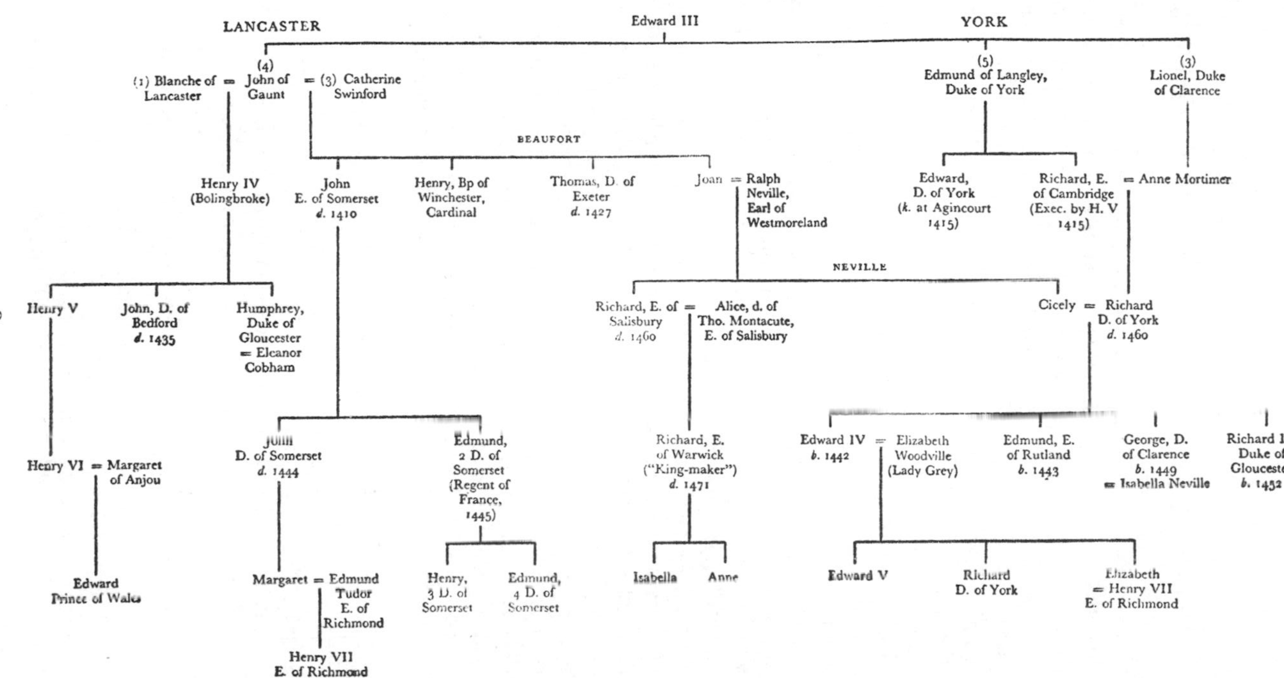

Appendix 3

"RECOLLECTIONS" IN *THE CONTENTION*

The Contention (the bad quarto of *2 Henry VI*) is, in the main, a defective version as reconstructed by a group of actors from what they could remember of the play as they had performed it. Where their memory failed or deceived them, they often introduced, by association of ideas, similar words and phrases from other plays in their repertoire. The clearest examples of these "recollections" in *The Contention* are given below, arranged according to the plays from which they were derived. In each case the phrase from the external "source" of the recollection is quoted first; then the passage, if any, in *2 Henry VI*, which the actors wished to reproduce; and last, the defective result as it appears in *The Contention*.

Recollections should be carefully distinguished (as they have not always been) from stock phrases in common use in the theatrical vocabulary of the age, and from direct imitations or quotations by one author of another.

In *The Contention* there is a further danger that some alleged recollections are really original Shakespeare, cut, censored, or otherwise omitted at some stage of transmission of the text. Such passages are apt to be dismissed, especially on a revision theory, as fossils of "pre-Shakespearean verse". To make matters more confused, they often contain, as they appear in *The Contention*, an element of recollection. A probable example is the "wild Onele" passage (*Cont.*, 539) quoted below in relation to *Edward II.*[1]

The text of *The Contention* is most conveniently consulted in volume IX of the Cambridge Shakespeare (1893). References are to the *pages* of that volume.

Most of the following recollections have been previously identified.

1 Henry VI

What ransom must I pay before I pass? *1 H 6*, v. iii. 73
Here shall they make their ransome on the sand,
2 H 6, IV. i. 10
And let them paie their ransomes ere they passe *Cont.*, 548

. . . vnto the house of York
From whence you spring by lineal descent. *1 H 6*, III. i. 165–6
. . . craving your opinion of my title,
Which is infallible, to England's crown. *2 H 6*, II. ii. 4–5

1. See Introduction, pp. xxi–xxii.

The right and title of the house of Yorke,
To Englands Crowne by liniall desent. *Cont.*, 528

Lionel Duke of Clarence, the third son
To King Edward the Third; *1 H 6*, II. v. 75–6
Edward . . . had seven sons . . . and the third, Lionel
Duke of Clarence . . . *2 H 6*, II. ii. 9 ff.
The third son, Duke of Clarence *2 H 6*, II. ii. 33
Lyonell Duke of Clarence, the third sonne to Edward
the third *Cont.*, 529 (twice)

3 Henry VI

And he that casts not up his cap for joy
Shall for the fault make forfeit of his head. *3 H 6*, II. i. 196–7
He that breaks a stick of Gloucester's grove
Shall lose his head for his presumption. *2 H 6*, I. ii. 33–4
That he that breakes a sticke of *Glosters* groue,
Shall for th'offence, make forfeit of his head. *Cont.*, 514
And he that casts not vp his cap for ioie,
Shall for the offence make forfeit of his head. *Tr. Tr.* 594

As I bethink me, you should not be king
Till our King Henry had shook hands with death.
3 H 6, I. iv. 101–2
And so think *I* Madame, for as you know,
If our King Henry had shooke hands with death, . . .
Cont., 538

Away! for vengeance comes along with them:
Nay, stay not to expostulate, make speed *3 H 6*, II. v. 134–5
Away, my lord! . . .
We shall to London get, . . . *2 H 6*, v. ii. 72, 81, 86
Make hast, for vengeance comes along with them,
Come stand not to expostulate, lets go. *Cont.*, 568

Richard III

As I intend to prosper and repent,
So thrive I . . . *R 3*, IV. iv. 397–8
as I intend . . . to thrive *2 H 6*, v. ii. 17
as I intend to prosper *Cont.*, 567

Titus Andronicus

Which dreads not yet their lives' destruction *Tit.*, II. iii. 50
that yet suspect no peril *2H 6*, III. i. 152
That dreads not yet their lives destruction *Cont.*, 537

Then sit we down, and let us all consult . . . of your safety
Tit., IV. ii. 132, 134
Then sit we downe . . . Let us consult . . . For safetie of . . .
Cont., 538

reverse the doom of death . . .
My everlasting doom of banishment *Tit.*, III. i. 24, 51
O Henry, let me plead for gentle Suffolk *2 H 6*, III. ii. 289
Oh Henry, reverse the doom of gentle Suffolkes banishment
Cont., 545

. . . lay hands on them . . . bind them sure; *Tit.*, V. ii. 159, 161
Lay hands upon these traitors *2 H 6*, I. iv. 44
. . . laie hands on them, and bind them sure, *Cont.*, 523

The Spanish Tragedy

I saw more sights than thousand tongues can tell,
Or pennes can write, or mortall harts can think.
S.T., I. i. 57–8
As free as heart can wish, or tongue can tell. *2 H 6*, IV. vii. 124
as . . . hart . . . thinke, or toong can tell *Cont.*, 558

Edward II

Nay, to my death, for too long have I lived *Ed. 2*, 2651
even to my death *Ed. 2*, 2331
welcome were my death *2 H 6*, II. iii. 14
Euen to my death, for I haue liued too long *Cont.*, 530

And levie armes against your lawfull king *Ed. 2*, 1516
oppose himself against his king *2 H 6*, V. i. 113
To leavy Armes against his lawfull King. *Cont.*, 565

Your love to Gaveston
Will be the ruine of the realme and you, . . .
And therefore, brother, banish him *Ed.*, *2*, 1010, 1011, 1013
they fear your highness death . . .
Makes them thus forward in his banishment.
2 H 6, III. ii. 249, 253
they feare the ruine of the realme
And therefore . . .
They wish you to banish him *Cont.*, 544

Nay, all of them conspire to crosse me thus
But if I live, ile tread upon their heads *Ed. 2*, 897–8
Follow I must, I cannot go before, *2 H 6*, I. ii. 61

But ere it be long, Ile go before them all
Despite of all that seeke to crosse me thus. *Cont.*, 515

Did you regard the honour of your name *Ed. 2*, 1323
As though your highnes were a schoole boy still
And must be awde and governd like a child *Ed. 2*, 1336–7
What, shall King Henry be a pupil still
Under the surly Gloucester's governance? *2 H 6*, I. iii. 44–5
And nere regards the honour of his name,
And still must be protected like a childe,
And governd . . . *Cont.*, 518

But hath your grace no other proofe then this? *Ed. 2*, 2611
Then you, belike, suspect these noblemen *2 H 6*, III. ii. 186
But have you no greater proofes than these? *Cont.*, 543

The wilde Oneyle, with swarmes of Irish Kernes,
Lives uncontroulde within the English pale, *Ed. 2*, 966–7
. . . rebels there are up . . .
The uncivil kernes of Ireland are in armes
2 H 6, III. i. 283, 310
The wilde Onele my Lords, is up in Armes,
With troupes of Irish Kernes that uncontrold,
Doth plant themselves within the English pale. *Cont.*, 539

Arden of Faversham

a sudden qualm came over my hart *Arden*, V. i. 316
Some sudden qualm hath struck me at the heart
2 H 6, I. i. 51
a sodain qualme came over my hart *Cont.*, 510

Hell fyre and wrathfull vengeance light on me *Arden*, I. 338
Mischance and sorrow go along with you! . . .
And threefold vengeance tend upon your steps!
2 H 6, III. ii. 300, 304
Hell fire and vengeance go along with you *Cont.*, 545

Appendix 4

PASSAGES IN *THE CONTENTION*, OMITTED OR VARIED IN THE FOLIO *2 HENRY VI*

I. i. 24–31; A2v; *The Contention* (Cambridge, 1893, vol. IX), p. 511:

Queene. Th' excessiue loue I beare vnto your grace,
Forbids me to be lauish of my tongue,
Least I should speake more then beseemes a woman:
Let this suffice, my blisse is in your liking,
And nothing can make poore *Margaret* miserable,
Vnlesse the frowne of mightie Englands King.

I. i. 136; A3v; *Cont.*, 511:

Card. ... As if our King were bound vnto your will,
And might not do his will without your leaue,
Proud Protector, enuy in thine eyes I see,
The big swolne venome of thy hatefull heart,
That dares presume gainst that thy Soueraigne likes.

After I. iii. 5; B2r; *Cont.*, 516:

2. Peti. ... For but for him a many were vndone,
That cannot get no succour in the Court,

I. iii. 37–41; B2v; *Cont.*, 517:

Suffolke. So now show your petitions to Duke *Humphrey*.
Villaines get you gone and come not neare the Court,
Dare these pesants write against me thus.

After I. iii. 210; B4v; *Cont.*, 521:

King. Then be it so my Lord of *Somerset*.
We make your grace Regent ouer the French,
And to defend our rights gainst forraine foes,
And so do good vnto the Realme of *France*.
Make hast my Lord, tis time that you were gone,
The time of Truse I thinke is full expirde.

I. iv. 1–22; B4v, C1r; *Cont.*, 521–2:

Enter *Elnor*, with sir *Iohn Hum*, *Roger Bullenbrooke* a Coniurer, and *Margery Iourdaine* a Witch.

Elnor. Here sir *Iohn*, take this scrole of paper here,
Wherein is writ the questions you shall aske,

And I will stand vpon this Tower here,
And here the spirit what it saies to you,
And to my questions, write the answeres downe.
She goes vp to the Tower.
Sir Iohn. Now sirs begin and cast your spels about,
And charme the fiendes for to obey your wils,
And tell Dame *Elnor* of the thing she askes.
Witch. Then *Roger Bullinbrooke* about thy taske,
And frame a Cirkle here vpon the earth,
Whilst I thereon all prostrate on my face,
Do talke and whisper with the diuels below,
And coniure them for to obey my will.
She lies downe vpon her face.
Bullenbrooke makes a Cirkle.
Bullen. Darke Night, dread Night, the silence of the Night,
Wherein the Furies maske in hellish troupes,
Send vp I charge you from *Sosetus* lake,
The spirit *Askalon* to come to me,
To pierce the bowels of this Centricke earth,
And hither come in twinkling of an eye,
Askalon, Assenda, Assenda.
It thunders and lightens, and then the spirit riseth vp.

I. iv. 38–9; C1r; *Cont.*, 522:

Bullen. Then downe I say, vnto the damned poule,
Where Pluto in his firie Waggon sits.
Rydyng amidst the singde and parched smoakes,
The Rode of *Dytas* by the Riuer Stykes,
There howle and burne for euer in those flames,
Rise Iordaine rise, and staie thy charming Spels.
Sonnes, we are betraide.

II. ii. 68–75; C4v; *Cont.*, 530:

War. Then Yorke aduise thy selfe and take thy time,
Claime thou the Crowne, and set thy standard vp,
And in the same aduance the milke-white Rose,
And then to gard it, will I rouse the Beare,
Inuiron'd with ten thousand Ragged-staues
To aide and helpe thee for to win thy right,
Maugre the proudest Lord of Henries blood,
That dares deny the right and claime of Yorke.

III. i. 282–7, 309–19; E1r, E1v; *Cont.*, 539:

Messen. Madame I bring you newes from Ireland,
The wilde Onele my Lords, is vp in Armes,
With troupes of Irish Kernes that vncontrold,
Doth plant themselues within the English pale,
And burnes and spoiles the Country as they goe. . .
Queene. . . . good Yorke be patient,
And do thou take in hand to crosse the seas,
With troupes of Armed men to quell the pride
Of those ambitious Irish that rebell.
Yorke. Well Madame sith your grace is so content,
Let me haue some bands of chosen soldiers,
And Yorke shall trie his fortune against those kernes.
Queene. Yorke thou shalt. My Lord of Buckingham,
Let it be your charge to muster vp such souldiers
As shall suffise him in these needfull warres.
Buck. Madame I will, and leauie such a band
As soone shall ouercome those Irish Rebels, . . .

III. i. 322–6; E1v; *Cont.*, 540:

Queene. Suffolke remember what you haue to do.
And you Lord Cardinall concerning Duke Humphrey,
Twere good that you did see to it in time,
Come let vs go, that it may be performde.

III. ii. 1–5; E2r; *Cont.*, 540:

Then the Curtaines being drawne, Duke *Humphrey* is discouered in his bed, and two men lying on his brest and smothering him in his bed. And then enter the Duke of *Suffolke* to them.

IV. i. 1–11; F1v; *Cont.*, 548:

Cap. Bring forward these prisoners that scorn'd to yeeld,
Vnlade their goods with speed and sincke their ship,

IV. i. 139–47; F2v; *Cont.*, 550:

Cap. Off with his head, and send it to the Queene,
And ransomlesse this prisoner shall go free,
To see it safe deliuered vnto her.
Come lets goe.

IV. ii. 21–30; F3r; *Cont.*, 550:

Nick. But sirrha, who comes more beside Iacke Cade?
George. Why theres Dicke the Butcher, and Robin the Sadler, and

Will that came a wooing to our Nan last Sunday, and Harry and Tom, and Gregory that should haue your Parnill, and a great sort more is come from Rochester, and from Maydstone, and Canterbury, and all the Townes here abouts, and we must all be Lords or squires, assoone as Iack Cade is King.

IV. ii. 113–15; F4[r]; *Cont.*, 552:

Kneele down Iohn Mortemer,
Rise vp sir Iohn Mortemer.
Is there any more of them that be Knights?
Tom. I his brother.
He Knights *Dicke Butcher*.
Cade. Then kneele down Dicke Butcher,
Rise vp sir Dicke Butcher
Now sound vp the Drumme.

IV. ii. 166–8; F4[v]; *Cont.*, 554:

Stafford. Well sirrha, wilt thou yeeld thy selfe vnto the Kings mercy, and he will pardon thee and these, their outrages and rebellious deeds?

Cade. Nay, bid the King come to me and he will, and then ile pardon him, or otherwaies ile haue his Crowne tell him, ere it be long.

After the end of IV. iii; F4[v]; *Cont.*, 554:

Cade. . . . for to morrow I meane to sit in the Kings seate at Westminster.

After IV. vii. 120–1; G2[r]; *Cont.*, 557:

Cade. Marry he that will lustily stand to it,
Shall go with me, and take vp these commodities following:
Item, a gowne, a kirtle, a petticoate, and a smocke.

After IV. vii. 119; G2[v], G3[r]; *Cont.*, 558:

Enter *Robin.*

Robin. O Captaine, London bridge is a fire.

Cade. Runne to Billingsgate, and fetche pitch and flaxe and squench it.

Enter *Dicke* and a Sargiant.

Sargiant. Iustice, iustice, I pray you sir, let me haue iustice of this fellow here.

Cade. Why what has he done?

Sarg. Alasse sir he has rauisht my wife.

Dicke. Why my Lord he would haue rested me,
And I went and entred my Action in his wiues paper house.
Cade. Dicke follow thy sute in her common place,
You horson villaine, you are a Sargiant youle,
Take any man by the throate for twelue pence,
And rest a man when hees at dinner,
And haue him to prison ere the meate be out of his mouth.
Go Dicke take him hence, cut out his toong for cogging,
Hough him for running, and to conclude,
Braue [=Brain] him with his owne mace.
Exet with the Sargiant.

IV. viii. 6–54; G3r; *Cont.*, 559:

Clifford. Why country-men and warlike friends of Kent,
What meanes this mutinous rebellions,
That you in troopes do muster thus your selues,
Vnder the conduct of this Traitor Cade?
To rise against your soueraigne Lord and King,
Who mildly hath his pardon sent to you,
If you forsake this monstrous Rebell here?
If honour be the marke whereat you aime,
Then haste to France that our forefathers wonne,
And winne againe that thing which now is lost,
And leaue to seeke your Countries ouerthrow.
All. A Clifford, a Clifford.
They forsake *Cade*.
Cade. Why how now, will you forsake your generall,
And ancient freedome which you haue possest?
To bend your neckes vnder their seruile yokes,
Who if you stir, will straightwaies hang you vp,
But follow me, and you shall pull them downe,
And make them yeeld their liuings to your hands.
All. A Cade, a Cade.
They runne to *Cade* againe.
Cliff. Braue warlike friends heare me but speak a word,
Refuse not good whilst it is offered you,
The King is mercifull, then yeeld to him,
And I my selfe will go along with you,
To Winsore Castle whereas the King abides,
And on mine honour you shall haue no hurt.

IV. ix. 1–21; G3v; *Cont.*, 560:

King. Lord Somerset, what newes here you of the Rebell Cade?

Som. This, my gratious Lord, that the Lord Say is don to death,
And the Citie is almost sackt.
King. Gods will be done, for as he hath decreede, so must it be:
And be it as he please, to stop the pride of these rebellious men.
Queene. Had the noble Duke of Suffolke bene aliue,
The Rebell Cade had bene supprest ere this,
And all the rest that do take part with him.
Enter the Duke of *Buckingham* and *Clifford*, with the Rebels, with halters about their necks.
Cliff. Long liue King Henry, Englands lawfull King,
Loe here my Lord, these Rebels are subdude,
And offer their liues before your highnesse feete.
King. But tell me Clifford, is there Captaine here.
Clif. No, my gratious Lord, he is fled away, but proclamations are sent forth, that he that can but bring his head, shall haue a thousand crownes. But may it please your Maiestie, to pardon these their faults, that by that traitors meanes were thus misled.
King. Stand vp you simple men, and giue God praise,
For you did take in hand you know not what,
And go in peace obedient to your King,
And liue as subiects, and you shall not want,
Whilst Henry liues, and weares the English Crowne.

IV. ix. 47–8; G3v; *Cont.*, 560:
King. Come let vs hast to London now with speed,
That solemne prosessions may be sung,
In laud and honour of the God of Heauen,
And triumphs of this happie victorie.

IV. x. 1–23; G4r; *Cont.*, 561:
Eyden. Good Lord how pleasant is this country life,
This little land my father left me here,
With my contented minde serues me as well,
As all the pleasures in the Court can yeeld,
Nor would I change this pleasure for the Court.

V. i. 88–95, 104–5; H1v; *Cont.*, 564:
Yorke. . . . Base fearefull Henry that thus dishonor'st me,
By heauen, thou shalt not gouerne ouer me:
I cannot brooke that Traitors presence here,
Nor will I subiect be to such a King,

That knowes not how to gouerne nor to rule,
Resigne thy Crowne proud Lancaster to me,
That thou vsurped hast so long by force,
For now is Yorke resolu'd to claime his owne,
And rise aloft into faire Englands Throane.

v. ii. 14–30; H2ᵛ, H3ʳ; *Cont.*, 567:

Yorke. Now Clifford, since we are singled here alone,
Be this the day of doome to one of vs,
For now my heart hath sworne immortall hate
To thee and all the house of Lancaster.
Cliffood. And here I stand, and pitch my foot to thine,
Vowing neuer to stir, till thou or I be slaine,
For neuer shall my heart be safe at rest,
Till I haue spoyld the hatefull house of Yorke.
Alarmes, and they fight, and *Yorke* kils *Clifford*
Yorke. Now Lancaster sit sure, thy sinowes shrinke,
Come fearefull Henry grouelling on thy face,
Yeeld vp thy Crowne vnto the Prince of Yorke.
Exet Yorke.

v. ii. 31–65; H3ʳ; *Cont.*, 567–8:

Alarmes, then enter yoong *Clifford* alone.
Yoong Clifford. Father of Comberland,
Where may I seeke my aged father forth?
O! dismall sight, see where he breathlesse lies,
All smeard and weltred in his luke-warme blood,
Ah, aged pillar of all Comberlands true house,
Sweete father, to thy murthred ghoast I sweare,
Immortall hate vnto the house of Yorke,
Nor neuer shall I sleepe secure one night,
Till I haue furiously reuengde thy death,
And left not one of them to breath on earth.
He takes him vp on his backe.
And thus as old Ankyses sonne did beare
His aged father on his manly backe,
And fought with him against the bloodie Greeks,
Euen so will I. But staie, heres one of them,
To whom my soule hath sworne immortall hate.
Enter *Richard*, and then *Clifford* laies downe his father, fights with him, and *Richard* flies away againe.
Out crooktbacke villaine, get thee from my sight,
But I will after thee, and once againe

When I haue borne my father to his Tent,
Ile trie my fortune better with thee yet.

Exet yoong *Clifford* with his father.

Alarmes againe, and then enter three or foure, bearing the Duke of Buckingham wounded to his Tent.

Before v. iii. 1; H3v; *Cont.*, 568:

Yorke. How now boyes, fortunate this fight hath bene,
I hope to vs and ours, for Englands good,
And our great honour, that so long we lost,
Whilst faint-heart Henry did vsurpe our rights:

Appendix 5

PARALLEL TEXTS OF III. ii. 299–411

F

Queen. Mischance and Sorrow goe along with you, III. ii. 299
Hearts Discontent, and sowre Affiiction,
Be play-fellowes to keepe you companie:
There's two of you, the Deuill make a third,
And three-fold vengeance tend vpon your steps
Suff. Cease, gentle Queene, these Execrations,
And let thy *Suffolke* take his heauie leaue.
Queen. Fye Coward woman, and soft harted wretch,
Hast thou not spirit to curse thine enemy... 307
Qu. Oh, let me intreat thee cease, giue me thy hand, 338
That I may dew it with my mournfull teares:
Nor let the raine of heauen wet this place,
To wash away my wofull Monuments.
Oh, could this kisse be printed in thy hand,
That thou might'st thinke vpon these by the Seale,
Through whom a thousand sighes are breath'd for thee.
So get thee gone, that I may know my greefe,
'Tis but surmiz'd, whiles thou art standing by,
As one that surfets, thinking on a want:
I will repeale thee, or be well assur'd,
Aduenrure to be banished my selfe:
And banished I am, if but from thee.
Go, speake not to me; euen now be gone... 351

Suf. Thus is poore Suffolke ten times banished, 356
Once by the King, and three times thrice by thee...
Qu. ... Aye me! What is this World? What newes are these? 380
But wherefore greeue I at an houres poore losse,
Omitting Suffolkes exile, my soules Treasure?
Why onely Suffolke mourne I not for thee?
And with the Southerne clouds, contend in teares?
Theirs for the earths encrease, mine for my sorrowes.
Now get thee hence, the King thou know'st is comming,
If thou be found by me, thou art but dead.
Suf. If I depart from thee, I cannot liue,
And in thy sight to dye, what were it else,
But like a pleasant slumber in thy lap? 389
Oh let me stay, befall what may befall. 401

Q

Queene. Hell fire and vengeance go along with you,
[From *Arden of Faversham.* See App. 3]

Theres two of you, the diuell make the third.

Fie womanish man, canst thou not curse thine enemies? . . .
Queene. No more. Sweete Suffolke hie thee hence to France,
Or liue where thou wilt within this worldes globe,
Ile haue an Irish that shall find thee out, } see 405–6
And long thou shalt not staie, but ile haue thee repelde,
[From *Ed. 2.* See App. 3]

Or venture to be banished my selfe.
Oh let this kisse be printed in thy hand, see 342–6
That when thou seest it, thou maist thinke on me.
Away, I say, that I may feele my griefe,
For it is nothing whilst thou standest here.
Suffolke. Thus is poore *Suffolke* ten times banished,
Once by the King, but three times thrise by thee. . .
Queene. . . . Oh what is wordly pompe, all men must die,
And woe am I for Bewfords heauie ende.
But why mourne I for him, whilst thou art here?
Sweete Suffolke hie thee hence to France,
For if the King do come, thou sure must die.

Suff. And if I go I cannot liue: but here to die,
What were it else, but like a pleasant slumber
In thy lap? [=389]
O let me staie, befall, what may befall. [=401]

Queen. Away: Though parting be a fretfull corosiue,
Ir is applyed to a deathfull wound.
To France sweet Suffolke: Let me heare from thee:
For wheresoere thou art in this worlds Globe,
Ile haue an *Iris* that shall finde thee out.
Suf. I go.
Qu. And take my heart with thee.

Suf. A Iewell lockt into the wofulst Caske,
That euer did containe a thing of worth,
Euen as a splitted Barke, so sunder we:
This way fall I to death.
Qu. This way for me. *Exeunt.*

Queen. Oh mightst thou staie with safetie of thy life,
Then shouldst thou staie, but heauens deny it,
And therefore go, but hope ere long to be repelde.

[From *Ed.* 2. See App. 3]

Suff. I goe.
Queene. And take my heart with thee.
She kisseth him.
Suff. A iewell lockt into the wofulst caske,
That euer yet containde a thing of woorth,
Thus like a splitted barke so sunder we.
This way fall I to death. *Exet Suffolke.*
Queene. This way for me. *Exet Queene.*